DATE DUE

~~JY 16 '98~~			
~~AY 30 '99~~			
~~AC 24 '00~~			
~~AG 3 '00~~			
~~OC 24 '00~~			
~~NO 14 '00~~			

studies in jazz

Institute of Jazz Studies
Rutgers—The State University of New Jersey
General Editors: Dan Morgenstern and Edward Berger

1. BENNY CARTER: A Life in American Music, *by Morroe Berger, Edward Berger, and James Patrick,* 1982
2. ART TATUM: A Guide to His Recorded Music, *by Arnold Laubich and Ray Spencer,* 1982
3. ERROLL GARNER: The Most Happy Piano, *by James M. Doran,* 1995
4. JAMES P. JOHNSON: A Case of Mistaken Identity, *by Scott E. Brown;* Discography 1917–1950, *by Robert Hilbert,* 1986
5. PEE WEE ERWIN: This Horn for Hire, *as told to Warren W. Vaché, Sr.,* 1987
6. BENNY GOODMAN: Listen to His Legacy, *by D. Russell Connor,* 1988
7. ELLINGTONIA: The Recorded Music of Duke Ellington and His Sidemen, *by W. E. Timner,* 1988
8. THE GLENN MILLER ARMY AIR FORCE BAND: Sustineo Alas/ I Sustain the Wings, *by Edward F. Polic;* Foreword *by George T. Simon,* 1989
9. SWING LEGACY, *by Chip Deffaa,* 1989
10. REMINISCING IN TEMPO: The Life and Times of a Jazz Hustler, *by Teddy Reig, with Edward Berger,* 1990
11. IN THE MAINSTREAM: 18 Portraits in Jazz, *by Chip Deffaa,* 1992
12. BUDDY DeFRANCO: A Biographical Portrait and Discography, *by John Kuehn and Arne Astrup,* 1993
13. PEE WEE SPEAKS: A Discography of Pee Wee Russell, *by Robert Hilbert, with David Niven,* 1992
14. SYLVESTER AHOLA: The Gloucester Gabriel, *by Dick Hill,* 1993
15. THE POLICE CARD DISCORD, *by Maxwell T. Cohen,* 1993
16. TRADITIONALISTS AND REVIVALISTS IN JAZZ, *by Chip Deffaa,* 1993
17. BASSICALLY SPEAKING: An Oral History of George Duvivier, *by Edward Berger;* Musical Analysis, *by David Chevan,* 1993
18. TRAM: The Frank Trumbauer Story, *by Philip R. Evans and Larry F. Kiner, with William Trumbauer,* 1994
19. TOMMY DORSEY: On the Side, *by Robert L. Stockdale,* 1995
20. JOHN COLTRANE: A Discography and Musical Biography, *by Yasuhiro Fujioka, with Lewis Porter and Yoh-ichi Hamada,* 1995
21. RED HEAD: A Chronological Survey of "Red" Nichols and His Five Pennies, *by Stephen M. Stroff,* 1995
22. THE RED NICHOLS STORY: After Intermission 1942–1965, *by Stanley Hester, Stephen Hester, Philip Evans, and Linda Evans,* 1996
23. BENNY GOODMAN: Wrappin' It Up, *by D. Russell Connor,* 1996
24. CHARLIE PARKER AND THEMATIC IMPROVISATION, *by Henry Martin,* 1996

This portrait is on permanent display in the Hemmens Auditorium, Elgin, Illinois, commemorating Benny Goodman's appearance there with the Elgin Symphony Orchestra, 21 November 1976.   (Photo, Jim Kutina)

Benny Goodman
Wrappin' It Up

by
D. Russell Connor

Studies in Jazz, No. 23

The Scarecrow Press, Inc.
Lanham, Md., and London
1996

SCARECROW PRESS, INC.

Published in the United States of America
by Scarecrow Press, Inc.
4720 Boston Way
Lanham, Maryland 20706

4 Pleydell Gardens, Folkestone
Kent CT20 2DN, England

British Cataloguing-in-Publication Information Available

Library of Congress Cataloging-in-Publication Data

Connor, D. Russell (Donald Russell)
Benny Goodman : wrappin' it up / by D. Russell Connor.
p. cm. — (Studies in jazz ; no. 23)
Includes bibliographical references and indexes.
1. Goodman, Benny, 1909- —Discography.   2. Goodman, Benny,
1909– .   3. Jazz musicians—United States—Biography.   I. Title.   II. Series
ML156.7.G66C6   1996   016.78165′092—dc20   95-39267   CIP

ISBN 0-8108-3102-3 (cloth : alk. paper)

CONTENTS

Acknowledgments   ix

Foreword by William F. Hyland   xi

Preface   xvii

Prologue   xix

Benny Goodman, 1910–1949   1

Benny Goodman, 1950–1995   75

The Savory Goodman Air Checks   135

Goodman Arrangements   155

Goodman Films, Videotapes   161

Memorabilia Price Guide   165

Necrology   167

Index of Tune Titles: Text   171

Index of Tune Titles: The Savory Goodman Air Checks   177

DEDICATION

To our grandchildren Alex, Kaitlin, Clare and Bennett,
in hopes that someday they'll grow to appreciate
the music of Benny Goodman.

ACKNOWLEDGMENTS

Over forty-odd years my bio-discographies have been enhanced by the contributions of Goodman fans world-wide. This one is no exception. Many of those named before offered information and advice again. Regrettably, some of them have passed on. They are missed.

New contributors have come forward. A few are cited in the text. Others include Jack Ames, Bob Barfoot, Dan Bied, Jack Browne, Rich Dondiego, Will Friedwald, Jens Jorn Gjedsted, Ben Hafey, Guy Hampson, Peanuts Hucko, Jerry Jerome, Arne Johnsrud, Harold Kaye, Norm Krusinski, Mort Linder, Maria Marshall, Charlie Morrison, Ulrich Neuert, Flip Phillips, John Prager, Art Rollini (deceased), Norm Saks, Harold Samuel, C. C. Sargent, Sue Satz, Al Stewart, Jim Stincic, Bob Stockdale, Louise Tobin, Joel Van Wambeke, Earl Vibbard, Mary Vibbert, Geoff Wheeler and Bob Zenter. My gratitude to all, and my apologies to some—one in Finland, another in Zimbabwe, for example—whose names have disappeared somewhere in my messy files.

Especially helpful have been Donna Connor, photography; and Dave Jessup, who compiled the Tune Indexes with the aid of his brother, Joel. Further, Dave proofread both my manuscript and the typeset, eliminating errata in both.

*

This is my fourth bio-discography on Benny Goodman; I have no plans for a fifth. Another will be warranted in future for two reasons. Interest in Benny is robust, attested to by the quantity of global releases of his recordings and the volume of mail I receive about them. And undoubtedly there will be new discoveries of his work.

I believe a successor Goodman bio-discography will best be a collaborative effort. My nominees for a partnership are Loren Schoenberg and Dave Jessup; both have accepted my charge. I will continue my research, forward to Loren and Dave data I develop or receive. They will respond to contributors. I urge all who have assisted me to cooperate with them so that they may add to Benny's legacy.

November 9, 1994

William F. Hyland
Shirley Deeter
Co-Executors

Susan Satz
Business Manager

Mr. D. Russell Connor
173 North Park Drive
Levittown, PA 19054

Dear Russ:

The news that an update of your remarkable Benny Goodman bio-discography will be published by Scarecrow Press was exciting for me to hear. I am sure Goodman fans throughout the world will have a similar reaction because the enjoyment of Benny's music has been enhanced for all of us through having at our fingertips your comprehensive history of his extraordinary recording career. I doubt that the professional output of any other jazz or classical musician has been documented more accurately and exhaustively. Thanks for all of your hard work and dedication.

Your 1988 edition, <u>Benny Goodman; Listen to His Legacy</u>, has been absolutely indispensable to the Estate since his death, just as the earlier editions were important to Benny himself when he needed to know the date of a particular recording or some other elusive fact. Hardly a day passes without a reference to <u>Legacy</u> by our business manager Susan Satz or myself as we encounter questions that can't be answered from Benny's files or from other available sources.   And when we truly are stuck, or something is of particular urgency, we pick up the phone, as you well know, and invariably get some help from you in solving our problem.

But, as you have suggested, let me tell your readers a bit more about the Benny Goodman Estate and how I got involved in it, and the remarkable interest in his music that persists down to the present moment.

I had been a part-time professional musician in the 1940's and early 50's, until a growing law practice made this double life too difficult. My instruments were the alto saxophone and clarinet, and like thousands of other reed players, my musical hero was Benny Goodman. In 1976, while I was serving a four year term as Attorney General of New Jersey, Benny was persuaded by a mutual friend to allow me to join him on clarinet in a concert in Waterloo Village in Stanhope, New Jersey. Our collaboration went quite well and led to our spending an increasing amount of time together, indulging in our mutual loves of music and fishing.

We would go to Canada, for example, and fish for salmon on the Miramichi River in New Brunswick, taking along not only our fly rods but our clarinets and music portfolios as well. Several times a day Benny and I set up our music stands in the lovely woods bordering our cabin and sight-read duets transcribed from works of Bach, Schubert and other great composers. We had similar sessions in Benny's home in Stamford, where on occasion we also jammed with some of his jazz sidekicks at birthday parties and other gatherings. And from time to time Benny would call and tell me to bring my horn to one of his Sextet concerts, where we would perform together. Sometimes his invitations to play with him in public were more unexpected, as when my wife Joan and I went to hear the Goodman Sextet at the Brooklyn Academy of Music. Knowing we were in the audience, Benny called me to the stage, handed me his own horn and stepped into the wings, leaving me to play a couple of tunes with his musicians. Pretty heady stuff!

On one very memorable occasion Joan and I went to Benny's home in Stamford to spend the weekend with him. When we arrived on Friday afternoon, he was practicing the Hindemith Clarinet Concerto with Harriet Wingreen, a fine pianist who is a member of the New York Philharmonic. Joan is an accomplished lyric soprano, and we had been preparing to give a performance a week or so later of Schubert's "Shepherd on the Rock", a lovely piece for soprano, clarinet and piano. Benny suggested that Joan and Harriet run through the music with him, but he was unable to locate the clarinet part. Clearly undaunted, Benny stood behind Harriet and over her shoulder transposed this somewhat difficult piece from the piano part, playing it perfectly until the very end, when his fingers got tangled up in the transposition of the accelerating climactic runs and everyone collapsed in laughter.

Over a period of time Benny began to talk with me about his business affairs. Occasionally at first, and then more regularly, he would ask me to assist with the legal aspects of a matter - perhaps the negotiation of a recording or television contract, or a tax problem. But Benny was a shrewd and thoroughly experienced businessman and needed very little help of this kind. However, he also was concerned about how his business affairs would be managed after his death, for he eventually asked if I would serve as co-executor and co-trustee of his Estate, along with one of his step-daughters, Shirley Deeter. With some reluctance I agreed to take on this responsibility because of our close friendship, even though I had discouraged doing this for other clients.

The will Benny executed shortly thereafter provided that all of his music arrangements, unreleased recordings and career memorabilia would be left to the Yale University School of Music, with which he had experienced many pleasant relationships in the past. He then asked me to visit Yale with him so that we could review with his good friend Dr. Harold Samuel, the Music Librarian there, the manner in which these materials would be organized and made available to students and others after his death. We went to

New Haven, Connecticut together on June 10, 1986 and had a very pleasant and useful visit with Dr. Samuel and his colleagues.

As I drove Benny back to Stamford at the end of our visit, he told me he was quite satisfied with everything he had seen and heard at Yale. I know this was a great comfort to him. But he also complained to me about being quite tired, and indeed he looked very weary by the time we reached his home in the late afternoon. I was quite worried about him. But, it was reassuring to get a telephone call from Benny the next morning and to hear that he was hard at work preparing for a "Mostly Mozart" concert at Lincoln Center on August 18th at which he was to perform the Mozart Quintet. His only complaint to me was that he also wanted to play a Brahms sonata, but had been discouraged from doing so by the "Mostly Mozart" people because it didn't strictly fit their traditional format.

The next evening Benny called to report with great enthusiasm that the August "Mostly Mozart" concert was sold out and that he had been asked to play another concert in that series in July. In the high register to which his voice often ascended when he was excited about something, Benny said: "You know, Bill, I think I'm going to play the Brahms!" Recalling how tired he had been just two days earlier, I replied: "Benny, why don't you make it easy on yourself and just play the same program for both concerts?" He was quiet for a moment and then said: "You're probably right. But let me think about it". Knowing Benny, I realized the subject was not necessarily closed. And I was right.

The next afternoon, Friday the 13th of June, I received a call at home from Benny's friend, Carol Phillips, with the dreadful news that Benny had died from an apparent heart attack in his New York City apartment an hour or so earlier. Thankfully his passing had been quite peaceful and Carol was with him at the end. I was stunned, of course. For a moment it felt as if the whole world had collapsed. I could only shudder with disbelief and grief. But, there were decisions to be made and things to do and I agreed to meet Carol at the apartment the next morning.

Joan and I arrived at Manhattan House about 9 o'clock on Saturday morning. Carol was there and asked me to put away Benny's clarinets, which remained where he had left them the previous morning at the end of what turned out to be his last practice session. His B-flat and A clarinets were both resting on the top of the grand piano in the living room, with his mother-of-pearl music stand in its usual rehearsal position nearby. Clarinet reeds by the dozens were scattered over the piano top and elsewhere throughout the room, as generally was the case when Benny was in the midst of what his daughter Rachel has called his never-ending "reed quest".

But then I took note of the music resting on the rehearsal stand. The last selection Benny had been playing before his fatal attack was the Brahms sonata, which he clearly was planning to perform at the July concert notwithstanding the reservations of the "Mostly Mozart" staff. I thought to myself how typical it was of Benny Goodman to feel so strongly about his music, right up to the very end. I remember shaking my head and muttering to myself: "Benny, you son-of-a-gun!" as I put his clarinets away in their cases.

Benny Goodman was buried in Stamford on June 15 at a private service attended only by his family and a few close friends. In the course of this simple ceremony I delivered a brief eulogy at the family's request.

Immediately after the funeral Shirley Deeter, Susan Satz and I began to familiarize ourselves with the active business affairs and files of Benny's New York office so that we could move promptly ahead with our work. Fortunately, Muriel Zuckerman, who had been Benny's indispensable secretary for much of his long career, was there to assist us in the early stages of our work. During the next several months, with the help of Benny's daughters, Rachel and Benjie, we inventoried all of the music arrangements, master tapes and other articles comprising the Yale bequest and turned them over to Harold Samuel. Perhaps the most precious items were the acetate recording disks from Benny's earlier years and about 400 reels of tape containing a good deal of material Benny felt was worthy of release to the public.

But some of these disks and tapes were in alarming stages of deterioration, either because they had a limited "shelf-life" or because they had been stored under less than ideal conditions. Dr. Samuel and I were intent upon saving as much of this unmined treasury of music as we could, and so he acted quickly upon my suggestion that Loren Schoenberg and Greg Squires be retained by Yale to organize and evaluate it. Loren is a well known New York City musician who also periodically had managed Benny's New York office. His assignment was to identify and collate the recordings suitable for release. Greg is a talented sound engineer in whom Benny had a great deal of confidence. His assignment was to transfer the more vulnerable recordings to modern tape and to remaster and prepare the best material for release. I also put Dr. Samuel in touch with Jeff Nissim, a young recording executive and Goodman fan who heads the Musical Heritage Society in New Jersey, which issues classical and jazz recordings under the MusicMasters label. Jeff had produced what turned out to be Benny's last studio recording sessions in January, 1986 and was enthused about being a part of this new project.

While Benny was interested in seeing Yale realize recording revenues that would help the Goodman archive be self-sustaining, he had stipulated that any proposed releases would first have to be approved by the Goodman Estate. One of my responsibilities, therefore, has been to preview all of the recordings selected for release in order to satisfy myself that the music in all respects would meet Benny's personal standards. Your editing of the liner notes for accuracy and in checking the proposed releases against material already sold by Benny in order to keep the project out of copyright trouble also has been very important to its integrity. These collaborative efforts, I am delighted to say, have resulted to date in nine MusicMasters releases of priceless Goodman music, which otherwise might have been lost forever. There is ample material left, I am told, for at least several more albums.

The other major component of the bequest to Yale was the almost 2,000 jazz or classical arrangements Benny had accumulated throughout his unparalleled career. The precedent for this bequest had been the gift to Yale by Benny in 1985 of twenty-nine other arrangements (or "charts" as they sometimes are called, although Benny seldom used that term). During his lifetime he also had given a substantial number of jazz arrangements to the New York City Public Library at Lincoln Center. The music that remained in his possession was carefully stored in file cabinets in Benny's office on East 66th Street, and I was delighted to find that in most cases the original scores had been preserved and were filed with the parts for the individual instruments. It was exciting to find manuscripts written for Benny by arrangers like Fletcher Henderson, Jimmy Mundy, Mary Lou Williams, Eddie Sauter, Tommy Newsom, Ralph Burns and Mel Powell, just to mention a few. This unique collection of arrangements, which comprises almost a half century of jazz history, is documented in The Benny Goodman Papers (Yale University Music Library 1988), a provisional catalog published at the end of the first stage of compilation of the Goodman Archival Collection. In few other places is the history of orchestrated jazz so helpfully available to researchers and others.

I don't know how Benny's musical legacy to Yale could have been implemented and made available to the public so promptly and thoroughly without the data you tediously accumulated over the years from so many diverse sources. Legacy was the compass that kept all of us from going astray.

As you know, some of the most popular selections played by Benny Goodman throughout his career were compositions he had authored, either alone or in collaboration with such other musicians as Charlie Christian and Lionel Hampton. These include such jazz standards as "Stompin' at the Savoy", "Airmail Special", "Don't Be That Way" and "Flying Home". Benny had copyrighted approximately 175 of these compositions and many of them paid handsome royalties. It was important for the Estate to assemble and maintain an accurate list of these copyrights so that it can be satisfied that renewals are being attended to and that proper royalties are being received. Once again, Legacy has been useful to us in performing this responsibility.

Benny's files and other business records ultimately were removed to my law office in Morristown, New Jersey, from which the Estate has continued to operate at a busy pace for the past eight years - monitoring royalties; licensing Benny's compositions or recordings for television shows, movies or theatrical productions;

attending to copyright matters; restraining unauthorized uses of the Goodman name and so on. Having the opportunity to assist in this important work has been one of the most satisfying experiences of my professional career.

Benny Goodman was one of the most unusual and unforgettable people I ever have known. The affection and kindnesses he exhibited to Joan and to me are among the most precious memories we have. There were times that the pressures of Benny's life and his quest for musical perfection may have made him seem to others a difficult and complicated person. But who among us is never difficult nor complicated? The high visibility of extraordinarily gifted people often magnifies their faults, especially in the eyes of those who have no basis for understanding the burdens those gifts can entail.

Benny never asked anything of a musician he didn't demand of himself. I never heard him play a careless phrase or approach a piece of music with anything less than the determination he displayed at his historic Carnegie Hall concert in 1938. Is it any wonder that he was impatient with those who settled for less?

Shortly after Benny was laid to rest in Stamford, I made a visit to his grave site to see that everything was in order. I found there, resting against Benny's headstone, warped in the heat of the sun, a 78 rpm recording of "Good-bye", his famous closing theme. I don't know who put it there and I never tried to find out. Perhaps it was someone from his family. But I prefer to think of the gesture as an anonymous remembrance on behalf of all of us who owe so much to the artistry of Benny Goodman.

Sincerely yours,

William F. Hyland

PREFACE

This volume sums up discoveries and releases of those Benny Goodman studio and location recordings that have materialized since publication of the author's *Benny Goodman: Listen to His Legacy* (Scarecrow Press, Metuchen, New Jersey, 1988). In chronological order, its text in part references specific pages and dates in that book. Although of use per se, this work is better employed in conjunction with *Legacy*.

Keyed references to *Legacy* obviate repetition of certain of its categories and indexes; those for Format, various abbreviations, Transcriptions, label credits, and Performing Artists are redundant, and thus are eliminated. (Whenever appropriate, dates, locales, personnels, labels, catalog numbers, and the like are detailed herein.) A new Index of Tune Titles is included. New listings for Arrangements and for Films/Videotapes, plus a Necrology, are indexed. Departures from past practice include a Prologue, which bears on the author's 31-year relationship with Benny Goodman; a Memorabilia Price Guide; and a special section on Air Checks that are known to exist, but are as yet unissued. The latter are indexed separately.

As heretofore, the focus of this bio-discography is on new material. Authorized and unauthorized releases that do nothing more than clone prior issues are in large measure omitted, provided that their liner notes give correct discographical detail. When in error, they are cited in the text.

RUSS CONNOR
December 1995

PROLOGUE

I miss Benny Goodman, much more so now than in the months immediately after his death. Then, I was absorbed in completing *Benny Goodman: Listen To His Legacy* and was enmeshed in a law suit over another book about him. Thus, although daily involved in matters related to him, I had little time to reflect upon his physical absence from my life.

I do not miss Benny Goodman because of his music. I likely have more of it on record and tape than anyone, can listen to him play whenever I choose. And, eerily, I can hear him speak whenever I wish, via tapes of his interviews. I don't do that very often.

I do miss him because of the fun we had together, wholly apart from music. We'd visit the auto show at the Coliseum: "Gonna buy a Rolls, Benny?" "Nah, who'd spend that kind of money for an automobile? You'd have to be crazy." We'd take in an exhibit at MOMA: "You have to realize, Russ, it's like jazz, the artist is expressing what he feels." "Yeah, but jazz I can understand." We'd argue about politics, he the liberal, I the conservative. We'd discuss books, his preference for non-fiction, mine for English mysteries. He made a wine buff of me, failed to make me a fisherman. The economy, our daughters, personalities in and out of show biz, sports, whatever appealed at the moment, all came within our purview. He was my Jewish man of catholic interests.

In a few pages following I reminisce about our times together. I trust the reader may get from them a sense of what it was like to be around this multi-faceted man, known to so many for his music alone.

FIRST MEETING, FIRST BOOK

By midyear 1955 I'd roughed in the discographical content of *BG—Off The Record*. I had original releases of those records issued under Benny's name, and their manufacturers had supplied data about them that I had requested. I had also amassed perhaps 600 Columbia-related recordings, many issued under fictitious names. (Here I was guided by a waist-high stack of mimeographed recording sheets, embracing 18 labels once under Columbia's aegis. Each label's set listed matrices in numerical/chronological order, label credits, tune titles and catalog numbers. Extrapolating from definite Goodman sides, I'd then acquired those records sequential to, both preceding and following, the unmistakable Goodmans.) A treatise on the "Whoopee Makers" by Carl Kendziora, recommendations from collectors, and general discographies added another 400-odd discs on non-Columbia labels to the candidates for inclusion in my manuscript.

Of those 1,000 "possibles," Benny was unquestionably present on some. To my ear, his was not the clarinet on many others, and I eliminated them. But there remained a few dozen about which I was ambivalent. Too, my biographical data had gaps in them, and some "facts" were unsubstantiated. Since I meant **BGOTR** to be a pioneering effort that would offer a biographical continuum between recording sessions—for which I coined the word, "bio-discography"—I was determined that both aspects be equally accurate. Further, courtesy dictated that Benny should be made aware that a book about him was in work. Hopefully to resolve the records in question, optimistically to confirm and add to the biography, and to inform Benny about my book, it was essential that I meet with him.

To my surprise, his address and telephone number—200 East 66th Street, Templeton

8-5280—were in the Manhattan directory. (Surely, celebrities had unlisted telephones? No, he was a working musician, open to offers, needed to be readily accessible. Besides, I was to learn he was now his own booking agent.) I phoned, got his secretary, Muriel Zuckerman. I explained why it was necessary that I interview Benny. Impossible just now, she said, he's in Hollywood for "The Benny Goodman Story." But he was expected back the end of August; if I would call then, and if Mr. Goodman were agreeable, she'd set up an appointment.

I did, Benny would see me, and Muriel set the date. Wearing my best suit, a new tie emblazoned with musical instruments—but no clarinet—I took the Pennsy to New York, taxied to the Manhattan House. Security buzzed the apartment, escorted me to an elevator, hit the button for the 21st floor. I rang the bell of B-2101, and Muriel admitted me. Her next words were shocking: "I'm sorry, Mr. Connor, Mr. Goodman's not here. He went downtown to have his hair cut."

You mean . . .? "On no, no, he wants to meet with you. He'd like you to come to the lobby of the St. Regis, you can talk there. And by the way, will you do me a favor? He forgot his clarinet; will you take it to him?" With that she handed me a black leather case, silver-mounted and engraved "Benny Goodman," and ushered me out.

So there in my hot hands was one of the most prized artifacts of the Jazz Era. What to do? They knew my name, true, but not my address or even my telephone number; Muriel hadn't asked for either, and I'd not volunteered them. If I went to Penn Station instead of the St. Regis, got the train back to Philly, they'd have the devil of a time finding me and Benny's clarinet. I thought, the hell with the book, take the clarinet and get out of town. But conscience—or something—got the better of avarice, and I headed for the hotel.

Freshly barbered, he was seated on a sofa in the busy lobby, ignoring the stares of passersby who obviously recognized him. He seemed to exude an aura of "Don't!," so no one approached him. Proffering the case almost as if it were a gift, I said, "Mr. Goodman, Miss Zuckerman asked me to bring you your clarinet. I'm Russ Connor." "Oh yeah, thanks. You're the guy writing the book, right? Sit down; what do you want to know?"

So began my first *nino a mano* encounter with Benny Goodman. It was then about 10:30 on a sunny September morning. I outlined the scope of my book, and in so doing evidently convinced him of my sincerity of purpose and my knowledge of his recordings. He relaxed, answered my questions as best he could, even put forward some things I'd not thought of. As time went on some courageous souls interrupted our conversation to ask Benny for autographs, requests he impolitely rejected. Annoyed by the intrusions, he signaled the bell captain, told him we wanted to move into the dining room, which had not yet opened for lunch, so we could have some privacy. The captain obliged immediately, seated us, closed the door as he left.

At noon the room opened to the public. Patrons wedging past our table might have caught some eyebrow-raising earfuls, to mix a metaphor. Asked about this band leader or that sideman, Benny might explode, "Oh, that son of a bitch!," and go on in like language about the subject's lack of talent, greed, sexual peculiarities, whatever. Inside stuff, and I lapped it up. But in the back of my mind I realized I'd better not put it in the book.

Benny had told Muriel he'd give me a half hour or so; we'd already consumed two. Thinking I'd be long gone, he'd invited Urbie Green to lunch, to go over the initial Park Recording Co. session, a few days ahead. Urbie joined us, Benny introduced me, ordered for the three of us. They chatted for a few minutes about the upcoming session, then Benny returned to our conversation. Poor Urbie could do nothing but sit and listen. The meal over, Urbie left and Benny and I talked until almost 1:30. Then he said, "I've got to go; I didn't realize it was so late." He authorized my access to his files whenever I could get to New York, just let Muriel know when I was coming. And he had a question for me: "How come there's no clarinet on that tie?"

Thus ended my first meeting with Benny Goodman, productive beyond my fondest expectations. By not swiping his clarinet—he gave me one later, anyway—I'd not only gained a wealth of information for my book, but I'd begun what turned out to be a close relationship with him that endured until the day he died. For some unfathomable reason he had accepted me at face value, something he rarely did with anyone or anything.

Muriel, and Benny's good friends Hal Davis and Jim Maher, all told me later that they were astonished that Benny had discoursed on old times and old records for three hours. Unprecedented, in their experience; like other musicians, Benny's focus was ever forward, not back into the past.

Surprising as that was, however, each found another aspect of our meeting beyond belief: Benny had picked up the tab for lunch.

*

Over the next two years I searched through Benny's files as often as I could. To my chagrin I learned that written records of his activities prior to the 1950s had been trashed. What files remained were chaotic, took too many of my precious few hours to find what I sought. As often as not I had to rely on Muriel's memory for specifics of even near-term events.

Benny was helpful. He listened to my tapes of questionable recordings, confirmed or denied his participation. He interceded if I got no reply to an inquiry I'd made to a record company. If he was to rehearse or record, he OK'd my presence. His aide, Jay Finegold, was to send me details of sessions I was unable to attend, and Benny's itineraries monthly. If he had a luncheon or dinner date with a "fellow you should know," he took me along.

He sought my opinions. He was thinking of hiring Joe Williams for his 1958 European tour; did I like him? Sure, but: it was common gossip then that Joe, flushed with deserved success, was "difficult to work with." Too, he was demanding, and getting, top dollar. The thought of two such strong personalities inevitably clashing, with big bucks involved . . . no. But I didn't want to imply that Benny couldn't control Joe, nor that Benny was, uh, cheap. Instead: "How about Jimmy Rushing? The Europeans are more familiar with him, would be more receptive to someone they know." Turned out well, Jimmy was a hit, and from then on Benny had confidence in my suggestions.

From time to time Benny challenged me. He once interrupted his incessant practicing to tootle a few bars of a tune that was familiar, but whose title eluded me. "Hah! That's 'You Forgot Your Gloves'—it better be in your book, for I made a record of it." He had, of course, waxed that obscure pop tune a quarter-century earlier (it was in my manuscript). Later I realized I'd witnessed a rare event; he seldom named a tune, almost always hummed it. My opinion of his much maligned memory rose several degrees.

And he put me to work. I began to write the biographical/discographical outlines in his press kits, updated them periodically. His mail was rife with requests for autographed photos, information, reeds he had used, etc. He gave me a slew of 5×7 prints, boxes of his stationery (but no reeds), had Muriel mail me the inquiries. I answered the letters, signed them and the photos, "Benny Goodman." There are a lot of bogus Benny Goodman signatures out there . . .

My wife and I were invited to his private gatherings in New York and in Stamford. As Benny's guests—all expenses paid—we and our two daughters had ringside tables or orchestra seats, with clearance to go backstage, to all engagements near Philadelphia. Would we like to vacation in St. Martin? He would "take care of" the plane tickets. Because of job and family responsibilities, and our limited finances, we could accept only some of Benny's invitations. Sensitive to our circumstances, Benny once sent me a check for $2,500, with a note reading, "Here, take Georgia someplace nice." I xeroxed that check . . . before I cashed it.

To have attained such status with this very wary man so quickly surprised a lot of people, myself most of all. That I was writing a book about him was a factor, of course; it touched his ego. But I've come to believe in main my rank in his esteem was because I didn't take advantage of our friendship, seldom asked him for anything except information. In his experience, I was a novelty. And I kept it that way until 13 June 1986.

BG-Off The Record was a vanity publication; I was its author, editor, financier, publisher and sole sales agent. Except for the one ad in *DownBeat* that I could afford, there was no paid promotion. But press reviews were laudatory, got me onto local radio and television shows, and over time I disposed of all 2,000 copies. At Benny's insistence, the U.S. Department of State bought 200 to distribute during his tour of the USSR, and he paid list price for several dozen. He had one re-covered in red leather with gold leaf appliqué, inscribed it "with my unbounded thanks," gave it to me at a small ceremony in the Rainbow Grill.

The book sold for $4.95. Now it's a collector's item, commanding $75–$110 from book-search dealers. I probably lost money on it.

But it did trigger a personal highlight. Gene and I had had lunch, went together to the rehearsal for Revlon's "The Big Party." Jess and Lionel were already there, Benny was not. We set up Gene's Slingerlands, and he handed me the sticks: "I know you can play, sit in with these guys." I did, but with brushes, and it went not too badly. I was having a ball when Benny arrived, took one look, said, "Well! I see we've got a new drummer." Sort of half a "ray," and I got off Gene's throne immediately, knocking it over in my haste. Everybody laughed, but I didn't care; I felt that now I was really in.

BOOK II, FINANCIAL ADVISOR

Benny kept busy, new releases appeared, collectors inundated me with questions, and I was soon at work on a second bio-discography. If and when, I was determined someone else would publish it. Contacts with Benny accelerated, my opinions again were sought. What did I think of Bobby Hackett? Loved him; good thing, too, for Benny had decided to give him a year's contract at $1,000 per week. Would I suggest some tunes the Quartet might record? I gave him a list of tunes they'd never cut, even included "High Society." Not the Quartet's bag, possibly, but I wanted to hear what Benny would do with that clarinet test piece. Suggestions accepted? None.

But I continued to bug Benny about his repertoire; I'd had enough of the same old tunes. Well, maybe; he had been considering some of the things Bix used to play, thought he might try them. And oh, yes, "Kansas City Kitty," that's one he'd like to sing. I made him some tapes of Bix's classics, with his groups and Frank Trumbauer's, tacked on the Original Memphis Five's "Kitty," Dick Robertson on vocal, Jimmy Dorsey on clarinet. Never adapted any of them to his own use.

Another angle: How about releasing some of the sides he'd made for Park Recording, material he owned outright? For example, the "Hawaiian sessions," not the greatest but some good McGarity and Sims. Nope, didn't like the tunes. Slight tangent: How about air checks? I had a flawless dupe of Swiss Radio's master tape of the marvelous 1959 Basel concert, surely that would raise those expressive eyebrows of his. Instead it raised his hackles, for I kept enthusing about how well he'd played ". . . with Red Norvo's group." Not interested. And, "That was MY band, and don't you ever forget it!"

However, my role as consultant entered a new dimension. I'd gone to work for the Federal Reserve Bank of Philadelphia, among other duties writing analyses of banking and business conditions for the bank's publications. Eventually I became a vice president, and Benny was impressed. More, as an investor (he had a $250,000 account with a Wall Street broker) he saw me as an insider who would know which way the Fed was pushing interest rates, which affected the stock market. True, I did attend the bank's board meetings, often wrote their minutes. But I was pledged not to reveal them, and I never did. Besides, local Feds don't set discount rates; they act when the Board of Governors "suggests" that they maintain, raise or lower them.

In fact, I had nothing at all to do with monetary policy deliberations. A new bank building was planned, and I became officer in charge of the $60 million project. Because I'd risen in Benny's esteem as a banker, I saw no reason to disabuse his mistaken concept of my job. To prepare for his frequent inquiries, I scanned the market news in the *New York Times* and the *Wall Street Journal* first thing every morning. When he called, I simply parroted their forecasts; when he read his copies of those papers, saw that they and I "agreed," he had to think, "Russ sure knows what he's talking about."

I had a vexing problem with installation and trial runs of the new building's extractor pumps, which were to deliver the bank's waste to the city's sewers. The same morning that my engineers informed me that they thought they'd solved the problem, Benny phoned. I hadn't had time to prep myself with the financial news, so—thinking of the now open waste conduits—I told him, "Well, Benny, today things seem to be going down the drain." I've wondered ever since just how much that piece of advice may have cost him.

To save publisher Arlington House the cost of composition, I typed *BG-On The Record* on camera-ready stock. Three different IBM type elements distinguished among biography, authorized releases, and—my innovation—air checks, first time such recordings appeared in a discography. Warren Hicks was inestimably helpful: he supplemented my research, edited my typescript, compiled the indexes. For these contributions he asked only to be named co-author. I got all the royalties . . . what there were of them.

The new book was published on Benny's birthday, 30 May 1969. Promoted by Arlington and critically praised, it was an early success, sold some 4,500 copies its first year. Benny was my unpaid press agent, boosting it on radio and TV talk shows, only "incidentally" publicizing his upcoming bookings.

First of two questions often asked about the book is, how many editions are there? Answer, one. Arlington eventually sold the rights to it, and some successor firms, plural, advertised their clones as a "new edition." Not so, content never changed. Multiple printings, yes. New editions, no.

The second is, how many copies were sold? At a guess, something between 18,000–20,000. Once *BGOTR-II* was out of Arlington's shop, it became impossible to get a count. Latter-day publishers ignored requests for sales statements, let alone royalty payments. Despite cease-and-desist orders from my attorneys, reprints were still being peddled into the 1990s. Clues to an Arlington "original," so to speak, are a dark blue (not black) cover, and the $10 price on the jacket.

In 1986, legal action caused all rights in the book to revert to me.

BG ALTERNATES, ARGUMENTS

In the 1970s, Sunbeam and other bootlegs began to fill up the bins in record shops, crowding out the few authorized LPs that paid Benny royalties. To decide whether Sunbeam could be sued successfully, I met with Benny, John Hammond, and a lawyer from the New York State Attorney General's office in Columbia's "Black Rock." A strategy similar to that of Glenn Miller's estate evolved, and John called in Columbia's legal eagles. It took them not 10 minutes to nix proceeding: no Federal law addressing record pirating existed, suit would have to be brought in California, Sunbeam's base, and that meant engaging local counsel; and chances of collecting damages sufficient to compensate for time, effort and money spent, seemed iffy at best.

In view of this experience, would Benny sanction releases by other than the major companies with which he regularly dealt? I had many hours' worth of unissued studio recordings and air checks from Benny's heyday, in my opinion some exciting music. I thought he might let me issue it, were I to do so legitimately.

I made him a proposal: He would get five percent of the retail price of every record sold. An agreement would be reached with any affected producer. Composers' royalties would be paid through the Fox Agency. Musicians' royalties would be processed through Local 802, AFofM, New York. Under these conditions Benny approved and introduced me to the treasurer of Local 802. There, after months of in-person, mail and telephone negotiations, I was stopped cold. The union insisted upon current scale for recordings made decades earlier. My cost estimates could accommodate the rates that obtained in the late '30s and early '40s, but not those current in the '70s. I argued that they would kill my project, and wouldn't it be better if the musicians, or their estates, got something rather than nothing? I lost that argument, as have many others.

A few years later my dormant project was revived by Stockholm's Anders Ohman, attorney, hobbyist producer of classical recordings, nonprofessional clarinetist who much admired Benny. Columbia's corporate affairs in Sweden were then in a state of flux. Anders led the team from his firm that was sorting them out, and he was on top of Swedish law governing recordings. Those statutes held records 25 or more years old to be in the public domain; thus he could issue my material legitimately, absent consent from any producer, and without payments to musicians. He believed eliminating those costs made the project feasible. I told Benny of this development, arranged a meeting between him and Anders in New York. They met, Anders assured Benny that he would be paid promptly, and that all composers' royalty requirements would be satisfied. Benny finally said OK, but: He wanted no royalties, and indeed wanted no association with the project.

Over time, a dozen Phontastic "The Alternate Goodman" LPs were issued. Production costs were higher than anticipated, distribution was spotty, sales were modest, and Anders just about broke even—when he could collect moneys due him. But he was esthetically pleased with his product, and collectors told me that they appreciated the releases. There was no word from Benny.

No word, that is, until the second week in September 1981. The first week, Benny was in Copenhagen for a night club gig. A fan brought the six "Alternate" LPs that had been issued by then to the club, asked Benny to autograph them. He erupted: "Six LPs! What in the hell is that Swede, and Connor, doing? I never expected anything like this!" He didn't call me long-distance, but he did immediately upon his return to New York. He was burning, reamed me but good. When he paused for breath, I tried to remind him that he'd agreed to the project, that they were legitimate releases, that he had refused our offer of royalties. That argument was rejected out of hand, he slammed down the phone, and I didn't hear from him again for months.

That was our only serious argument during our 31-year relationship. I regret that I caused it; and Benny, wherever you are, I'm sorry. But you did say OK.

BENNY BADMAN

I got mad at Benny, too. For instance—

Benny's tapes were in rental storage at 50th and Broadway; the building had new owners, and he lost his lease. He, Muriel and I went there to take inventory, found total disarray, eventually gave up. Benny groused because he'd wasted half a day. While I stood in pouring rain to hail a cab, he and Muriel stayed in the doorway. False alarms, they'd run into the street, get as wet as I was. Benny's blood pressure rose. Success at last, we taxied to his apartment. I outfumbled Benny for the fare, his ill humor peaked. He pulled out a couple of dollars, dug for a handful of coins . . . then tossed the lot onto the front seat, ignoring the cabbie's outstretched palm. Shouting, "Who the hell do you think you are, Mr. Big Shot!", this massive driver got out, started after Benny. The doorman got between them, and I hustled a resistant Benny into the foyer, Muriel leading the way. "Yo, Benny . . .," I shook my head in disgust. He just smiled. With satisfaction.

In the late '70s, early '80s, Benny fired Muriel more than once, at times for just cause; deteriorating health affected her work, she made mistakes, some of them costly. I would intercede, remind Benny of Muriel's long faithful service. So I wasn't surprised when she called one day in tears; he'd canned her again, she didn't know why, he'd given her no explanation. I phoned Benny, and he told me what had happened. He owned a rundown bungalow on a small but valuable lot near his Stamford home. In lieu of a pension, he had promised the property to Muriel when she retired. I was aware of this, knew that, anticipating the future, she sometimes let friends stay in the cottage. Benny didn't object until . . . He had as house guests a relative and her "companion." Increasingly annoyed with them— "They're the only ones now using the pool, and they're too damned lazy to clean it!"—he told them to get out. Broke, with nowhere to go, they appealed to Muriel. Sure, no problem, use my place. Benny eventually found out; incensed, he told Muriel she was through, but didn't tell her why. I remonstrated with him, told him that this time he was entirely in the wrong. He did rehire Muriel but never forgave her.

It was obvious that Benny needed someone to backstop Muriel, so I induced him to hire Loren Schoenberg. I had "known" him since he was 10, when he wrote me of his admiration for Benny and his ambition to become a professional musician. I kept track of his progress—constant study, proficiency as a saxophonist, a budding arranger. He would be ideal for Benny, who'd never had an office assistant who knew music. But perhaps Loren's eager display of that knowledge irritated Benny for, as with Muriel, he fired Loren several times, and I would intercede. Once, in my presence, he flayed Loren, among other things told him he knew nothing about music. Loren fled, and I braced Benny: come on, the kid does know music, and you know he knows it. Besides, if you must criticize him, do so privately. "Well, I want him out of here. If I give him hell while you're here, maybe he'll quit, and I won't have to fire him." Yes, I thought, and also not have to give him severance pay, nor get hit by the state for unemployment comp. But even my courage had limits, and those thoughts remained unspoken.

In the end, Benny prevailed. His last big band was really Loren's, who had organized it, led it, got it what few jobs he could for several years before Benny took over. After the 7 October 1985 Marriott Marquis TV'er, an exhausted Benny rested in his dressing room, admitted no one, then left the hotel for a private dinner party. With Benny unavailable, the media turned to Loren, duly reported his comments. The next day Benny read the papers . . . and fired Loren for the last time. Yo, Benny . . .

BENNY POORMAN

There were many times that I pitied Benny, no matter his talent, fame, wealth and assured rank in history. Too often was I with him when pain almost overwhelmed his iron resolve to ignore it. One occasion that's etched in my memory is a black August night in the seventies, on the muddy fairgrounds at Stanhope, New Jersey. Although still summer, sheets of rain driven by a cold wind made me glad of my lined raincoat, sorry I'd not worn boots. I found Benny in a heated trailer a half hour before the concert, twisting and turning in a futile effort to relieve his aching back. "It was pure hell riding down here, I just couldn't get comfortable, took forever because of the rain, and now I've gotta play in a God-damned tent." Cut it short, I advised, go home early. But no, he played for an hour and a half, and the audience never realized how much he was suffering. When the concert was over—no encores—he exited quickly through the rear of the flapping tent. I left through the entrance, circled around back to see how he was holding up. He was nowhere in sight but Muriel was, motioned me to follow her into a small tent nearby. There he was, bent double on a low stool, half hidden in an overcoat, his arms wrapped around his chest. "Russ, do you have any Demerol, anything like that?" For personal reasons I did carry some phenobarbital tablets. I shook a few out of the vial, told him to take one, it might help, it couldn't hurt. He sat up, grabbed three or four, chewed and swallowed those bitter pills with nothing to wash them down. Saying nothing, he weakly waved his thanks, shrank back into the fetal position. Knowing that those sedatives would do little for his condition, frustrated because I had nothing better to offer this man who'd become a large part of my life, I left without another word.

Once, in Philadelphia, I didn't feel sorry for Benny at all, for his pain was self-inflicted. He came to town before noon in March 1974 for an evening concert. Sol Schoenbach, an old friend who'd performed with Benny in the early thirties, took Benny and me to lunch at the Famous Deli, Fifth and South, notorious for its highly spiced Jewish cuisine. Sol, who then headed the Settlement Music House, was a regular customer and was warmly welcomed. Benny's presence caused a sensation, and the management urged the three of us to sample just about everything on the menu. (I settled for an omelet, to everyone's derision.) When the feast was over, the management invited Benny and Sol—but not me—back for dinner, and they enthusiastically accepted. Thus I wasn't the least bit surprised when I visited Benny backstage an hour before the 8:00 P.M. start. There he was, lying flat on the floor, bloated with gas, gulping air and squeezing his belly, trying desperately to belch. Did I have any Tums, anything like that? No, I did not. "I know," burped Benny, turning to his aide Jeff Wilson, "Zoot always has a bottle of Scotch. Ask him for a glassful for me." Leaving the door to Benny's dressing room open, Jeff crossed the narrow passageway to a smaller room where Zoot was "preparing" for the concert. Clearly audible to us, Jeff said, "Mr. Sims, Mr. Goodman would like a glass of your whiskey." Equally distinct was Zoot's reply: "Tell him to go fuck himself, get his own bottle!" Benny just looked up at me, shrugged whatta ya gonna do? The concert was a little late in getting started.

CAN'T KEEP A GOODMAN DOWN

Events in the years bridging the late seventies, early eighties, disheartened Benny, daunted his customary optimistic outlook. They began with the deplorable 40th Anniversary concert. They would not end until he recovered from heart surgery.

I fault Benny for the failed concert, a commercial success but an artistic flop. In the months preceding it, he came to realize that, despite his disclaimers, it would be compared with his 1938 triumph; he knew full well he could not come close to that. Seeking to escape accountability for the disparity, he distanced himself from the concert. He holed up in his island retreat, let a sideman acquaint pickup personnel with new charts and each other. Understanding, however, that it would be his reputation under scrutiny, he returned to New York in time for frantic rehearsals just three days before the curtain went up. Too little and too late, his belated effort could not salvage the concert.

It almost did. The first half was concisely structured, satisfactorily paced. Relieved, I said to myself, "By God, he's going to pull it off!" But he did not, could not, and the second half deteriorated progressively. Gaps between performances grew in frequency and length; the audience began to decamp. Backstage, recording engineers were distraught: "Come on, Benny, get on with it; we're running out of tape!" Finally, *Good-Bye,* and the ordeal was over. Later, he asked me, "Well, what do you think?" I knew how to play that game: "Well, Benny, what do YOU think?" He merely shrugged, and so did I.

The critics' scathing reviews adversely affected sales of the London album, further jolting Benny; he'd hoped it would be the hit release he'd not had in years. Thus began the winter of his discontent.

Eighteen days after the disappointing concert, Benny suffered a truly crushing blow: Alice died. Benny was devastated. Not only had he lost a loving wife and gentlewomanly companion of nearly 36 years, the mother of his children, but no longer could he turn to her for the incisive candor, sage counsel, and unfailing support that no one else could give him. I commiserated with him the day after Alice was cremated. I think it was the only time I ever saw him near tears.

Insignificant in light of Alice's demise, the pictorial biography, *Benny—King Of Swing* (William Morrow & Co., 1979), nevertheless added to Benny's malaise. Although a critic found it to have been "hastily patched together," in one sense it'd been in work a decade earlier when Benny was given a $10,000 advance for a new life history. Two writers recommended to him submitted outlines; Benny rejected both. Was I interested? No. The project lay dormant until Stanley Baron suggested a different approach: Let photographs tell your story, keep the text to a minimum, eliminate that problem. Benny liked the idea, and an appeal to the public brought in a torrent of photos. Added to Benny's stock, Benny, Stan and I had about 5,000 from which to choose. Simultaneously, Stan commissioned an English author to produce a modest text. We all thought it trite, unsuitable; I found it rife with errors. I corrected the mistakes, Stan rewrote the text. The pictures were fine, but not even Stan's efforts could resuscitate the words. (The Englishman sued Stan for altering his copy!) As a result the book got short shrift from the critics, sold poorly, was soon remaindered, and Benny had another loser. Ossa upon Pelion.

Benny had worked infrequently in the five months prior to the 1978 Carnegie fiasco. Seeking solace in music after Alice's demise, he let it be known he was open to offers. They poured in from promoters who knew Benny's concerts were sellouts. He accepted many, booked more classical dates than in the past; guest appearances eliminated the many hassles attendant assembling his own groups, and he felt that the classics would challenge him as jazz now did not. His sidemen, although excellent musicians, seldom inspired him, it was usually the other way 'round. There were times when the jazz came alive, but they were too few to dispel his dolor.

His associates through the years say Benny rarely, if ever, drank to excess, certainly not on the job. Socially, in my experience, he never did. A Scotch now and then, a cognac, but his preference was fine wine, and he delighted in introducing his friends to the great chateaux. (At dinner one evening at his Century Club, Benny recommended a vintage Bordeaux to Jim Maher and me. We opted instead for a sweet sherry, Harvey's Bristol Cream. He was disgusted with both of us.) But on occasion in 1980 he did drink too much—while performing. For instance, his guest shot on "The Tonight Show" in January, and a Jazz Festival, Boston, in March. (He told me later he'd never been so drunk in his life as he was that night in Beantown. To hide his condition, he turned over the bulk of the concert to the vocal group, Rare Silk, who exhausted their repertoire to fill the engagement.) Undoubtedly, mental and physical anguish—loneliness because of Alice's demise, incessant sciatic pain—were factors in his intemperance. But there was another: he found little joy in jazz, "just knew" he would not play well. That's "would," understand, not "could"; there's a difference.

Perceiving that a full schedule alleviated neither his solitude nor his pain, Benny tapered off in 1981, curbed his itinerary still more in 1982—until its end, another down year for him. He had hoped performers he introduced—e.g., the guitarist Cal Collins, the vocalists Debi Craig, Rare Silk—would become stars, and that he'd be credited for their discovery. None made it. Heeding the opinions of his office aides (Loren Schoenberg in '82, the nonmusician Wendy Chamberlain in '83), Benny transferred random tracks from tapes he owned to cassettes, personally tried to sell them to major, then lesser, record companies. All turned him down. I realized the full measure of his loneliness one morning in May '82, the day after his concert in Philadelphia's Academy of Music. It was a date he tried to cancel—something he often did in those days. But since I'd been involved in the negotiations, I cajoled him into appearing, reminding him that it was for a charity. We had a late snack in the Ritz-Carlton, he went to his room, and I assumed he'd return to New York with some of his sidemen on the morrow. But that morning he called my office: could I "give him a hand," get him to the train station? I requisitioned a bank car and a driver, picked Benny up at the hotel. We carried his case and a heavy valise to the car, then into the station and down an escalator to the platform. There we were stopped; only Metroliner ticket holders could proceed, and we gave Benny his luggage. Stoop-shouldered because of their weight, all alone, he shuffled slowly to the marked arrival point, and I thought to myself: "Is this what the King of Swing has come to?" It hit me pretty hard.

Word got around about Benny's attempts to wriggle out of contracts, so promoters shied away from seeking his services. Since he'd decided to work less, that didn't bother him, he was confident he could always get jobs he wanted. But fewer dates made it harder to hire sidemen he preferred, for they sought regular employment elsewhere. Besides, they'd all heard that Benny was more "difficult" than ever, and some made excuses to refuse his offers. One was more forthright: Benny especially liked to work with Zoot Sims, who he felt inspired him to play better. Contacted for a series of Kool Jazz concerts, Zoot exploded, "Is he there? No? Well, you tell him for me that I don't want to work for him, I don't EVER want to work for him!", and slammed down his receiver.

I don't know what Benny had done to Zoot to cause such animosity. But I do know the source of friction between Benny and Teddy Wilson at the Kool Jazz Festival, June 1982. That began a decade earlier, when producers of the Timex TV'er insisted Benny hire Teddy, who consequently demanded, and got, $10,000 from Benny, many times his usual pay, then showed up drunk for the dress rehearsal. Benny never forgave nor forgot, hired Teddy from then on only when it was unavoidable, overtly ignored him at Kool Jazz. Nor did Lionel Hampton escape Benny's ill humor at Kool Jazz. Lionel had been performing regularly, was in good form, drew the audience's plaudits the first show. Backstage between shows, he also commanded the media's attention. Neglected, Benny did his best—worst?—to disrupt the Hamp's interviews, mugged, waved his arms in the background, as the TV cameras tried to focus on Lionel. It was awful. Appalled at his behavior, I told Benny no, I would not stay for the second show, went home.

Benny's deportment didn't improve during what would prove to be his final overseas tour, July 1982. He would disappear, telling no one where he was going; promoters called his New York office, frantically seeking his whereabouts, asking, is he going to show up? He cancelled one concert, gave no explanation. By phone, he fired Muriel Zuckerman and Loren Schoenberg . . . again. He sniped at his sidemen continually, alienating each in turn. But one of them got even, sort of: Benny always assigned someone to carry his clarinet case. The task usually fell to the pianist, who had no instrument of his own to tote. Determined not to be Benny's caddy this time, John Bunch took along a second suitcase, empty, demonstrated he just couldn't manage the Buffet, sorry.

Two events late in 1982 brought about a sea change in Benny's attitude and conduct. He had gotten other awards earlier in the year, but national recognition at Kennedy Center, Washington, in December made an impression on him. More importantly, about a month earlier, he'd met and begun a relationship with Carol Phillips, CEO of an affiliate of Estee Lauder, Clinique. (She provided Benny with samples of those cosmetics, which he providently gave as Christmas gifts one year!) Bright, attractive—"and she's a good dancer, too"—Miss Phillips merits much of the credit for making Benny's few remaining years happy ones.

First half of the eighties was traumatic for me, too. During my last years at the Fed—I took early retirement in '84—I'd begun my third Goodman bio-discography. Intent upon having it in print while Benny was still with us, I accepted the first offer made to me from one Eugene Frank, a publisher whose catalog included some music-related books. His associate was a commercial bank officer, and in retrospect I think that's what convinced me to sign on with Frank, despite Gene Goodman's warning that Frank had an unsavory reputation around New York.

I fed Frank the beginning chapters while I finished the manuscript. Our agreement was that Frank would typeset my copy when received, forward it to me for final approval. His first sending told me I was in trouble, for the typeset was incredibly bad. Whole paragraphs were missing; others were transposed out of context. Wrong fonts made it impossible to distinguish studio recordings from air checks. Material not mine was randomly inserted. Misspellings and other typos were in almost every line. Alarmed, I phoned, then sent registered letters, telling Frank he'd nullified our agreement; there was no response. When I learned Frank was going to publish the book on his own, Bill Hyland, Benny's attorney, told Frank to cease and desist via registered mail and courier deliveries. Ignoring all, Frank published the atrocity in 1984, and we were off to court.

The battle lasted almost two years, cost me some $35,000 out-of-pocket for five law firms acting in my behalf in hearings before the American Arbitration Association, the Superior Court in New Jersey, and the Supreme Court in New York. Benny was supportive throughout, deposed for me, offered to lend me whatever I needed to carry on. (He also had an alternative suggestion: "Y' know, Russ, it'd be a helluva lot cheaper to have him knocked off, probably for less than a thousand." I think he was only half kidding.) We prevailed in all venues. Among other considerations: Copyright reverted to me. All copies were to be destroyed, neither advertised nor sold (Frank had been seen peddling the book out of a supermarket cart on Broadway). I was awarded $60,000 in damages.

But I never collected a dime; Frank conveniently died of a heart attack, and his estate was bankrupt. In notifying me of Frank's death, record dealer/collector/friend Artie Zimmerman wrote, "And no one came forward to claim his body." Didn't surprise me a bit.

My wife and I visited Benny in October 1983, and it was manifest that the year had been a good one for him. He was upbeat, gracious, solicitous, "a real charmer," as Georgia put it. We had lunch at Oscar's, who usually catered Benny's parties. We went to a shoemaker, Benny carrying a paper bag containing shoes he wanted resoled. We shopped at a florist's for a bouquet for Wendy Chamberlain: "She's been a great help to me." Georgia left to do her own thing, and Benny and I strolled back to the apartment for some small talk. He hadn't been working much, so I asked him how things shaped up for the rest of year. His answer surprised me, for he rarely spoke of his ailments. Well, his back was giving him hell, a knee hurt, but what really troubled him were his fingers. For some reason, probably arthritis, they just wouldn't move fast enough over the clarinet, he might have to cancel some dates. Maybe he'd consult a different doctor; whatever, he'd work through it, not to worry. I left, reassured, pleased that he was in such good spirits.

Thus I was stunned when Wendy called just before Thanksgiving. "Benny's sick, real sick, it's his heart, he's in the hospital. He wants you to know, but you're not to tell anyone else." I told Georgia, of course, and we both asked ourselves the unanswerable, why is this happening to Benny now, just when things have turned around for him? Despite progress reports from Wendy, we worried until mid-December, when Benny called. To aid his recovery, he was staying with his good friend Dr. Localio and his wife at their farm in Massachusetts. First, he wanted to know how *we* were — imagine! — and then he described his operation and confinement in considerable detail. Finally, "But I made it, I'm OK. I hope to see you after the first of the year." We enjoyed Christmas 1983 more than we had hoped we would.

WRAPPIN' IT UP

When my retirement became effective, Benny asked me to come to work for him. It was a generous offer, good salary, expenses, live in the apartment. And a kind and thoughtful one, too, for he knew my legal fees were skyrocketing, and I could use the money. But I said no: "Benny, we've been friends for a long time, and I won't jeopardize our relationship. I'm as used to being a boss as you, and I'm just as stubborn as you. There'd come a time when we'd disagree, and neither of us would give in. Then what, a big hassle, and all the years of our friendship down the tubes? No, let's keep things as they have been. I'll come to New York whenever you need me, do what I can to help, but thanks anyway."

And I did. Once again, I was his "financial advisor": Alice's will had set up trust funds for Rachel and Benjie with Benny as executor. Should he release the funds to them now or retain control until they attained the ages specified, his choice? Do it now, they're both big girls. How about mortgaging the house in Stamford, put the proceeds into stocks, the head of MCA told him the market's going to hit 2,000? No, too risky; speculation's for youngsters, safety's for us, CDs are paying double digit interest. (This was the early '80s, remember.)

I tried to put his files in order, catalog his tapes in the apartment (most were at Stamford), with minimal success. I took phone calls from people he didn't want to speak with, answered some of his correspondence, again forging his signature. I updated his press kit, which precipitated our only argument (Legacy, page 307). I prepared the provenance transmittals for arrangements he donated to the New York Public Library. And I wrote speeches for him. (One that he delivered before the Chicago Historical Society was kind of cute, got him some national publicity.) In sum, I was his "Russ-of-all-trades," did what had to be done.

In these last few years, Benny was introspective, more so than I'd ever known him to be in the past. He was not nostalgic about his successes, although we did reminisce about his 1937–38 band, in his view, "The best; we did things no one else could. Why, we used to laugh about Fletcher's band, playing the same arrangements he'd made for us. There was no comparison." I said I envied him, fronting that band, listening to it night after night. That puzzled him: "Well, no, I wasn't a spectator, you know. Leading a band's hard work, you don't stand around admiring what you're doing. Some nights, when that band just exploded, I'd think, 'My God, where did that come from!' But most of the time I didn't reflect on how good they were, because it's what I expected of them."

Benny was well content with his life and career, expressed but few regrets. He was ever sorry that his father had not lived to see his sons fulfill the ambitions he had had for them. He was fairly bitter about Alice's mother squandering much of the family fortune on a religious sect, decimating the inheritances that eventually would go to her grandchildren. And he deplored the now insignificant role of the clarinet in popular music, its small voice ineffectual, and so dispensed with, in groups comprised mainly of amplified rhythm instruments.

For the first time ever in my experience, and a dire signal to me, Benny mused about his future place in history. He dismissed the honorary degrees conferred upon him, the uncounted awards he'd received; who would remember them, when he could not? Benny, your music will be your monument. No, tastes change, music's ephemeral, he wanted something physical, permanent. He knew what it should be, and it was denied to him: "That Avery Fisher Hall in Lincoln Center, that should have been named after me. I did a lot for Lincoln and the Library (the Center's part of the New York Public Library), and I deserved it. But Fisher gave them $10 million, and I can't compete with that. I spoke with Alice Tully about it (there's also an Alice Tully facility at the Center), and she said money's the answer. The hell with it."

That was a huge disappointment for Benny, and it's why he stopped donating his arrangements to the Library, began to give them to, then willed them to, Yale University. His Archives there is his tangible memorial, but hey, I for one think his music may outlast it.

During one of my last visits, I asked Benny something I'd long thought about, the wellspring of improvisation: "Benny, take a tune like 'After You've Gone,' one I've heard you play hundreds of times. Your solos are never exactly the same, but usually there's a pattern to them, and I can anticipate what you'll play next." Raised eyebrow: "You can? I can't." "Ah, that's just it. Every now and then you'll rip off a chorus unlike anything I've heard you do before. What flashes through your mind to make you play that particular combination of notes?" He sat silent for some time, obviously searching for an answer. "You know, I don't know. I'm not aware of thinking about what I'm going to play. Or if I do actually think about it, it's so fast that I'm not conscious of it. I just play, and what happens, happens."

Until some behavioral psychologist comes up with a scientific explanation for the *fons et origo* of improvisation, I have one word for it: Genius.

And with that, "Good-Bye," Benny Genius.

BENNY GOODMAN, 1910–1949

15 April 1910, Cook County, IL

Genealogical research by collector George Blau reveals the status of the David Goodman family on 15 April 1910, the date of the decennial census of Cook County, Illinois. On that day the Goodmans were living in a rented flat at 1342 Washbourne Avenue, Chicago. The only other tenants of those premises was the family of Simeon Potowsky.

In addition to the address cited above, the census data are:

David Goodman, age 36 (born c. 1874). Born Russian Yiddish. Occupation: operator-pants. Cannot read or write. Immigrated 1892, married 13 years (c. 1897).
Dora Goodman, age 36 (born c. 1874). Born Russian Yiddish. Immigrated 1892.
Lena Goodman, age 12. Born Maryland.
Louis Goodman, age 11. Born Maryland.
Morris Goodman, age 9. Born Maryland.
Ida Goodman, age 8. Born Illinois.
Effie Goodman, age 6. Born Illinois.
Harry Goodman, age 3. Born Illinois.
Fred Goodman, age 2. Born Illinois.
Bennie Goodman, age 10 months. Born Illinois.

*

Census content consists of responses to questions put by interviewers, who usually accept the answers without further attempt at verification. Information proffered may not always be factual; memory may be faulty, or, for whatever reason, responses may be falsified deliberately. But if these—verbatim—census data are accurate, they revise and add to published intelligence about Benny, his parents, and his brothers and sisters. They specify the years when his parents were born, when they came to the United States, and when they married; and by interpolation, when they moved from Baltimore to Chicago. They tell us sister Ethel was called "Effie" at home, and that the youngest son's name was given as, "Bennie," a spelling he came to detest.

According to Eugene (Gene) Goodman, his mother's maiden name was, Grunzinski. He believes his father's name was originally "Guttman," for two reasons: Gene has searched the scrolls at Ellis Island, New York's port of entry for immigrants, for a "David Goodman," without success; and a branch of the family, living in South America, spells the name, "Guttman."

Obviously not named in this census are Irving, born in 1914; Gene, born in 1916; and the last of the Goodman children, Jerome, born in 1923, all in Chicago.

Also unnamed is sister Mary, about whom Benny says in his autobiography, ". . . the youngest girl, Mary, who was born just before me. I was still very young when she had an accident that resulted in a tumor of the brain. She died at seven, so I don't remember much about her" (*The Kingdom Of Swing,* Stackpole Sons, 1939, page 16). Was the omission of her name an oversight? Or is Benny's recollection wrong? According to Ida, still feisty and still living in Chicago, Benny is mistaken. Ida is adamant that the ill-fated Mary was born a year after Benny.

15 February 1927, Chicago

On this date a formal Benjamin Goodman entered into a contract with Melrose Bros. Music Co., Inc., for publication of his ". . . one book of one-hundred or more saxophone and clarinet breaks." As compensation, our Benjamin was to be paid royalties of ". . . Five Cents for each copy sold . . . at wholesale, and actually paid for by the purchaser . . . and No % of all moneys received by (Melrose) from or on account of the use of such composition."

Almost two years later—8 February 1929—Glenn Miller and Bennie Goodman were treated a bit more generously by the Melrose Bros. A new contract for their composition **Room 1411** promised each of them ". . . .01¢ cents for each sheet music copy of piano arrangement of the composition sold (and paid for) . . . and 16½% of all moneys received (by Melrose) . . . for mechanical reproduction (principally as) piano player word rolls."

These were prosperous times, remember, pre-Depression, and everybody was getting rich . . . but not off the Bros. Any wonder, then, that Benny was, uh, frugal in later years when he signed on his sidemen? Frank Melrose had taught him well.

26 April 1928, New York (ref: page 3)

Liner notes for the CD, RcaBB 3136-2-RB err in respect take 4, matrix BVE 43540, **Singapore Sorrows.** Take 4 is from this date, not 6 April 1928.

15 October 1928, New York (ref: page 4)

Liner notes for the CD, RcaBB 3136-2-RB err in respect take 3, matrix BVE 47742, **Buy, Buy For Baby (Or Baby Will Bye Bye You).** Take 3 is from this date, not 1 October 1928.

Typo: Correct first issue for matrix BVE 47743 to, VI 21743 A.

3 December 1928, New York (ref: page 5)

Typo: Correct first issue for matrix BVE 49220 to, VI 21827 B.

26 December 1928, New York (ref: page 6)

An experienced collector continues to insist that take C, matrix 3588, **Let Me Be Alone With You,** is issued on CA 9045, as by The Lumberjacks. Despite repeated comparisons of this claimed alternate to the certain take B, the author and other of his associates fail to discern any difference between the two.

14 January 1929, New York (ref: page 7)

An English LP, RETRIEVAL FJ-122, offers a non-vocal take of the Hotsy Totsy Gang's **Futuristic Rhythm,** transferred from a test pressing. (To date, this non-vocal version has not surfaced on the BrF/BrG A-8149 issues.) Revise the listing in Legacy to include it:

HOTSY TOTSY GANG   14 January 1929, New York

Personnel as per Legacy.

E 29064	BR 4200, et al (clt solo)
	Futuristic Rhythm - voc (Smith Ballew)
E 29064-G	**LP:** RETRIEVAL FJ-122 (clt solo)
	Futuristic Rhythm (no voc)

8 February 1929, New York (ref: page 8)
   Legacy errs in attributing the LP, BIO 1, to the three tunes recorded this date. Instead, credit the LP to the same three tunes on the Mills session of March 1929, pages 8 and 9, q.v.

5 March 1929, New York (ref: page 8)
   Liner notes for the CD, RcaBB 9986-2-RB, incorrectly list take 2 for **My Kinda Love;** take is -3.

9 May 1929, New York (ref: page 9)
   Good audio-quality transfers of **Companionate Blues, Campus Crawl** and **Wild And Wooly Willy** are on the English LP, RETRIEVAL FJ-129.

Poss. 19 June 1929, New York (ref: page 10)
   Non-vocal takes of both tunes recorded this date as by "Carl Fenton's Orchestra" have been discovered on a German Brunswick 78; both takes are inscribed, G. Revise Legacy's listing to include them:

CARL FENTON'S ORCHESTRA   poss. 19 June 1929, New York

Personnel as per Legacy.

E 30035	BR 4421, et al (clt solo)
	What A Day! - voc Dick Robertson
E 30035-G	BrG A-8350 (clt solo)
	What A Day! (no voc)
E 30036	BR 4421, et al (clt solo)
	Maybe-Who Knows - voc Dick Robertson
E 30036-G	BrG A-8350 (clt solo)
	Maybe-Who Knows (no voc)

   Gustave (Gus) Haenschen, who employed the "Carl Fenton" pseudonym for some of his many 1920s Brunswick-based recordings, was a 23-year member of the board of trustees of Ithaca College, Ithaca, New York. A lengthy biography in the 13 April 1992 edition of **The Ithaca College News** outlines his illustrious half-century career in music. In it, Gus is quoted as naming Benny especially, ". . . as one of the guys he had hired as a studio musician," solidifying Legacy's listing of him for this date.

? 10 August 1929, New York (ref: page 10)

Revise the caption of the Vitaphone film to "Ben Pollack and his Park Central Orchestra," and credit Benny with the clarinet solo on **My Kinda Love.** Note that Jack Teagarden doubles on xylophone (!), and that Harry Goodman plays string bass, not tuba. Visual evidence thus belies Harry's 27 April 1991 assertion (q.v.) that he played tuba only, never string bass, while with Pollack.

9 June 1930, New York (ref: page 16)

A test pressing in prime condition adds a non-vocal "A" take to the final tune recorded on this Lanin session. Unfortunately, the absent vocal is not replaced by clarinet soli, but rather by two trumpet soli by Mannie Klein, surrounding a tenor solo that's unlikely Benny's. Then Jack Teagarden again contributes two soli, quite different than his in the vocal version. Revise Legacy's listing to include the test:

SAM LANIN   **9 June 1930, New York**

Personnel as per Legacy.

W 404216-A	UNISSUED-Test Pressing (clt lead)
(W 490085-A)	**Rollin' Down The River** (no voc)
W 404216-B	PaA PNY34104, et al (clt lead)
	Rollin' Down The River - voc Scrappy Lambert

2 August 1930, New York (ref: page 17)

The post-publication release, MERITT LP 24, adds one track to Legacy's display of this Nichols session. (A typo in the liner notes gives matrix "XE 35546," instead of the correct, XE 33546.) Position this addition to follow matrix XE 33545-A:

RED NICHOLS AND HIS ORCHESTRA   **2 August 1930, New York**

Personnel as per Legacy.

XE 33546	**LP:** MER 24
	("HEAT" Program-?)
	After You've Gone (clt solo)

Note that the "Heat" announcer calls the tune, "After You're Gone."

19 February 1931, New York (ref: page 23)

Matrix E 36108-A, **Things I Never Knew Till Now,** Loring "Red" Nichols and his Orchestra, is also on LP, MCA 1518 and SB 137.

25 August 1931, New York (ref: page 31)

Matrix W 351089-1, **This Is The Missus,** Jack Whitney & His Orchestra, is also on LP, TOM 16.

28 October 1931, New York (no ref)

Check No. 12094, in the amount of $44.00, was issued this date by the Columbia Phono-graph Company, Inc., Special Account, to one Ben Goodman. Benny endorsed the check and deposited in his account in The Corn Exchange Bank & Trust Co., Jackson Heights branch, which received payment from the issuing bank, Manufacturers Trust Company, on 4 November 1931. The check bears the notation, "Services for week ending Oct. 23, 1931." Not bad, for a week's work in this depth-of-the-Depression year.

Winter, 1931–1932, New York (ref: page 35)

Programs 15, 16, 17 and 18, "The Blue Coal Minstrels," likely were recorded on Armistice Day, 11 November 1931. No broadcast date for any of the transcriptions is known.

c. 1932–1933, New York (ref: page 36)

One track on two just-discovered Western Electric 12-inch transcriptions by "The Westernaires" solidifies Legacy's personnel listing for their **Puttin' On The Ritz;** W-E No. 483's **Lazy Day** includes an unmistakable Goodman clarinet solo. Revise Legacy's listing to include it:

THE WESTERNAIRES   c. 1932–1933, New York

Personnel as per Legacy, but see note.

6349-2	**12" ET:** W-E Wide Range Transcription, No. 478 **Puttin' On The Ritz** (clt solo)
6354-2	**12" ET:** W-E Wide Range Transcription, No. 483 **Lazy Day** (clt solo)

(Omitted in Legacy's instrumentation listing for **Puttin' On The Ritz** is a bass saxophone. It is not in evidence in **Lazy Day**.)

Lazy Day is the first of the two tracks on No. 483; the second track is **We Just Could-n't Say Goodbye.** The two tracks on W-E No. 486 (matrix 6357-2) are **Whisper Waltz** and (The) **Night Shall Be Filled With Music.** None of these three latter performances of-fers any evidence of Benny's participation.

26 January 1933, New York (ref: page 36)

Columbia's massive Bing Crosby retrospective release—CO 44229, four LPs/three CDs—falsely claims first issue of the B take of **I've Got The World On A String;** the LP, JASS 7, preceded it.

2 October 1933, New York (ref: page 37)

Take 1, matrix W 265149, **In De Ruff,** Joe Venuti and his Blue Six, is issued on LP, PHON 7659, the first of three consecutively-numbered LPs in a box set. That track is NOT included in a companion two-CD set, numbered PHON 7659/7660.

18 October 1933, New York (ref: page 38)

Take 1, matrix W 265165, **Ain't-Cha Glad?**, Benny Goodman and his Orchestra, is issued on LP and CD, PHON 7659.

? 14 November 1933-27 March 1934 (ref: pages 39, 40)

Continuing research by specialist Mike Kirsling suggests that the WOR broadcasts of "The Taystee Breadwinners" programs were transcribed by Columbia much later than the speculative air dates cited in Legacy would indicate. Likely RECORDING dates, according to Mike, are:

Program No.	2:	19 February 1934	
Program No.	4:	23 February 1934	
Program No.	8:	5 March 1934	
Program No.	9:	7 March 1934	(matrix 301441)
Program No.	10:	9 March 1934	(matrix 301442)
Program No.	12:	16 March 1934	
Program No.	13:	19 March 1934	(matrix 301446)
Program No.	14:	23 March 1934	(matrix 301447)
Program No.	16:	2 April 1934	
Program No.	21:	19 April 1934	

Note that Mike's research also supplies four previously unknown matrices. Note, too, that the DeMarco Sisters' tracks in the album, RAD 3MR-3, are not from "Taystee Breadwinners" programs, do not include Benny Goodman.

BILL DODGE, February/March 1934, New York (ref: page 43)

Possibly because of contractual entanglements, the World Broadcasting System released transcriptions recorded for it by certain band leaders under pseudonyms, not their true names. These often followed a pattern: the first initials of the leaders' names became the first initials of the aliases. Thus, "Bert Castle" for Bob Crosby, "Russ Norman" for Red Norvo, for example. Collector Dave Weiner makes the interesting suggestion that "Bill Dodge" may have stemmed from Benjamin David . . . Goodman.

14 August 1934, New York (ref: page 317)

Thanks to Art Rollini, details of the earliest known air check by a Benny Goodman orchestra are now available: A 15-minute broadcast from Billy Rose's Music Hall was recorded for Art by the National Recording Company, 2 West 46th Street, New York, on this date.

Two turntables were used to transcribe the program onto two 12-inch acetates, recorded inside-out on both sides @78 rpm. Side "A" of the first disc begins the broadcast; Side "A" of the second continues it. Side "B" of the first disc has the next segment, then Side "B" of the second continues it. There is no overlapping, which causes some minor gaps, and the two discs have different tonal qualities.

Art criticizes the band for its faulty intonation, so early in the evening (program began at 7:15 p.m.). Nevertheless, there are excellent soli by Benny, Art, Jack Lacey and (likely) Jerry Neary. No violins are audible. The band swings.

Noteworthy are Benny's use of **Good-Bye** for both the opening and the closing themes; only the second extant vocal by Ann Graham; a unique big band rendition of **Nagasaki;** and an announcer's hard-sell description of the delights—and low prices—of the Music Hall.

Although a Philip Morris spot commercial precedes the opening theme, Benny's broadcast had no sponsor.

SUSTAINING BROADCAST   WNEW Radio   14 August 1934, Billy Rose's Music Hall,
New York

Personnel similar to that of 16 August 1934, Legacy page 44.

Good-Bye (opening theme - voice over)
All I Do Is Dream Of You
Blue Interlude
Pardon My Southern Accent - voc Ann Graham
Nagasaki (arr HH)
Good-Bye (closing theme - voice over)

5 January 1935, New York (ref: page 46)
Correct the title to, **Serenade FOR a Wealthy Widow,** and the credit to SB 100, not "104."

23 January 1935, New York (ref: page 46)
Oddity: A copy of CO 3012-D, matrix COW 16600-2, has been discovered bearing the title, **Toccata In E Flat,** instead of **Dodging A Divorcee.** Questions: Was this Reggie Foresythe's original title? Is this record the first issue? Did Columbia change the title for subsequent releases? Or is the label simply a mistake? The author has been unable to get any answers.

26 January 1935, New York (ref: page 47)
Correct the credit for **That's A Plenty** to SB 100, not "104."

2 February 1935, New York (ref: page 47)
Correct the title to, **I Guess I'll Have To Change My Plan** (singular).

23 February - 4 May 1935, New York
Essential to discographical research, among other sine qua nons, are the contributions of authorities in the field . . . and patience. In 1989, Jerry Valburn advised that additional acetates from "Let's Dance" broadcasts had been discovered. Five years later, Gus Statiras supplied transfers of those acetates for the express purpose of inclusion in this work, plus details of their origin: Recorded by an amateur, they were sold by his widow to a doctor in Albany, New York, who "just happened to be" a Goodman enthusiast.

The array below is in both chronological and program order, based on playlists of all of the "Let's Dance" broadcasts. There is this caveat, however: Goodman, Murray and Cugat repeated their 15-minute segments several times each Saturday evening, in order to accommodate time zones across the U.S. On occasion, if seldom, they altered their order-of-performance slightly, sometimes substituted one tune for another.

Audio quality of the transfers ranges from good to excellent. Note that 23 February's **I Was Lucky** is likely the same performance as that on the LP, SB 150 (Legacy, page 48); absence of soli impedes comparison. Also, 9 March is the uncertain, but probable, date of **King Porter Stomp.**

"LET'S DANCE"   NBC Radio Network   *23 February - 4 May 1935, New York*

Personnels as per Legacy for the respective dates.

23 February:
Sweet Georgia Brown
I Was Lucky - voc Helen Ward (SB 150)

9 March:
King Porter Stomp

13 April:
If The Moon Turns Green - voc Ray Hendricks

20 April:
Let's Dance (theme - very much up-tempo)
Bugle Call Rag (n/c)
Pardon My Love - voc Helen Ward - to station break
I Surrender, Dear
Hunkadola

27 April:
Three Little Words (n/c)
Japanese Sandman
Right About Face - voc Helen Ward (arr SM)
Farewell Blues - to station break

4 May:
I Know That You Know
I'm Livin' In A Great Big Way - voc Helen Ward
She's A Latin From Manhattan - voc Helen Ward
When My Baby Smiles At Me - voc Toots Mondello (arr SM)
Every Little Moment - voc Helen Ward - to station break
Let's Dance (theme - few bars only)
I Got Rhythm
The Dixieland Band - voc Helen Ward
Clouds - voc Ray Hendricks (n/c)
Star Dust
Walk, Jennie, Walk

4 April 1935, New York (ref: page 51)
    Released in late 1991, a three-CD set, hyperbolically titled "The Birth Of Swing," of-
fers several previously unissued takes from Benny's Victor era. ADD the first of these alternates to the display in Legacy:

BENNY GOODMAN AND HIS ORCHESTRA   **4 April 1935, New York**

Personnel as per Legacy.

BS 89516-2   **CD:** RcaBB 61038-2, et al
                          Hunkadola

6 April 1935, New York (ref: page 51)
    At The Darktown Strutters' Ball is issued on LP & CD, PHON 7659.

Summer 1935, Palomar, Los Angeles
    A post-Legacy release, the LP MERRITT 504, includes one track that excited Berigan enthusiasts: **Sometimes I'm Happy**, reputedly an air check from the Palomar while Bunny was in Benny's band. Unquestionably it is the Goodman orchestra, it features a trumpet solo; but its tenor solo is unmistakably Vido Musso's. Since Vido joined Benny some 10 months after Bunny's departure, the trumpet solo is not Berigan's.
    A few comparisons quickly dated this air check correctly: it is the CBS broadcast from the Madhattan Room, 2 December 1936, Legacy, page 64. ADD the LP to that entry.

27 September 1935, Hollywood (ref: page 54)
    Unremarked by many Goodman collectors is a previously-unissued take in a June 1995 RcaBB CD release titled, "Bunny Berigan/The Pied Piper (1934–40)." (Three other Goodman Victor tracks on the CD, all from 1 July 1935, are dupes of the original 78s.) ADD this one to Legacy's listing:

BENNY GOODMAN AND HIS ORCHESTRA   **27 September 1935, Hollywood**

Personnel as per Legacy.

BS 97015-1   **CD:** RcaBB 66615-2, et al
                          Santa Claus Came In The Spring - voc Joe Harris

24 January 1936, Chicago (ref: page 56)
    The three-CD set, RcaBB 61038-2, erroneously cites "take 2" for matrix BS 96568, **Stompin' At The Savoy,** Benny Goodman and his Orchestra. No; the take is 1A, per VI 25247 A, et al.

March/April 1936, Chicago (ref: page 57)
    The "M-1" Hammond acetate of the Trio's **My Melancholy Baby** is issued on the EP, PHON BG PH86. The EP was first offered as a $5.00 "bonus" to purchasers of the album "The Permanent Goodman," PHON 7659-7661. The EP also includes additional initial issues that are noted herein, as they occur chronologically.

29 March 1936, Chicago

A cache of 152 16-inch NBC Reference Recordings, most of them in remarkably good condition, were made available to the author for his identification and evaluation in the summer of 1993. Some of the acetates, either glass- or aluminum-based, bear descriptive labels, and some do not. Recorded at 33-1/3 rpm, standard groove, each side of a disc accommodates about 15 minutes of program material. The great majority of them transcribe sustaining broadcasts by an impressive array of the big bands, 1936–1941. There is one especially noteworthy broadcast, the latest in the lot, 9 September 1943, q.v.

Among the earliest is an NBC production, "Swingtime At NBC," broadcast from 8:00–9:00 p.m., Sunday, 29 March 1936. Its theme is that new phenomenon, "swing music"—what is it?, do you like it?, and et cetera. Originating in NBC's studios in the RCA Building, New York, with remotes from Chicago and Hollywood, examples of swing are provided by Frank Froeba's piano solo, a duet by guitarists Dick McDonough and Carl Kress, and a vocal medley by the Kay Thompson Rhythm Ensemble; and by orchestras led by Ray Noble, Red Norvo, Adrian Rollini, Stuff Smith, Meredith Willson . . . and Benny Goodman.

Fittingly (after some introductory dialogue and background music by Red Norvo's Swing Septet), "Benny Goodman, the King of Swing, makes the case for America's most controversial music," and opens the program. And save for Red Norvo's concluding offering, Benny bookends the broadcast:

"SWINGTIME AT NBC"   NBC Radio Network   29 March 1936, Congress Hotel, Chicago
Personnel as 20 March 1936 (page 57).

Stompin' At The Savoy
The Dixieland Band - voc Helen Ward
Dear Old Southland

For other Goodman transcriptions from this treasure trove, see under dates of 15 January 1940, 24 February 1941, 22 October 1941, and 9 September 1943 herein.

All of the Goodman ETs are now in Benny's Archives at Yale. Excerpts from them are slated for eventual release in the Yale/MusicMasters series.

"The Elgin Revue," 7 April 1936, Chicago

A ten-inch Presto acetate, recorded both sides @78 rpm, has several faults. Flipped over and back several times, its multiple tracks are not in program order. Two seconds-long excerpts preclude identifying a tune, fail to name a speaker. Its surface noise ranges from prominent to merely annoying. But it also has its virtues. It is dated, as so many acetates are not. Its surface noise abates during the principal performances. It offers an entire rendition complete with vocal, too frequently disdained by instrumental-oriented amateur recordists. And it provides an archetypal treasure: the first extant air check by the Benny Goodman Trio.

A reasonable order-of-performance of the disc's contents is:

"THE ELGIN REVUE"   NBC Radio Network (disc via WEAF, New York)   7 April 1936,
Chicago

Orchestra personnel as per Legacy, 20 March 1936. Helen Ward, vocal.
TRIO: Benny Goodman, clt; JESS STACY, p; Gene Krupa, d.

. . . intro, non-BG material
. . . few bars, Benny & the band, unidentifiable tune
. . . Eddie Dowling (?), remarks

7 April 1936, continued

7 April 1936, continued
Someday Sweetheart - orchestra - to time check (intro missed)
Get Thee Behind Me, Satan - voc Helen Ward
I'm Gonna Sit Right Down And Write Myself A Letter - TRIO
Let's Dance (closing theme) - to signoff

2 May 1936, Grand Rapids, MI (ref: c. page 58)
The band didn't relax on its off nights at the Congress Hotel; this Sunday, it made it a seven-day week at the Civic Auditorium, Grand Rapids.

26 May 1936, New York (ref: page 58)
Sing Me A Swing Song, from this "Elgin Revue," is also on LP, SB 149.

27 May 1936, New York (ref: page 58)
Take 2, matrix BS 101255, **House Hop,** is also on LP, BlD T-1015.

13 August 1936, Hollywood (ref: page 60)
Typo: Correct first issue of matrix PBS 97713 to, VI 25387 B.

21 August 1936, Hollywood (ref: page 60)
The two other authentic first-issue alternate takes in the three-CD set, RcaBB 61038-2, should be ADDED to the display in Legacy:

BENNY GOODMAN AND HIS ORCHESTRA   **21 August 1936, Hollywood**

Personnel as per Legacy.

PBS 97748-2	**CD:** RcaBB 61038-2, et al **St. Louis Blues**
PBS 97750-2	**CD:** RcaBB 61038-2, et al **Love Me Or Leave Me**

Take 2, matrix PBS 97752, the Quartet's **Moon Glow**, is also issued on LP, BlD T-1015.

1 September 1936, Atlantic City, NJ (ref: page 61)
Chris Griffin recalls Ziggy Elman's joining the band at the Steel Pier: "Ziggy was so loud, it was like he was pressing the button on a bus horn. Zeke Zarchey and I were talking about it, and Benny overheard us. Next thing we know, Benny's talking to Ziggy. Benny says something like, 'Hey, Pops, you don't have to play so loud; take it easy, willya?' And Ziggy says, 'Benny, I didn't ask for this job. I was real happy with Alex Bartha, and I can go back to him anytime I want.' Benny backed right off, so from then on, Zeke and I played louder!"
Revise the locale of the 1 September 1936 "Camel Caravan" broadcast to the Steel Pier in Atlantic City, not New York, as cited in Legacy.

4, 11 November 1936, New York

Three home-recorded acetates provide a tantalizing glimpse of Margaret McCrea's subbing for Helen Ward at the Madhattan Room, then Helen's return after a three-week absence. Although the discs are not dated, program logs, showing the tunes in sequence, strongly suggest dates for Margaret's performances, and pinpoint Helen's return.

Unfortunately, only one of Margaret's contributions is complete; the other three are partials, once again illustrating the custom of amateur recordists to save their acetates for instrumentals by sacrificing vocals. Nevertheless, Margaret's credentials as a top-flight band vocalist are confirmed; she sings very well, especially on the incomplete **Midnight Blue.** Were it complete, for it's a gem.

SUSTAINING BROADCASTS   CBS Radio Network　　　　　*4, 11 November 1936, Hotel Pennsylvania, New York*

Instrumental personnel as Legacy, 16 September 1936. Margaret McCrea, voc.

4 November 1936:

Let's Dance (theme)
I've Found A New Baby
You're My Best Bet - voc Margaret McCrea (n/c)
Body And Soul - TRIO (Benny, Teddy, Gene) (intro defective)
It's Delovely - voc Margaret McCrea (n/c)
Good-Bye (theme)

11 November 1936:

Three Little Words
There's Something In The Air - voc Margaret McCrea
At The Darktown Strutters' Ball
Midnight Blue - voc Margaret McCrea (n/c)

18 November 1936, New York

Upon her return, Helen sings two of the three tunes Ella Fitzgerald recorded anonymously for Benny on the 5 November 1936 Victor session. As if to celebrate her homecoming, both are complete:

SUSTAINING BROADCAST   CBS Radio Network　　　　　*18 November 1936, Hotel Pennsylvania, New York*

Personnel as per Legacy, 16 September 1936.

Let's Dance (theme)
Jingle Bells
Goodnight My Love - voc Helen Ward (arr JM)
Oh, Lady Be Good! - (arr FH)
Take Another Guess - voc Helen Ward

19 November 1936, New York (ref: page 63)

Two alternate takes from this session are available on CDs from at least two producers, Columbia and King Jazz (It); liner notes for the latter claim an antecedent issue, Masters of Jazz 32, which has been unobtainable by the author. ADD the certain releases to the display in Legacy:

TEDDY WILSON AND HIS ORCHESTRA   19 November 1936, New York

Personnel as per Legacy.

B 20290-2   **CD:** CO 47724, KJ(It) 171FS
                                 Pennies From Heaven - voc Billie Holiday

B 20291-2   **CD:** CO 47724, KJ(It) 171FS
                                 That's Life I Guess - voc Billie Holiday

(The Columbia issue may also have been released via cassette, less likely via LP. If so, they will carry the same catalog number as the CD.)

Tails out of schul:

Toward the twilight of her career, Billie had a modest gig in Pittsburgh, PA. While she was in town, major Goodman collector Ken Crawford interviewed her. Naturally, Ken asked Billie about Benny. She spoke glowingly about her relationship with him, beginning with: "Benny? Oh, Benny! He was the best fuck I ever had!" In like vein, Billie also confided that in her experience Sid Catlett richly deserved the descriptive appellation, "BIG."

During its March 1980 "Teddy Wilson Festival," WKCR-FM, New York, broadcast extensive taped interviews with the eloquent Mr. Wilson. Admitting that his recordings with Billie enhanced his career, Teddy continued: "But as I said, my excitement was with the musicians on the date, I wasn't particularly a fan of Billie Holiday." Then, after naming female vocalists he did admire, he emphasized: "But I wasn't particularly a Holiday fan, at all."

Another non-preference, on a near-deified jazzman, Benny to the author: "Jo Jones? No, no, we didn't think much of him at all." That's an orchestral, not an editorial, "we."

2 December 1936, New York (ref: page 63)

After decades of fruitless search, an alternate take of the Trio's **Tiger Rag** has been found. But it is not on a commercial release; it is the first of six Goodman small-group tracks on the "A" side of a 16-inch AFRS transcription. (The other five are dubs of issued records. The "B" side is devoted to Bobby Hackett.)

Arguably, it could be take 1, from the 18 November 1936 session. But because of its structural and ambient similarity to the original release, VI 25481 B, take 2, the ET track is more likely the otherwise-unissued take 3 from this 2 December 1936 studio date. ADD it to the display in Legacy:

BENNY GOODMAN TRIO   2 December 1936, New York

Personnel as per Legacy.

BS 03064-3   **ET:** AFRS Music Transcription Library No. P-S-49, matrix SSL-
                                 3569, Track 1
                                 Tiger Rag

9 December 1936, New York (ref: page 64)

Because of a 17-second running-time difference cited in their liner notes for **Gee! But You're Swell,** the LPs RcaBB AXM2-5532 versus SAVILLE 212, some collectors assume that the takes are not the same. Not so; both are take 1, as per VI 25486 B et al. Time stated in the RcaBB release is simply wrong.

From this session: The T-2435-1 test dub, **Smoke Dreams,** is issued on the LP, BlD-T-1015.

6 January 1937, New York (ref: page 64)

A glaring error in Legacy falsely lists the big band rendition of **Stompin' At The Savoy** from this broadcast as issued on the DR. JAZZ LP. No; its track is the Quartet's performance of the same tune from the "Camel Caravan" program of 23 March 1937 (Legacy, page 68). The author should never have made this mistake, for he made the original tape transfers from the source acetates.

The Dr. Jazz releases (LP and cassette) were later made available on CD, on the Dr. Jazz, Columbia and ZETA(Fr) labels.

30 January 1937, New York

The 30 January birthday of President Franklin D. Roosevelt, who was crippled by infantile paralysis, was marked each year by a funds drive to combat the disease. An hour-long broadcast of dance band remotes from across the U.S. promoted the Fourth Annual Infantile Paralysis campaign. Benny Goodman and his Orchestra closed the program from the Madhattan Room:

SUSTAINING BROADCAST   Major radio networks   30 January 1937, Hotel Pennsylvania, New York

Orchestra personnel as per Legacy, 27 January 1937.

Ridin' High (n/c - to signoff)

23 March 1937, New York (ref: page 68)

As noted previously herein, it is the Quartet's **Stompin' At The Savoy** from this date's "Camel Caravan" broadcast that is issued on the DR. JAZZ and related releases, not the full band rendition of 6 January 1937 (Legacy, page 64).

Milt Yaner, as, substituted for ailing Hymie Schertzer on this program.

13 April 1937, New York (ref: page 68)

Bill Savory's comprehensive review of his Goodman air check acetates, for purpose of inclusion in this work, discovered a misassignment in the Columbia "Benny Goodman—Jazz Concert No. 2" album: Its track of **Minnie The Moocher's Wedding Day** is not from this date's "Camel Caravan" program, as he once believed. Rather, it is from the WNEW "Make Believe Ballroom" broadcast of 29 April 1937 (Legacy, page 68).

This date's **Minnie The Moocher's Wedding Day** is unissued, and is thus included in the section on Savory's Goodman air checks, as of 13 April 1937.

29 April 1937, New York (ref: page 68)

As noted above, reassign the CO air checks album's **Minnie The Moocher's Wedding Day** to this date's WNEW broadcast.

11 May 1937, New York (ref: page 68)

Another CO air checks album reassignment: Its track of **Let's Dance**—Benny whistles the final two bars—is not from this date's "Camel Caravan" program. It is from a 23 March 1937 sustaining broadcast from the Madhattan Room, and is included in the section on Savory's Goodman air checks, together with other performances from this previously unlisted 23 March 1937 broadcast.

6 July 1937, Hollywood (ref: page 70)

Take 3, matrix PBS 09570, **Can't We Be Friends?**, is also issued on the LP, BlD T-1015. Correct Legacy's take 2 listing of the catalog number for the same matrix to, VI 25621.

TIME-LIFE reissued its STBB03 album on compact disc, TL TCD0003. Unfortunately, the CD has the common take 2s for its tracks of **Sing, Sing, Sing,** instead of the more desirable -3/-1 coupling on TL's original release.

October 1937 - January 1938, New York

Interviewed by Lloyd Rauch on his WHRU-FM (New York) radio program, guitarist Allen Hanlon reveals that he substituted for Allan Reuss on several occasions during the winter of 1937/1938. Reuss's absences were because, first, ". . . he (Reuss) got married and took a few days off," and later when Reuss was ill. Hanlon says that he was in the band for one or more "Camel Caravan" programs, as well as for some sustaining broadcasts from the Hotel Pennsylvania. He does not claim to have made any of the RcaVictor studio sessions. Hanlon recalls that Reuss returned to the band "early in November."

Hanlon also mentions that Reuss was unable to be on time for a rehearsal for the 16 January 1938 Carnegie concert, and that in response to Reuss's frantic phone call, he, Hanlon, once again filled in for him.

29 October 1937, New York (ref: page 76)

An alternate take of matrix BS 015577, the Quartet's **Vieni, Vieni**, is issued on CD, RcaBB 2273-2-RB and associated releases. Liner notes state that this previously unissued take was pressed from the original metal stamper, and that it is inscribed, "take 2." Take 2 is, of course, the take number inscribed in the original-issue 78, VI 25705 A. Neither RCA nor the author has a convincing explanation for this confusing duplication.

ADD the release to the display in Legacy:

BENNY GOODMAN QUARTET   **29 October 1937, New York**

Personnel as per Legacy.

BS 015577-alt	**CD:** RcaBB 2273-2-RB, et al
	Vieni, Vieni

"21" November 1937, LIFE MAGAZINE (ref: page 76)

An uncorrected typo misdates the band's "Life Goes To A Party" spread. Change it to 1 November 1937.

12 November 1937, New York (ref: page 77)

Previously-unissued take 2 of matrix BS 017042, **Camel Hop,** is available on CD, RcaBB 66155-2, and associated releases. ADD it to the display in Legacy:

BENNY GOODMAN AND HIS ORCHESTRA   **12 November 1937, New York**

Personnel as per Legacy.

BS 017042-2   **CD:** RcaBB 66155-2, et al
                     Camel Hop

Note that the liner notes give erroneous matrix numbers for both tracks of **Camel Hop** and both tracks of **Life Goes To A Party.** Those listed in Legacy are correct.
    See also this release under date of 16 February 1938, herein.

3 December 1937, New York (ref: page 78)
    Take 2, matrix BS 017454, **If Dreams Come True,** is also issued on the LP, BlD-T-1015.

16 January 1938, New York (ref: page 81)
    Neglectfully omitted from Legacy's list of 78 rpm releases for the Carnegie Hall concert is a 12-inch "promo" sent to disc jockeys. Two-sided, it consists of voice tracks Benny recorded on an unknown date in fall 1950. Accompanying it was a script that suggested dialogue for station personnel. ADD to Legacy's array:

"BENNY GOODMAN INTRODUCES . . ."   **Fall 1950, New York**

Benny comments on selections from the concert.

XP 45712-1A   **12" 78:**   1. Don't Be That Way
                                     2. Blue Reverie
                                     3. Life Goes To A Party

XP 45713-1A   1. Body And Soul
                                     2. Avalon
                                     3. Swingtime In The Rockies
                                     4. Conclusion

    Also: Correct the parenthetical credit for the 78, CO DJ XCO45711, to (17), not the misprinted "(8)".

16 February 1938, New York (ref: page 82)
    Previously-unissued take 2s of both matrices recorded this date are on the CD, RcaBB 66155-2 and associated releases. ADD them to the display in Legacy:

BENNY GOODMAN AND HIS ORCHESTRA   **16 February 1938, New York**

Personnel as per Legacy.

BS 019831-2   **CD:** RcaBB 66155-2, et al
                     Don't Be That Way

BS 019832-2   **CD:** RcaBB 66155-2, et al
                     One O'Clock Jump

Note that the CD's liner notes' discography introduces a new tenor saxophonist to the Goodman personnel roster, one "BABY" Russin.

See also this CD under date of 12 November 1937, herein.

9 March 1938, New York (ref: page 83)

Typographical error: For the first issue of matrix BS 021127-2, **Please Be Kind,** change the catalog number to LP, VI LPM6702.

12 March 1938, New York (ref: page 84)

The air check, **Sweet Sue—Just You,** is issued on LP, PHON 7660, but is not included in the companion CD.

The air check, **The World Is Waiting For The Sunrise,** is issued on EP, PHON BG PH86.

25 March 1938, New York (ref: page 84)

Liner notes for the CD, RcaBB 2273-2-RB, et al, incorrectly list take 2 for matrix BS 021629, **Dizzy Spells.** The take is -1, same as that for the original issue on VI 25822 A. See parenthetical note at the end of the display in Legacy for this session.

22 April 1938, New York (ref: page 85)

The test pressing, "2359," **Feelin' High And Happy;** and take 2, matrix, BS 022488, **Why'd Ya Make Me Fall In Love?,** are issued on the LP, BlD T-1015.

1 May 1938, Boston (ref: page 86)

A 16-page program for the 1 May 1938 Symphony Hall, Boston, concert reveals that Bobby Hackett was on hand for the **I'm Coming, Virginia** pastiche he'd played at Carnegie Hall. Irving Kolodin's extensive text is at least the equal of the liner notes accompanying Columbia's release of the 16 January 1938 concert.

12 May 1938, Allentown, PA

Correction: Following his 11 May 1938 appearance in Philadelphia, Benny did not go directly to New York's Roseland Ballroom. On the 12th, the band performed at Dorney Park, Allentown, PA. The Roseland engagement began on Friday the 13th.

Dorney Park is an amusement park, still operating today. Then as now it had the usual complement of "thrill rides," plus a ballroom. In the mid-1930s, the park featured a name band every Thursday, a local group every Saturday. The reason for this programming was economic: The name bands charged more on weekends and holidays, less on their "traveling days" through the week.

Dorney Park's ledger sheet for the period 21 April through 30 June 1938 reveals that Benny was paid top dollar during that 11-week spread, $1,250. He drew the biggest crowd, 1327 paid, 110 complimentary, admissions. At a ticket price of $1.10 (including tax), Dorney made a gross profit of $76.99 on the Goodman gig.

The park's experience with the other name bands it employed that spring and summer is below, in the order of band fee; paid/comp admissions; ticket price; profit (+) or loss (−):

Hal Kemp (21 April)	$1,000.	774/61	$1.10	$226.29–
Sammy Kaye (28 April)	750.	1096/67	1.10	346.80+
Louis Armstrong (5 May)	800.	282/82	1.10	516.80–
Red Norvo (19 May)	500.	271/60	.85	190.48–
Kay Kyser (26 May)	1,000.	674/70	1.10	328.00–
Bunny Berigan (2 June)	see note	383/61	.75	12.85+
Count Basie (9 June)	250.	342/30	.50	79.09–
Paul Tremaine (16 June)	200.	165/30	.50	117.50–
Casa Loma (23 June)	700.	722/92	1.10	22.71+
Sammy Kaye (30 June)	500.	319/78	1.10	181.10–

NOTE: Berigan's asking price was $400. But Dorney's management insisted that it would pay him only a percentage of the paid admissions, up to $400. Bunny's pay for the gig was $142.15!

31 May 1938, New York (ref: page 87)
Correction: The closing theme, **Good-Bye,** listed as from this date on LP, BlD 5001/2, is from the broadcast of 7 June 1938, not 31 May.

7 June 1938, Cleveland (ref: page 87)
As noted above, **Good-Bye** is issued on LP, BlD 5001/2.

21 June 1938, Boston (ref: page 88)
The air check, **Paradise,** is issued on LP, SB 152. This is a reassignment from the broadcast of 28 March 1939, page 97, q.v.

11 July 1938, New York (ref: page 88)
A 1994 discovery in RcaVictor's (now BMG Music's) vaults is an unissued take of **Could You Pass In Love?,** matrix BS 024021. ADD it to the display in Legacy:

BENNY GOODMAN AND HIS ORCHESTRA   **11 July 1938, New York**

Personnel as per Legacy.

BS 024021-1   UNISSUED - Tape
                              Could You Pass In Love? - voc Martha Tilton

8 August 1938, New York (ref: page 89)
The test pressing, take 1, matrix BS 024472, **You Got Me,** is issued on the LP, BlD T-1015.

12 August 1938, New York (ref: page 89)

Typographical error: The correct matrix for **When I Go A Dreamin'** is BS 024493-1(2).

13 September 1938, Chicago (ref: page 90)

The LP, SC 1019, omits the opening theme for this broadcast; its initial track is **Changes.**

20 September 1938, Kansas City (ref: page 91)

The bootleg LP release for the air check, **Space, Man,** is SB 152, not SB 151.

Bumble Bee Stomp, this broadcast, is also on the LP, SB 152. It is not from the broadcast of 11 October 1938. SB 152's liner notes misdate this air check.

Parenthetical note in re this broadcast: Correct LP credit to SC 1020, not 1021, and note that it omits the opening theme.

11 October 1938, Chicago (ref: page 91)

Delete the LP credit, SB 152, for **Bumble Bee Stomp** from this program. See preceding entry, 20 September 1938.

The DRJ 40350, SC 1021 and SB 152 tracks of **Bumble Bee Stomp** are identical, all from the "Camel Caravan" broadcast of 20 September 1938. The true 11 October 1938 rendition includes trombone soli not in the Kansas City version.

12 October 1938, Chicago (ref: page 91)

Liner notes for the CD, RcaBB 2273-2-RB, and associated releases, erroneously cite take 2 for its track of matrix BS 025879, **'S Wonderful.** Its take is 1, same as that on the original issue, VI 26090 A.

25 October 1938, New York (ref: page 92)

Add to this "Camel Caravan" program repartee between Benny and jazz critic Hughes Panassié (who once said Benny's clarinet playing reminded him of birds twittering), and announcer Dan Seymour; plus another song by Kate Smith, backed by her own trio, The Ambassadors:

"CAMEL CARAVAN"   CBS Radio Network   *25 October 1938, New York*

. . . conversation, Goodman, Panassié, Seymour
(When The Moon Comes Over The Mountain - voc Kate Smith w/trio, band in coda

December 1938, New York

Jerry Jerome replaced Bud Freeman the end of November. He knew the other sidemen, who accepted him readily, and Benny seemed pleased with his work. All was going smoothly until an unfortunate event precipitated a crisis. Let Jerry tell the tale:

"I'd only been with the band a few weeks, and as a new boy I kept a low profile, just doing my job, not asking for any favors. We were in the Waldorf then, and one day Benny announced a rehearsal for 10:00 a.m. the next morning, and warned everybody to be on time. Well, my grandfather had just died, his funeral was that next morning too, and I had to go. So I approached Benny with some apprehension, told him what had happened, and said I was sorry, but I'd have to miss the rehearsal. He didn't say a word, merely nodded, and I thought, well, that was easy. When the last set was over that night, and everybody was headed out, Benny waved me over. I thought he might want to extend sympathy, something like that, but what he said floored me: 'Hey, Pops, can you get out of that thing tomorrow?' I'll never forget that; and I did go to the funeral."

Jerry has a fund of stories about Benny. Here's another:

"Remember pea shooters when you were a kid? Tin tubes, maybe 10 inches long, wooden mouthpiece, put a pea or a bean in them, blow real hard, zap somebody a couple of yards away? Well, we were playing a theater gig in Cincinnati (ed. note: Elby Theater, May 1939), and Hymie, Chris and I found some in a novelty store there. But these were kind of special, came with little paper parachutes. Blow them straight up, they'd open up, float down real nice. So, during a show, the three of us shot them up, and the audience started laughing, pointing at the stage. Benny, facing front, didn't know what was happening, and he got real flustered. Finally he turned around to the band, said loud enough for the P.A. system to pick up, 'What the hell's going on? Is my fly open or something?'"

One more, again from the Waldorf, winter 1939:

"For some reason nobody understood, we weren't drawing big crowds at the Waldorf. The management brought in a society band to spell us, even put in a milk bar for teenagers. Then it hired Paul and Grace Hartmann, a kind of comic magic act. Paul was clever, had some good tricks; one was, he'd get a scarf or something from the audience, fold it over a lighted cigar. You'd think he'd burn a hole in it, but no, he'd open it up, and it was good as new. Well, we backed their act, and one night Paul asked Benny for the silk handkerchief he always wore in the breast pocket of his jacket. Benny, who'd seen the trick many times, faked reluctance, then gave it to him. Paul blew the ashes off his cigar, wrapped that expensive handkerchief around it, waved it around while Benny feigned horror. Finally, Paul whipped the hankie open for all to see, and there's a great big hole burnt right in the middle of it! Benny couldn't believe it."

15 December 1938, New York (ref: page 93)

Matrix BS 030702, **Bach Goes To Town,** as issued on TIME-LIFE releases, is take 3, not take "2," an error in Legacy. It is difficult to differentiate among the (now) three issued takes because Henry Brandt's fully-scored arrangement affords little space for improvisation. But one can detect minute variations in the three recordings at their respective 15- and 115-second running times.

DELETE the TL credit from take 2; ADD TL credits as take 3 to the array in Legacy:

BENNY GOODMAN AND HIS ORCHESTRA   **15 December 1938, New York**

Personnel as per Legacy.

BS 030702-3	**LP, Cas:** TL STBB03. **CD:** TL TCD0003
	Bach Goes To Town

15 December 1938, continued

15 December 1938, continued

One track on a 1995 RcaBluebird release warrants its purchase: The previously-unissued take 2 of matrix BS 030704, **Undecided.** ADD it, too, to Legacy's array for this 15 December 1938 session:

BS 030704-2   **CD:** RcaBB 66549-2, et al
                               Undecided

23 December 1938, New York (ref: page 94)

Observant collectors have questioned Legacy's twice-listed take 2's for matrices BS 030390, **It Had To Be You,** and BS 030391, **Louise.** Both are in the 12 December 1938 display, both as issued via the LP, RcaBB AXM2-5568, both credited to 12 December per the album's liner notes. Both take 2's again appear in the display for the 23 December 1938 session, but in parentheses signifying "unissued," together with take 3's for each. The question is, which date is correct for those tracks on the RcaBB release?

The author is unable to answer, because source material is ambiguous: A handwritten "AXM2-5568" for both matrices is on a RcaVictor "Records By . . ." form dated 12 December. In seeming contradiction, typewritten take 2's (and 3's) are on a like form dated 23 December. No help from them. Speculatively, what may be the case - although it doesn't resolve the duplication - is this:

It Had To Be You and **Louise** were the only tunes recorded during a three-hour, 45-minute session on 12 December. At all odds, each must have been waxed several times. Then assume that Benny, on playback, chose one take of each as "best effort," and they were assigned take 1's of preference. His alternate choices from this session then became take 2's. When he cut both tunes again on 23 December, and again listened to their playbacks, his 12 December take 1's retained their positions as his favorites. But his 12 December take 2's were supplanted by superior performances on 23 December, and they now became his take 2 selections.

Discography is less an exact science than, say, DNA blood tests, certain defense counsel notwithstanding. At times we should simply enjoy the music, ignore the mystery.

3 January 1939, New York (ref: page 94)

Let's Dance is issued on CD, PHON 8817. See 17 January 1939 entry below for further comment about this release.

9 January 1939, New York

An anecdote has sultry Libby Holman engaging Benny, Lionel, Teddy and Gene, and Billie Holiday and Helen Ward, to help celebrate her son's birthday this evening in her Manhattan apartment. The festivities reportedly lasted until nine o'clock the next morning.

Helen remembers the party quite differently: "It wasn't that way at all. Libby had a house, not an apartment, an impressive place uptown, even had a circular driveway in front. She'd made a lot of money on her own, and she'd married into the Reynolds tobacco family, could afford anything she wanted. None of the boys in the original quartet was there; how would I forget them? Billie and I weren't 'hired,' we were there as guests because Libby liked the way we sang. We each did a couple of songs, accompanied by a pianist whose name I can't recall. It wasn't a birthday party, just a gathering of some of Libby's friends; Fanny

Brice, Clifton Webb, and the very social, very wealthy Jimmy Donohue were some of the people there. I was just a kid then, and Jimmy embarrassed me no end; he did a strip tease, took all his clothes off. I didn't know where to look, couldn't wait to get out of there."

Can't wait to read Helen's autobiography; should be a blockbuster.

11/12 January 1939, New York (ref: page 95)

Take 2, matrix BS 031446, **The Blues,** was first issued on the LP, BlD T-1015, later on CD RcaBB 9986 and associated releases, and on RcaBB 7636, all formats.

17 January 1939, New York (ref: page 95)

In December 1992 PHONtastic released three CDs that embrace nine "Camel Caravan" broadcasts from the Johnny Mercer first-half 1939 era, three programs per disc. Each CD has as its initial track **Let's Dance** from one program, and **Good-Bye** as its final track from another. Opening and closing themes of the other broadcasts on a given CD are omitted. Certain other performances are also deleted; these are noted herein under the relevant broadcast dates. Commercials and much dialogue are also left out. But most of the music is retained, and the transfers are satisfactory.

PHON CD 8817 includes the "Camel Caravan" program of 17 January 1939, with these exceptions: **Let's Dance** is spliced in from the broadcast of 3 January 1939, and **Good-Bye** from 17 January is omitted.

24 January 1939, New York (ref: page 96)

A typographical error lists "v" (violin) for Andre Petri. He was the pianist who accompanied Szigeti.

Sans both themes and **Clair De Lune,** this "Camel Caravan" is on the CD, PHON 8817.

31 January 1939, New York (ref: page 96)

Sans the opening theme and **Hold Tight,** this "Camel Caravan" is on the CD, PHON 8817. **Basin Street Blues** is also on the CD, PHON XMCD 92.

This broadcast is also on STAR-LINE cassette 61033, which substitutes **Deep Purple** from 28 February 1939 for **Umbrella Man,** and omits **Good-Bye.**

21 February 1939, Newark, NJ (ref: page 96)

Sans **Them There Eyes** and **Good-Bye,** this "Camel Caravan" is on the CD, PHON 8818.

Save for **Good-Bye,** this broadcast is also on STAR-LINE cassette 61182. **The World Is Waiting For The Sunrise** is also on the CD, PHON XMCD 92, and on STAR-LINE cassette 61142.

28 February 1939, Detroit (ref: page 97)

Sans both themes, this "Camel Caravan" is on the CD, PHON 8818.

Deep Purple and **I Cried For You** are on STAR-LINE cassettes 61033 and 61142, respectively.

14 March 1939, Pittsburgh, PA (ref: page 97)

Carelessly omitted from Legacy's array: **You Turned The Tables On Me** - vocal Martha Tilton, immediately precedes **Sent For You Yesterday And Here You Come Today.**

21 March 1939, Washington, DC (ref: page 97)

Sans **Let's Dance** and **Limehouse Blues,** this "Camel Caravan" is on the CD, PHON 8818.

Deep Purple is on STAR-LINE cassette 61142.

28 March 1939, Akron, OH (ref: page 97)

Sans **Good-Bye,** this "Camel Caravan" is on the CD, PHON 8819. **Clap Your Hands** is also on the CD, PHON XMCD 92.

As noted previously (21 June 1938, q.v.), delete the LP, SB 152, **Paradise,** from the display in Legacy.

18 April 1939, Louisville, KY (ref: page 98)

Sans both themes, **And The Angels Sing** and **'T'Ain't What You Do,** this "Camel Caravan" is on the CD, PHON 8819.

The Man I Love is on STAR-LINE cassette 61142.

25 April 1939, Asheville, NC (ref: page 98)

Sans **Let's Dance,** this "Camel Caravan" broadcast is on CD, PHON 8819. **Opus 3/4** is also on STAR-LINE cassette 61142.

16 May 1939, Cleveland, OH (ref: page 99)

The Sheik Of Araby is on STAR-LINE cassette 61142.

23 May 1939, Columbus, OH (ref: page 99)

I Got Rhythm is on STAR-LINE cassette 61142.

30 May 1939, Cincinnati, OH (ref: page 99)

Tea For Two and **Stompin' At The Savoy** are on STAR-LINE cassette 61142.

20 June 1939, Boston (ref: page 100)

China Boy is on STAR-LINE cassette 61142.

10 August 1939, Los Angeles (ref: page 102)

With this session, Phontastic issued the first in a set of 12 LPs titled, "The Alternate Goodman." In 1993/1994, Phontastic reprised those LPs on 10 CDs, two each in five albums titled, "Goodman—The Different Version." The great majority of tracks are common to both series, but there are some substitutions among the CDs. These are detailed herein as they occur.

DELETE unauthorized credit "NOST 1004" from matrix LA 1947-B, **There'll Be Some Changes Made.**

16 August 1939, Los Angeles (ref: page 103)

Liner notes for multi-format CO 40651 err in specifying take B for its track of matrix LA 1951, **Stealin' Apples.** Its take is C.

13 September 1939, New York (ref: page 104)

Omitted in error: The breakdown, matrix CO 25350, **One Sweet Letter From You,** is issued on LP, PHON 7606.

The first unnumbered take of matrix CO 25351, **Down By The Old Mill Stream,** initially released on LP, PHON XM79, is also issued on LP and CD, PHON 7660.

A word of explanation about the LP, PHON XM79:

Throughout Legacy and this tract, attributions are made to various Phontastic 12-inch LPs, seven-inch LPs, EPs and CDs that bear atypical catalog numbers. Representative of them are such PHON releases as XM79, VELP 1, BGEP 01, XM-MLP80, XM-EPH81, et alia. These are limited-edition issues distributed by PHON producer Anders Ohman to his close friends and associates. They commemorate special events: Christmas, family birthdays, a tribute to a friend's wife, celebration of an associate's wedding, and the like.

Invariably, each includes one or more Goodman tracks, often otherwise unissued, of a studio recording and/or an air check. Unadvertised, never sold, these esoteric discs challenge the best efforts of Goodman collectors to acquire them. However, some have also been commercially released in Phontastic's CD reprise of its "Alternate Goodman" series, and these are noted herein.

2 October 1939, New York (ref: page 105)

Delete the LP, CO KG31547, from the Legacy listing for matrix WCO 26133-A, **Rose Room (In Sunny Roseland).** Proofreading failed to detect this sneaky insertion by an unappointed "editor." Unfortunately, there are others.

6 October 1939, New York (ref: page 105)

The Sheik Of Araby was performed by the Trio, not the "TRO."

20 October 1939, New York (ref: page 106)

Among the most surprising recent Goodman discoveries are four two-sided Columbia Reference Recording 12-inch acetates that add a total of six extant takes to the studio sessions of 20 and 24 October 1939. Search of Columbia's vaults failed to find them, for a very good reason: They were in private hands.

Two of the discs have a Goodman recording on one side, non-Goodman material on their reverse sides. The other two discs offer Goodman recordings on both sides. Three of the six sides are inscribed either "B. Goodman" or "Benny Goodman"; all six sides are absent matrix/take designations. Each take's order-of-performance is undeterminable; each is arbitrarily assigned as having preceded the "A" take for its matrix.

The two Goodman one-side-only CO Ref's are from the 20 October session. ADD them to the display in Legacy.

BENNY GOODMAN AND HIS ORCHESTRA   **20 October 1939, New York**

Personnel as per Legacy.

WCO 26194-alt   UNISSUED - CO Ref
                          Make With The Kisses - voc Mildred Bailey

WCO 26196-alt   UNISSUED - CO Ref
                          I Thought About You - voc Mildred Bailey

23 October 1939, New York (ref: page 106)

Delete LPs BRO/RADR 100 from the credits for, **Absence Makes The Heart Grow Fonder.**

24 October 1939, New York (ref: page 106)

In whole or in part, the most extensively reissued Goodman recording is **Let's Dance,** matrix WCO 26202-A, recorded this date. For years the author sought an alternate take, with the active cooperation of a succession of Columbia's producers. Their efforts went unrewarded because—as for the session of 20 October 1939, q.v.—an alternate was in a private collection, was not in Columbia's inventory. Its recent acquisition marked "paid in full" to decades of search.

The flip side of the CO Ref that gives us **Let's Dance** is an almost complete alternate take of **That Lucky Fellow.** The other two-sided CO Ref cited under date of 20 October provides a second alternate of **That Lucky Fellow,** this take complete; on its reverse is an alternate take of **Bluebirds In The Moonlight.**

ADD all below to the display in Legacy, arbitrarily as preceding their respective "A" takes, for their order-of-performance is unknown.

BENNY GOODMAN AND HIS ORCHESTRA　　　　　　　　**24 October 1939, New York**

Personnel as per Legacy.

WCO 26202-alt	UNISSUED - CO Ref **Let's Dance**
WCO 26203-bkdn WCO 26203-alt	UNISSUED - CO Ref UNISSUED - CO Ref **That Lucky Fellow** - voc Mildred Bailey
WCO 26204-alt	UNISSUED - CO Ref **Bluebirds In The Moonlight** - voc Mildred Bailey

Typo: For matrix WCO 26204's credits, make that ET, not "EP," for both AFRS transcriptions in Legacy's array.

4 November 1939, New York (ref: page 107)

Epileptic ephemera: The orchestration backing Mildred Bailey's rendition of **Scatter-Brain** is arrestingly different from Eddie Sauter's familiar chart. Further, she misspeaks the lyrics, singing, "I know I'll end up EPILEPTIC"—twice—instead of "apoplectic." On the 2 December 1939 "Camel" broadcast she gets it right in her second chorus, first singing "apolectic," finally, "apoplectic."

22 November 1939, New York (ref: page 107)

Available earlier to a few collectors via tapes of a Columbia Reference Recording, the "B" take of matrix WCO 26288, **Peace, Brother!,** was released to the public in 1995. ADD it to the listing in Legacy, as waxed prior to the "A" take:

BENNY GOODMAN AND HIS ORCHESTRA   **22 November 1939, New York**

Personnel as per Legacy.

WCO 26288-B   **CD:** CO 66198, et al
                     Peace, Brother! - voc Mildred Bailey

9 December 1939, New York (ref: page 108)
   The air check **Madhouse** is also on LP, SB 149.

31 December 1939, New York (ref: page 109)
   The air check **Till Tom Special** was initially issued on LP, JAA 42. In 1991, it and other Goodman material that had been released on the LPs JAA 23, JAA 42, et al, were reissued on a Vintage Jazz Classics CD, VJC 1021-2. See entry herein for 13 April 1940, for a new air check on that CD.

15 January 1940, New York (ref: page 109)
   Discovered in 1993, two glass-base NBC 16-inch transcriptions, each with a running time of 15 minutes, capture the complete short-wave broadcast to Scandinavia. The ETs are in excellent condition, the performances well recorded and quite attractive. Among the highlights are two Sextet renditions, and good soli by Benny, Ziggy, Toots and Johnny Guarnieri, on the big band numbers.
   Note that Chris Griffin, at this time a studio musician in New York, replaces Johnny Martel, possibly for this broadcast only. His is the intro to **King Porter Stomp.** The Sextet personnel is announced as including one Art "Benson," bassist . . .

SHORT-WAVE BROADCAST   via NBC   15 January 1940, Rockefeller Center, New York
Orchestra personnel as per Legacy, 27 December 1939, except CHRIS GRIFFIN, tpt, replaces Martel. Sextet as per Legacy, 20 December 1939.

Let's Dance (theme)
Scatter-Brain
Indian Summer - voc Helen Forrest
Bach Goes To Town
Star Dust - SEXTET
King Porter Stomp
All The Things You Are - voc Helen Forrest (arr EdSau)
Flying Home - SEXTET
One O'Clock Jump
Good-Bye (theme)

16 January 1940, New York (ref: page 109)
   In summer 1993 Phontastic began to re-release on CD its "The Alternate Goodman" set of 12 LPs. The CD series is titled, "Goodman—The Different Version." Volume I includes newly-discovered take B of matrix WCO 26419, **Squeeze Me.** This previously unknown alternate is free of the mechanical faults that mar the A take's test pressing.
   ADD it to the display in Legacy:

BENNY GOODMAN AND HIS ORCHESTRA   16 January 1940, New York

Personnel as per Legacy.

WCO 26419-B   **CD:** PHON 8821
Squeeze Me

7 February 1940, New York (ref: page 110)

Take A, matrix WCO 26495, **Gone With "What" Wind,** first issued on the LP, BID T-1009, is now available on multi-format CO 40846 and CBSFr 460.612.

13 April 1940, Los Angeles (ref: page 111)

The CD, VJC 1021-2, adds a previously unissued air check to this broadcast from the Cocoanut Grove in the Hotel Ambassador:

SUSTAINING BROADCAST   NBC Radio Network   *13 April 1940, Cocoanut Grove, Los Angeles*

Personnel as per Legacy, 19 March 1940, SEXTET.

*Soft Winds - SEXTET (**CD:** VJC 1021-2)*

"3 July 1940," Los Angeles (ref: page 112)

Collector Dave Weiner cites an oversight in Legacy: Personnel listing should have read, "Personnel as March 19; Christian on g." etc. (Charlie has a solo in **Li'l Boy Love,** preceding the coda.) And we'll remind one and all that the correct date of this World Broadcasting System-recorded session is 25 June 1940; see Legacy, p. 317.

17 August 1940, Cedar Grove, NJ

While Benny was recuperating from surgery, Ziggy Elman joined Joe Venuti's orchestra, prior to signing on with Tommy Dorsey. An NBC broadcast by the "Virtuoso of the Violin" this date from Frank Dailey's Meadowbrook features Ziggy fraliching through his **And The Angels Sing** as a highlight of a 20-minute program.

28 October 1940, New York (ref: page 113)

All four Septet recordings from this session are also issued on the LP, JAA 42, and on the CD, VJC 1021-2.

In parentheses concluding the Legacy displays for this session, and that of 7 November 1940, are unfair and inaccurate references to the Swedish LP, JD 7997. The author was misinformed as to the provenance of its included tracks. JD 7997 was transferred directly from first-generation tapes of the source acetates, supplied to producer Carl Hallstrom by the transcriptions' owner, Les Zeiger. Our apologies to Carl.

See herein under date of 7 November 1940 a 1993 CD produced by Hallstrom, whose contents are transferred from the master tapes cited above.

7 November 1940, New York (ref: page 113)

Post-publication releases alter and add to Legacy's display for this Sextet session. Noteworthy are the multi-format Columbia issue, CO 40846, and the Danish Jazz Unlimited CD, JUCD 2013. The latter replicates some of the tracks on producer Carl Hallstrom's earlier LP, JD 7997.

Revise Legacy's listing as follows:

BENNY GOODMAN AND HIS SEXTET
FEATURING COUNT BASIE

7 November 1940, New York

Personnel as per Legacy

CO 29027	**LP:** JAA 6. **CD:** JUCD 2013
CO 29027	**LP:** CO G30779, et al. **CD:** JUCD 2013
CO 29027-4	**LP:** CO G30779, et al. **CD:** JUCD 2013
CO 29027-Bkdn	**CD:** JUCD 2013
CO 29027-1	CO 35810, et al
CO 29027-2	CO 35810, et al
	Wholly Cats

(An additional Columbia release, CO CG33566, officially designates the third complete take, above, as take 4.)

CO 29028	**LP:** JAA 6. **CD:** JUCD 2013
CO 29028	**LP:** CO G30779, et al. **CD:** JUCD 2013
CO 29028-1	CO 35810, et al. **CD:** JUCD 2013
	Royal Garden Blues

The 1987 multi-format Columbia release, CO 40846, offers a previously unknown take, next, which it designates as, take 2:

CO 29029-1	CO 35901, et al
CO 29029-2	**LP, Cas, CD:** CO 40846, CBSFr 460.612
	As Long As I Live

Omitting the almost four minutes of chatter and miscellaneous rehearsal on the master tapes between matrices CO 29029 and CO 29030, the CD, JUCD 2013, then tracks the balance of this session in full. The acetates from which the masters for matrix CO 29030 were transcribed are worn, and their surface noise is audible on the CD. It does not detract from the worth of the CD, however, which offers to the public unspliced performances.

Track 8 of the CD is continuous, from the rehearsal relevant to matrix CO 29030 through conversation that ends the session. Its 27:31 running time is separated into its salient elements to distinguish among its partial and complete renditions.

7 November 1940, continued

7 November 1940, continued

CO 29030 (a)	**CD:** JUCD 2013. **LP:** JAA 6 *
CO 29030 (b)	**CD:** JUCD 2013. **LP:** JAA 6 *
CO 29030 (c)	**CD:** JUCD 2013. **LP:** JAA 6 *
CO 29030	**CD:** JUCD 2013
CO 29030 (d)	**CD:** JUCD 2013. **LP:** JAA 6 *
CO 29030	**CD:** JUCD 2013
CO 29030-1	CO 35901, et al. **CD:** JUCD 2013
	Benny's Bugle

* See Legacy for details of the spliced takes issued on the LP, JAA 6, Side 2/Track 1, and Side 2/Track 4. Unlettered designations are rehearsals between complete takes, and are now issued on the CD, JUCD 2013.

13 November 1940, New York (ref: page 114)

An unpardonable error in Legacy has Helen Forrest married to Harry Jaeger. Helen was indeed married to a drummer, but he was Al Spieldock, not Jaeger. It may be recalled that Helen and Al also recorded together, on the Lionel Hampton Victor sessions of 10 May 1940 and 17 July 1940.

For a further note on Spieldock herein, see 15 December 1943.

Matrix CO 29064, **Henderson Stomp:** Delete the LP, FR Series, from credits for take 1, add it to the unnumbered take immediately following take 1, as issued on LP, BID T-1009.

This previously unnumbered take is now designated as take 2, per assignment by a Columbia release post-publication. The entry for this take now is:

BENNY GOODMAN AND HIS ORCHESTRA   **13 November 1940, New York**

Personnel as per Legacy.

CO 29064-2	**LP:** BID T-1009, FR Series, CO 40834, CBSFr 460.829.
	Cas, CD: CO 40834, CBSFr 460.829
	Henderson Stomp

29 November 1940, New York (ref: page 114)

Take 1, matrix CO 29178, **Cabin In The Sky,** has been discovered on the original-issue 78, CO 35869.

10 December 1940, New York (ref: page 114)

Rumored extant for years, the elusive acetate of Benny's guest appearance on this "We The People" broadcast has at last surfaced. Sponsored by Sanka Coffee, the cut begins with a few introductory bars by Mark Warnow's orchestra. Next, Benny chats with music critic Deems Taylor about Benny's upcoming debut with the Philharmonic-Symphony Orchestra of New York. Then Benny introduces his Septet, and they play. Unfortunately, the disc runs out during Benny's final solo. But the audio quality is excellent, and Christian gets a chorus and a half.

"WE THE PEOPLE"   CBS Radio Network   *10 December 1940, New York*

Benny Goodman clt; Cootie Williams, tpt; George Auld, ts; Count Basie, p; Charlie Christian, g; Art Bernstein, b; Harry Jaeger, d.

Flying Home (n/c)

12 December 1940, New York (ref: page 115)

An acetate that affords no clues as to its origin offers Benny and a symphony orchestra performing Claude Debussy's **First Rhapsody For Clarinet.** It is known that the Debussy opus was included in the Carnegie Hall program this date, and thus this performance is so assigned. Uncertain, however, is whether it or the Mozart composition were broadcast; both may have been privately recorded for an unknown purpose.

"NBC SYMPHONY ORCHESTRA"   ? NBC Radio Network ?   12 December 1940, New York

Benny Goodman, clt, and the Philharmonic-Symphony Orchestra of New York, John Barbirolli conducting.

First Rhapsody For Clarinet (Debussy)

19 December 1940, New York (ref: page 115)

Delete the false, undetected insertion of the LP, CBS 62581, from all credits for matrix CO 29259, **Breakfast Feud.**

Prompted by the post-Legacy release of multi-format CO 45144, **Breakfast Feud** was reevaluated. In its entirety, substitute the following for matrix CO 29259:

BENNY GOODMAN AND HIS SEXTET   **19 December 1940, New York**

Personnel as per Legacy.

CO 29259	**LP:** JAA 6 (Side 1, Track 7)
CO 29259-4	**LP:** JAA 6 (Side 2, Track 5). **LP, Cas, CD:** CO 45144
CO 29259-"3"	**LP:** JAA 6 (Side 2, Track 7–partial; see note)
CO 29259-Bkdn	UNISSUED - CO Safety
CO 29259-Bkdn	UNISSUED - CO Safety
CO 29259-"2"	**LP:** JAA 6 (Side 2, Track 7–partial; see note)
CO 29259-1	**LP:** CO G30779, SONY SOPZ4-6, CBS 67233, SONY 56AP 674-6, BID-T-1004. **CD:** JUCD 2013
	Breakfast Feud

(Unnumbered take is, in fact, a rehearsal.
(CO 29259-4 is a single, unspliced take. CO 45144 designates it as take 4.
(CO 29259-"3": JAA 6, Side 2, Track 7, uses this take as its base, then splices into it a guitar solo from take "2." Thus the unadulterated take "3" is Unissued.
(CO 29259-Bkdn: The first-listed breakdown is identifiable by Benny's remark, "My mistake." It is Unissued.
(CO 29259-Bkdn: The second-listed breakdown is identifiable by Benny's remark, "Aw, c'mon, boys." It is Unissued.
(CO 29259-"2": As noted above for CO 29259-"3," JAA 6, Side 2, Track 7, splices a guitar solo from this take into its base take "3." Thus, the unadulterated take "2" is Unissued.
(CO 29259-1: Take 1 is inscribed onto the test pressing of this performance (it does not appear on microgroove releases). LP BID T-1004's track of matrix CO 29259 is take 1; its liner notes are in error.

19 December 1940, continued

19 December 1940, continued

Multi-format CO 45144's liner notes are confused in regard its track of matrix CO 29261, **Gilly.** They correctly designate it as take 2. But then they mistakenly credit the initial release of take 2 to the EP, CoE SEG C11. Not so; the CoE SEG C11's track of **Gilly** is the unnumbered take for matrix CO 29261, per attributions in Legacy. And note that ALL FOUR takes of **Gilly** (including the breakdown) are on the CD, JUCD 2013, per Legacy's listing.

20 December 1940, New York (ref: page 116)

The first-listed unnumbered take of matrix CO 29274, **I'm Always Chasing Rainbows,** is issued on LP, BID T-1015.

The second-listed, unissued take of matrix CO 29275, **Somebody Stole My Gal,** although almost complete, should be correctly classified as a breakdown.

"20 December 1940, New York" (ref: page 116)

This notice of a 1990 Columbia release is inserted here simply for convenience's sake, Legacy's Index reference to the tune, **Somebody Stole My Gal.**

In October 1989 the author received preview tapes of a proposed Columbia release, was asked for his comments and specifications of dates, matrices and takes, personnel. Save for **Somebody Stole My Gal,** all of the tracks were readily identifiable. Its structure and tenor saxophone soloist were different from those of the four available takes of matrix CO 29275, 20 December 1940. Further, they were different from all other performances of the tune in the author's collection, whether studio recordings available on record or ET, or air checks on acetate or tape.

The author immediately sought information about this studio recording of **Somebody Stole My Gal** from the producer. None was forthcoming. The release's liner notes offer no discographical detail.

There are several distinct differences between this previously-unissued take of **Somebody Stole My Gal** and any or all of the four takes of matrix CO 29275. The tenor saxophone soloist is not George Auld. There is but one tenor saxophone solo, not two separated by an ensemble passage; Benny takes what had been the second tenor solo. And although this new cut is taken at a faster tempo, its running time is longer than any of the matrix CO 29275 takes.

In the author's opinion, this tenor saxophonist is Vido Musso, Auld's successor in the band. Auld departed in June 1941, Musso joined in July 1941, remained through May 1942. If the author's identification of Musso is correct, then this recording of **Somebody Stole My Gal** could have been recorded on any of the Columbia studio sessions in this time span.

A further delimiting factor appeals to the author. He doesn't believe the drummer here is Sid Catlett. Ralph Collier replaced Catlett in time for the Columbia session of 21 October 1941. Nine big-band sessions follow, ending with the Columbia studio session of 14 May 1942. The assignment here thus lies in any of the ten orchestral Columbia sessions between 21 October 1941 and 14 May 1942. The author's preference is for one of the earlier dates, rather than any of the later ones.

With little hope of now getting from Sony/Columbia the true facts, we go out on a limb with:

BENNY GOODMAN AND HIS ORCHESTRA   21 October 1941 - 14 May 1942, New York

Personnel for this period as per Legacy, including Vido Musso, ts.

- 0 - **CD, Cas:** CO 45338, CO 53774
Somebody Stole My Gal

15 January 1941, New York (ref: page 116)
A CD issued in 1993 offers two previously unlisted takes of **Breakfast Feud** from this session. Its release also revises the makeup of two spliced LPs, and alters the order-of-recording for matrix CO 29512. Substitute the following for the display in Legacy:

BENNY GOODMAN AND HIS SEXTET
FEATURING COUNT BASIE   **15 January 1941, New York**

Personnel as per Legacy.

CO 29512	**CD:** JUCD 2013 - Track 14
CO 29512	**CD:** JUCD 2013 - Track 15
CO 29512-2	CO 36039, et al. **CD:** JUCD 2013 - Track 16
CO 29512-1	**LP:** PHON 7612, BID T-1006. **LP, Cas, CD:** CO 40846, CBSFr 460.612. **CD:** JUCD 2013 - Track 17
CO 29512-S^1	**LP:** CO CL 652, et al - Note A
CO 29512-S^2	**LP:** CO G30779, et al - Note B
	Breakfast Feud

A.   CO CL 652: Intro through Basie's solo, JUCD 2013 - Track 15; Christian's 1st solo, matrix CO 29259-1, session of 19 December 1940; Christian's 2nd solo, JUCD 2013 - Track 15; Christian's 3rd solo, matrix CO 29512-2, this session; Auld's solo to completion, JUCD 2013 - Track 15.

B.   CO G30779: Intro through Christian's 1st solo, JUCD 2013 - Track 14; Christian's 2nd solo, JUCD 2013 - Track 15; Christian's 3rd solo, matrix CO 29512-2, this session; Christian's 4th solo, to completion, matrix CO 29512-1, this session.

The Smithsonian Institution's CD, RD033-A519477's track of **Breakfast Feud** has five Christian soli. Liner notes ascribe the first three as from CO CL 652; the fourth, matrix 29512-2; and the fifth, unspecified, as "from CO G30779." The author does not have this CD, and so is unable to verify these identifications. The CD also offers **I Found A New Baby,** mx CO 29514-1.
Typo: CO 36039, not "36029," for **I Found A New Baby**.

15 January 1941, New York (ref: page 117)
Multi-format CO 45144 mistakenly cites take 1 for its track of matrix CO 29519, **Gone With What Draft.** Take is -3.

21 January 1941, New York (ref: page 117)
Delete one listing, "UNISSUED - TAPE," from the array for matrix CO 29530, **Time On My Hands.** Further review proves it to be the same take issued on LP, PHON 7612.

Liner notes for multi-format CO 48902 err in assigning its track of matrix CO 29531-1, **You're Dangerous,** to "28 January 1941." Correct date is 21 January.

28 January 1941, New York (ref: page 117)

The previously-unnumbered complete take of matrix CO 29578, **Bewitched,** as first issued on LP, PHON 7615, is now designated as take 2, per multi-format CO 40834's liner notes (companion releases, CBSFr 460.829).

17 February 1941, New York (ref: page 118)

Delete **Let The Doorknob Hitcha** from this listing, reassign it to 24 February 1941, q.v. The author did not, and does not, have a log of this "What's New?" broadcast, and made his assignments in Legacy on the flimsy evidence of post-dated acetates.

19 February 1941, New York (ref: page 118)

The third complete take of matrix CO 29755, **Scarecrow,** first issued on LP, BlD T-1009, is also on multi-format CO 40834 and CBSFr 460.829. Columbia's liner notes err, cite this take as, -1. Also for **Scarecrow,** delete the FR Series credit from the true take 1, add it to the unnumbered take first issued on LP, TL STLJ05. Arbitrarily, TL STLJ05 identifies its track as, "take 2."

There is a redundancy in Legacy's array for **Yours.** The first credit line—PHON 7615—and the third credit line—"UNISSUED - Tape"—are one and the same take. In proper order of performance, assign PHON 7615 to what now becomes the second credit line.

24 February 1941, New York (ref: page 118)

For unknown reasons, NBC's engineers "lifted the needle" whenever any dialogue cropped up as they recorded this "What's New?" broadcast. Thus the opening theme is interrupted as soon as the announcer begins, "The makers of . . .". When his voice-over spiel finishes, the theme resumes. This practice persists throughout, resulting in a music-only transcription about two/thirds the length of what was a 30-minute program. Save for the themes, however, all other performances are complete, compensate in part with excellent audio for the absent commentary.

These Reference Recordings revise Legacy's listing. As noted under date of 17 February herein, **Let The Doorknob Hitcha** is from this 24 February broadcast. And the putative **What's New—It's You(?)** was not performed on this Old Gold show, is relegated to an unknown date.

Substitute the following in its entirety for the array in Legacy:

"WHAT'S NEW?" WJZ Radio (NBC)   *24 February 1941, New York*

Personnels as per Legacy.

Let's Dance (theme)
Frenesi
The Moon Won't Talk - voc Helen Forrest
Let's Dance (historical evolution, to complete Henderson arrangement)
Yours - voc Helen Forrest
(The Fives - Basie w/rhythm - NO BG
*Gone With What Draft - SEPTET (**LP:** TRIB-no #)*
Let The Doorknob Hitcha
Let's Dance (theme)

"AMERICA IN SWINGTIME," Spring 1941, New York (ref: pages 317, 318)

Consensus of opinion is that it was Vic Berton's brother, not his son, who MC'd this broadcast.

4 March 1941, New York (ref: page 119)

Multi-format CO 40834 et al mistakenly list the track of matrix CO 29865, **Solo Flight,** as "take 1." It is take 2.

13 March 1941, New York (ref: page 119)

Take 1, matrix CO 29942, **A Smo-o-o-oth One,** first issued on the LP, BlD 1004, is also on multi-format CO 45144.

Multi-format CO 40846 et al err in identifying the track of matrix CO 29943, **Good Enough To Keep (Airmail Special),** as the spliced recording first issued on the LP, CO CL 652. It is not; it is the unspliced take 2, first released on the LP, PHON 7615.

28 April 1941, New York (ref: page 120)

Misinformation continues to vex collectors about the bogus "Swedish" LP, the un-numbered TRIB, ascribing its track of **Air Mail Special** to Benny's "What's New?" broadcast this date. No; the TRIB track is a dub of Jimmy Mundy's V-Disc 701. No Goodman, and no Charlie Christian, either; the guitarist is believed to be Irving Ashby.

5 May 1941, studio, New York (ref: page 121)

Don't Be That Way (no matrix assigned), first issued on the LP, PHON 7616, is also on multi-format CO 45338.

15 August 1941, Chicago (ref: page 124)

Liner notes for SONY/CO CD 53422, ignoring the LP, PHON 7616, falsely claim its track of matrix CCO 3950-1, **Elmer's Tune,** to be "previously unissued." In company with other major label producers, Sony refuses to acknowledge prior releases on unauthorized labels.

20 August 1941, Chicago (ref: page 124)

Benny was unhappy with the audio engineering in Columbia's Chicago studios, hastily summoned Bill Savory to participate, "give them a hand." As souvenirs of the event, Bill has a rehearsal take of matrix CCO 3951, **The Birth Of The Blues,** and three introductory takes of matrix CCO 3982, **I See A Million People (But All I Can See Is You).** ADD them to Legacy's display as preceding the respective Columbia releases, all as "UNISSUED Acetate."

Benny was also annoyed with John Hammond during this session. With Helen Forrest on notice, John kept bugging Benny to hire Billie Holiday, get rid of Peggy Lee, who "just cahn't sing, Benny, she really cahn't." Benny put a stop to that by throwing a chair at his future brother-in-law.

Delete from Legacy's listing its "(reputedly FR series)" credit for take 1, matrix CCO 3980, **Clarinet A La King,** reassign the Franklin Mint track to take 2, same matrix, as first issued on the LP, PHON 7616.

14 September 1941, Cedar Grove, NJ (ref: page 125)

The air check **Take It** is issued on the CD, VJC-1032.

17 September 1941, Cedar Grove, NJ (ref: page 125)

Inadvertent omission: The air check, **A Smo-o-o-oth One,** immediately precedes **Something New.**

25 September 1941, New York (ref: page 126)

In order to pinpoint additions and other changes to the Legacy array for this session, data below are separated into those identically-numbered matrices that were recorded with drums, and without drums.

WITH drums:

The first-listed take of matrix CO 31363, **How Deep Is The Ocean,** is issued on LP, BlD T-1015.

The last full take of matrix CO 31364, **The Earl** (immediately preceding the tune title), is issued on EP, PHON BG PH86. As noted earlier in this tract, the EP is complementary to the album, PHON 7659-7661.

WITHOUT drums:

The first complete take of matrix CO 31363, **How Deep Is The Ocean,** first issued on LP, PHON 7616, is also on multi-format CO 40834 and CBSFr 460.829. Columbia's liner notes now designate this performance as take 2.

ADD the release, FR Series, to matrix CO 31364-1, **The Earl;** and DELETE the same release, FR Series, from the matrix CO 31364-2, **The Earl.**

DELETE SONY 20AP-1486 from the listing for take 2, matrix CO 31367, **Let's Do It (Let's Fall In Love).** See also entry herein for 21 October 1941.

4 October 1941, Cedar Grove, NJ (ref: page 127)

Delete credit, LP: JOY 1097, from the air check, **Caprice XXIV Paganini.**

21 October 1941, New York (ref: page 128)

A newly-discovered Columbia "safety" reveals that, as for the 25 September 1941 session, three breakdowns preceded an acceptable take of **Let's Do It.** Prior to this coincidence, however, two complete takes were recorded. The array for matrix CO 31367, this date, now becomes:

BENNY GOODMAN AND HIS ORCHESTRA   **21 October 1941, New York**

Personnel as per Legacy.

CO 31367	UNISSUED - Tape
CO 31367	UNISSUED - Tape
CO 31367-bkdns	UNISSUED - Tape (3 consecutive aborted attempts)
CO 31367-3	**LP:** VELP 1, PHON 7617
CO 31367-4	OK 6474, et al, plus: **LP:** SONY 20AP-1486
	Let's Do It (Let's Fall In Love) - voc Peggy Lee

(Credit for the SONY 20AP-1486 album was inadvertently misassigned to take 2, matrix CO 31367, 25 September 1941, in Legacy.)

21 October 1941, continued

21 October 1941, continued

Columbia's multi-format 53422 errs in assigning "take 3" to its track of **Shady Lady Bird.** Take is -2, as first issued on LP, PHON 7617.

Caveat emptor: Ignore offers of a tape of **Buckle Down Winsocki,** proffered as a live performance via a broadcast of 22 August 1942, location unspecified. It's a dub—and partial, at that—of the common 78 release, CO 36429.

22 October 1941, New York (ref: page 128)

NBC was the network of origin for this broadcast from the Ice Terrace Room, revealed by its Reference Recordings embracing the full half hour. Substitute this array in its entirety for the listing in Legacy:

SUSTAINING BROADCAST   NBC Radio Network   22 October 1941, Hotel New Yorker,
New York

Personnel as per Legacy.

Let's Dance (theme)
Caprice XXIV Paganini
I See A Million People - voc Peggy Lee
*Moon And Sand (**LP:** FAN 19-119)*
Superman
Who Can I Turn To? - voc Tommy Taylor (arr EdSau)
Something New
I Don't Want To Set The World On Fire - voc Peggy Lee
A Smo-o-o-oth One
Let's Dance (theme)

26 October 1941, New York (ref: page 128)

The Quartet's air check **You And I** is on the LP, SB 158.

28 October 1941, New York (ref: page 129)

Take 2, matrix CO 31610, **Limehouse Blues,** first issued on the LP, BlD T-1004, is included in multi-format CO 44437.

Note that the 7" LP, "EPH82," is a PHONtastic release.

27 November 1941, New York (ref: page 130)

CBS Special Products cassette BT 17817, titled "Christmas With The Big Bands," includes a take from this session listed in Legacy as, "UNISSUED-Tape." Copyrighted in 1984, the cassette likely has a companion LP; if so, it has not been located. Nine other tracks on the cassette are non-Goodman Columbia recordings.

In 1992, Sony Music Special Products replicated and re-released the album on CD, retaining the catalog number 17817. This suggests that a putative LP would also bear that catalog number. For first-release collectors, the cassette, and possibly the LP, are primary issues.

Neither the cassette nor the CD offers discographical data. Because the previously-unissued take is an authorized release, and because it was the third complete take recorded, it is arbitrarily designated as take "3." In order-of-performance per Columbia master tapes, the array for matrix CO 31811 now is:

BENNY GOODMAN AND HIS ORCHESTRA   27 November 1941, New York

Personnel as per Legacy:

CO 31811-bkdn	UNISSUED - Tape
CO 31811	**LP:** PHON 7617
CO 31811	UNISSUED - Tape
CO 31811-bkdn	UNISSUED - Tape
CO 31811-bkdn	UNISSUED - Tape
CO 31811-"3"	**Cas:** CoSP BT 17817. **CD:** SonySP A 17817. **LP:** ? CoSP 17817 ?
CO 31811-bkdn	UNISSUED - Tape
CO 31811-1	OK 6516, et al
	Winter Weather - voc Peggy Lee & Art London (arr MP)

(Note that the CD was also made available for Christmas 1994 and 1995.)

10 December 1941, New York (ref: page 131)
Deliberately ignoring the LP, PHON 7620, the SONY CD CO 53422's liner notes cite its track of take 1, matrix CO 31945, **Not A Care In The World,** as "previously-unissued."
Also for PHON 7620: Delete its credit in Legacy for the second breakdown of matrix CO 31946, **You Don't Know What Love Is.** This take was aborted when Lou McGarity fluffed his trombone solo, and Benny illustrated how it should be played . . . on his clarinet. Programmed for inclusion in this LP, it was inadvertently omitted, and is correctly designated as, "UNISSUED-Tape."

24 December 1941, New York (ref: page 131)
A scratchy Columbia "safety" adds a breakdown to matrix CO 32052 preceding the issued take. The array for the matrix now is:

BENNY GOODMAN (& HIS) SEXTET   24 December 1941, New York

Personnel as per Legacy. Note that Mel Powell also plays celeste, in addition to piano.

CO 32052-bkdn	UNISSUED - Tape
CO 32052-1	OK 6553, et al
CO 32052	**LP:** PHON 7620, BID 1002
	Where Or When - voc Peggy Lee

Typographical errors: 78 credit for matrix CO 32052-1, **Where Or When,** should be CO 38281, not "38821." And make it OK 6553 for the first issue of matrix CO 32051, **Blues In The Night.**

15 January 1942, New York (ref: page 132)
Correction: The LP, JOY 6015, should be credited to take 2, matrix CO 32240, **If You Build A Better Mousetrap,** not to take 1.

4 February 1942, New York (ref: page 133)

The previously-unissued take B, matrix 76989, **Mood At Twilight,** is included (together with all five previously-issued takes) on record 19, Side A, of the pricey MOSAIC MR23-123 album. Affected matrix is:

MEL POWELL AND HIS ORCHESTRA   **4 February 1942, New York**

Personnel as per Legacy.

76989-A	CMS 544B, et al, plus **LP:** MOSAIC album MR23-123
76989-B	**LP:** MOSAIC album MR23-123, record 19, Side A
	Mood At Twilight

5 February 1942, New York (ref: page 134)

As a warmup for the 5 February 1942 session, Benny and the band ad-libbed snatches of several traditional Dixie tunes, ending with the redoubtable **Muskrat Ramble.** Their high jinks were captured on a Columbia "safety."

Add FR Series to the credits for take 1, matrix CO 32383, **A String Of Pearls.**

The second full take of matrix CO 32383, **A String Of Pearls,** is issued on the LP, BID T-1015.

Sharp-eared collector Dave Jessup questioned whether the two LPs credited in Legacy for the "breakup" recording of **Ramona** are identical, both take -2 of matrix CO 32385. Review confirmed his finding that they are indeed different, although they do have an element in common:

The 12" LP, Blu-Disc 1006, is a true transfer of the breakup, take -2 of matrix CO 32385. The 7" 33 LP, Columbia's "bonus record," is not; it is spliced. It combines the first half of take -1 (as per CoArg 20.323 B), through Benny's chorus, with the second half of take -2 (as per Blu-Disc 1006), to conclusion. These determinations are validated by comparisons to Columbia's "safeties." Thus CO ZLP 13905 reverses the splices that make up the **Ramona** track on the LPs, CO GL 523 et al. Bonus record? Make that bogus record.

So that there is no misunderstanding, matrix CO 32385 is reconstituted in its entirety. Note that Benny's intro fluff—the fourth breakdown, marked below with an asterisk—preceding matrix CO 32385-2, is also on CO ZLP 13905, an oversight omission in Legacy.

Substitute the following for the array in Legacy.

BENNY GOODMAN AND HIS ORCHESTRA   **5 February 1942, New York**

Personnel as per Legacy.

CO 32385	**LP:** PHON 7620
CO 32385-bkdn	UNISSUED - Tape
CO 32385-bkdn	UNISSUED - Tape
CO 32385	UNISSUED - Tape
CO 32385-bkdn	UNISSUED - Tape
CO 32385-bkdn*	**7" 33:** CO ZLP 13905. **LP:** BID 1006 (Benny's fluff)
CO 32385-2 [a]	**LP:** BID 1006
CO 32385-1 [b]	CoArg 20.323 B, et al
CO 32385-S^1	**LP:** CO GL 523, et al
CO 32385-S^2	**7" 33:** CO ZLP 13905
	Ramona (arr EdSau)

(CO GL 523 splices the first half of mx CO 32385-2 [a] above—through Benny's chorus—to the second half of matrix CO 32385-1 [b] above. CO ZLP 13905 splices the first half of matrix CO 32385-1 [b] above—through Benny's solo—to the second half of matrix CO 32385-2 [a] above.)

"SYNCOPATION," February 1942, New York (ref: page 134)

Clips of Benny from the "untitled blues" epilogue of "Syncopation," seen in the 1993 PBS-TV presentation, "Benny Goodman: Adventures In The Kingdom Of Swing," prompt further explanation of his contributions to the motion picture. This restatement is made possible by Ken Crawford, whose unmatched collection of jazz films includes the only known complete print of "Syncopation" held privately.

As stated in Legacy, Benny recorded his soli with his own rhythm section, not with the "All-American Jazz Band." He is never seen together with them in the film, although adroit splicing integrates his soli flawlessly. In one full-group sequence an actor, "Paul Rickey," his back to the camera, appears to play a clarinet. (Could he have been the clarinetist Paul RICCI?) Adding to the illusion of Benny's seeming to play with the group is the set's jungle motif behind him, common to the sequences showing the full group. Manifestly, then, Benny's soli were filmed, not simply recorded on acetate.

An inference that Benny recorded separately can be drawn from a still photograph shot in the Fox-MovieTONE (not ". . . town") studios. In it he looks on while makeup technicians groom Gene Krupa and Harry James for the movie. Gene wears a bow tie with his tux jacket, as do all the others when they are on screen. Benny, however, has on a business suit, with it a four-in-hand tie. This argues that he was not then going to play with the group, else he would have been similarly dressed. When seen in the film, Benny is formally clad, with bow tie. Thus, recorded separately, via film.

Neither pianist Howie Smith, substituting for poll winner Eddie Duchin, nor bassist Bobby Haggart is on screen with the "All-Americans." And both are omitted from the film's credits, although the author's long-ago information had them participating. Only poll winners Goodman, James, Jenney, Venuti, Barnet, Rey and Krupa are visible in the epilogue.

As noted in Legacy, "Syncopation" was released 22 May 1942—to various RKO-Radio theaters in the United States. At one or more of them, a souvenir album was given to patrons, to mark the premiere. Its jacket is extant, but it does not describe the contents, and they are unknown.

10 March 1942, New York (ref: page 135)

The SEXTET recording of matrix CO 32594, **The World Is Waiting For The Sunrise,** first issued on the LPs, BlD 1002 and PHON 7644, is also released on multi-format CO 44437, which designates this take as, -3.

12 March 1942, New York (ref: page 135)

Inadvertent omission: Matrix CO 32600 (no take #), **Before (Rachmaninoff Special),** as credited to the LP, PHON 7644, was also released on the LP, BlD T-1006. (For those who lack either LP, this unnumbered take was also included in the 1993 CD, PHON 8823).

5 April 1942, Atlantic City, NJ

Confirming a speculative report in Legacy (page 136), an eyewitness collected Dick Haymes's autograph, plus others of those in the Goodman orchestra, Sunday, 5 April 1942, on the Steel Pier, Atlantic City. This advances Haymes's brief sojourn with Benny by almost two months. It does not, however, explain why Art London recorded with the band on 14 May. It's possible Dick was a "special added attraction" for the desirable Easter weekend engagement at the Pier.

14 May 1942, New York (ref: page 136)

The second complete take of matrix CO 32796, **Take Me,** listed in Legacy as "UNISSUED - Tape," was in fact issued on the LP, JOY 6015, when the book was published. To position that LP in its order-of-performance, per the Columbia master tapes, the matrix is arrayed in its entirety:

BENNY GOODMAN AND HIS ORCHESTRA   **14 May 1942, New York**

Personnel as per Legacy.

CO 32796	UNISSUED - Tape
CO 32796-bkdn	UNISSUED - Tape
CO 32796-bkdn	UNISSUED - Tape
CO 32796	**LP:** JOY 6015
CO 32796-bkdn	UNISSUED - Tape
CO 32796-1	**LP:** PHON 7644. **CD:** PHON 8824
	Take Me - voc Art London

A spectator asserts that Paul Geil, tpt, and Johnny McAfee, bar, were present for this session. They are not named in Columbia's personnel list.

17 June 1942, New York (ref: page 137)

The first take of matrix CO 32923, **Serenade In Blue,** listed in Legacy as, "UNISSUED - CO REF," was released via CO CD 66198 in 1995. Liner notes erroneously identify its take as, "1," which properly belongs to the initial issue of this tune on the 78, CO 36622.

"Lawrence Stearns" (ref: page 137)

"Stearns's" baptismal name is Alfred Sculco. A student at Juilliard, Al tried to earn tuition money via record dates in Manhattan, but was denied them because of Local 802's residency requirement. Seeking any means to overcome that obstacle, he eventually found a Local 802 card-holder, a drummer about to be drafted, willing to sell his union card for $100. Al bought it, assumed the drummer's name—Lawrence Stearns.

Recovered from a stroke, when last heard from Al was "doing well." He doesn't know whatever became of the real Lawrence Stearns.

27 July 1942, New York (ref: page 137)
Two Blu-Disc LPs, T-1015 and T-1016, were released after Legacy's text had been typeset; for that reason their contents were necessarily omitted. References to them are elsewhere in this work. Blu-Disc T-1015 affects two matrices this date, which now become:

BENNY GOODMAN AND HIS ORCHESTRA   27 July 1942, New York

Personnel as per Legacy.

CO 33048	**LP:** BID T-1014
CO 33048-bkdn	UNISSUED - Tape
CO 33048	**LP:** BID T-1015, plus: **LP:** PHON 7661. **CD:** PHON 7660, PHON 8824
CO 33048-1	CO 36652, et al, plus: **LP:** SONY 20AP-1486, FR Series, CO 44158, CO 45338. **Cas, CD:** CO 44158, 45338
CO 33048-2	VD 233 B, et al, plus: **45:** CO 13-33305. Delete **LP,** SONY 20AP-1486
	Why Don't You Do Right (?) - voc Peggy Lee

CO 33049	**LP:** BID T-1015
CO 33049-bkdn	**LP:** BID T-1015
CO 33049	**LP:** BID T-1014. **CD:** PHON 8824
CO 33049-bkdn	UNISSUED - Tape
CO 33049	**LP:** BID T-1014
CO 33049-1	CO 36699, et al, plus: **LP, Cas, CD:** CO 44158
	After You've Gone

Correct PHON 8824's liner notes ascription for its track of **Why Don't You Do Right(?)** to Blu-Disc T-1015, not T-1014.

September 1942, Hollywood (ref: page 139)
The acetate, **You're Out Of This World,** is confirmed as an out-take from the United Artists film, "The Powers Girl."

Mid-October 1942, New York (ref: page 139)
Trumpeter Al Sculco, aka "Lawrence Stearns," advises that Jimmy Zito, not Conrad Gozzo, replaced Al at the Hotel New Yorker. Zito was in but briefly, soon replaced by Gozzo. Also, Legacy's personnel credits enter trombonist Earl LeFave a few weeks too early. LeFave left Sam Donahue 1 November to go with Benny.

1 November 1942, New York (ref: page 140)
Rhapsody In Blue is on CD, VJC 1034, and also on Italian CD, HUNT 534. For another track on HUNT 534, see under date of 14 November 1943, herein.

December 1942, New York (ref: page 140)

Revise the band's personnel for "Stage Door Canteen" to substitute trombonist Miff Mole and saxophonist Joe Rushton for Jack Jenny and Ted Goddard, respectively; both are identifiable in still photos. And substitute an unidentified saxophonist for Al Klink. The movie is available on an indifferent-quality commercial videotape, MURRAY HILL 873443.

Paramount Theater, 1942/1943, New York (ref: page 141)

The Public Broadcasting System's "Frank Sinatra: The Voice Of Our Time," televised in 1991, includes a seconds-brief sequence of Sinatra's appearance with Benny at the Paramount. A clip from a newsreel, it occurs about eight minutes into the telecast. From the wings, Benny and a few sidemen are shown on stage, then Sinatra enters. Picture only, no sound.

"The Cresta Blanca Carnival"/YOUR BROADWAY AND MINE, both:? 10 January 1943, New York (ref: page 141)

Transferred from acetates in fair quality, the 45-minute "Cresta Blanca Carnival" is on cassette, RADIO YESTERYEAR 18163. It revises the listings in Legacy for all relevant entries for the broadcast, in several respects:

Broadcast date is 13 January 1943, a Wednesday (Morton Gould had told the author that, so far as he could recall, the broadcasts were on Sunday evenings.)

Rose Room was performed early in the broadcast; **Rhapsody In Blue** was the program's finale.

The untitled duet, Benny and an unknown pianist, is NOT from the "Carnival." Possibly the "10 January 1943" date inscribed on this acetate is correct for this performance, but now from an unknown source.

Rhapsody In Blue is the only track on the YOUR BROADWAY AND MINE ET from the "Carnival." All other material on it is excerpted from different programs.

13 February 1943, Chicago (ref: page 141)

On this Saturday evening Benny ". . . and his celebrated orchestra . . ." played a one-nighter at the famed Trianon Ballroom, Cottage Grove at 62nd Street in the Windy City. (Relief band was Eddy Howard's.) Thus the Trianon is the locale of the "Spotlight Bands" broadcast of 13 February.

14 March 1943, Hollywood (ref: page 142)

That incomplete air check likely is, **The Great LIE,** not ". . . Guy." No arrangement under either title is in Benny's Archives at Yale.

March/April 1943, Hollywood (ref: page 143)

Revision/addition: TCF 141 offers "Brazil," by a studio orchestra and chorus; its reverse, TCF 142, waxes a two-part "You Discover You're In New York." Neither side includes Benny; and TCF 239/240 remains undiscovered.

The film, "The Gang's All Here," which long had eluded collectors, was televised on the American Movie Classics cable channel in January 1994, and later in that year.

16 July 1943, Hotel Astor, New York (ref: page 144)

Their owner assures the author that the air checks cited this date (paragraph following the same-date listing of the "Broadway Bandbox") are extant; he offers no advice as to their audio quality. An unsigned and unattributed arrangement of **Mexico Joe** is in Benny's Archives at Yale.

"? January - 9 December 1943," New York (ref: page 145)

As suggested in Legacy under this heading, the acetate of **Henderson Stomp** is an alternate take of the release on V-Disc 159 A, recorded 9 December 1943. It is the last extant take of the tune, two complete takes and two breakdowns having preceded it. For complete details of the V-Disc session, see herein under date of 9 December 1943.

9 September 1943, New York

The final pair of the NBC Reference Recordings described herein under date of 29 March 1936 are labeled, "Benny Goodman Audition." Recorded before a live audience, they constitute a music-and-quiz program NBC and Benny hoped to sell as a half-hour weekly broadcast titled, "Music Is My Business." (Transcriptions' running time is 24:20.)

Although both an announcer and Benny separately state that there will be a succeeding program—". . . Until next Thursday evening when Benny will again bring you . . ." and "See you next week . . ."—we have no evidence of a successor, nor that a sponsor was obtained.

Nor can we be sure that this audition was in fact broadcast. NBC labels on other of the 152 transcriptions infallibly list either the Red or Blue network, or the station of origin. Labels here have neither. Broadcasts on the other ETs usually conclude with station identification or network identification, NBC chimes; they're absent here. And the hour of the audition—11:15–11:45 p.m.—is almost unprecedented for a commercial (sponsored) broadcast.

Withal, Benny enjoys himself as quizmaster, does a good job, on this most unusual addition to Benny's air checks:

"MUSIC IS MY BUSINESS"   *NBC (Radio Network ?)*   *9 September 1943, NBC Studios,*
New York

Band personnel as 17 August 1943 (page 144), except unknown d.
QUARTET: Goodman, Stacy, Reuss, Weiss

Let's Dance (theme)
At The Darktown Strutters' Ball
(. . . contest)
In My Arms - voc Benny Goodman, band
Sunday, Monday And Always - voc Ray Dorey
(. . . contest)
Three Little Words - QUARTET
(. . . contest; instrumental soli, band in coda, Put Your Arms Around Me, Honey)
Bugle Call Rag
Good-Bye (theme)

25 September 1943, Ithaca, NY (ref: page 146)

Correction: Catalog number of the GOL LP is 15082, not "15078."

After You've Gone and **Three Little Words** are also on LP, SWH 46.

9 October 1943, New York (ref: page 146)

Misplaced credit: **Honeysuckle Rose,** not the theme, is on JOY 1073.

16 October 1943, New York (ref: pages 146, 318)

Minnie's In The Money is incomplete on the Columbia Reference Recording of this broadcast; its beginning, through most of Benny's vocal, is missing. A home-recorded acetate is complete, but its audio quality is only fair.

13 November 1943, New York (ref: page 148)

Oh, Lady Be Good! is issued on a seven-inch LP, PHON MX EPH83.

14 November 1943, New York

False claim: The Italian CD, HUNT 534, includes the NBC Symphony Hour's broadcast of **An American In Paris,** this date. Its liner notes assert that Benny Goodman and Earl Wild performed. Not true: clarinetist was a member of maestro Toscanini's regular complement, and the pianist was Bernardo Segall.

17 November 1943, New York (ref: page 148)

Delete credit of the LP, SWT 103, for **I've Found A New Baby.**

Honeysuckle Rose, Mission To Moscow, and **I've Found A New Baby,** same performances as those on AFRS ONS No. 53, are on an acetate dated 15 November. If this earlier date is correct, two possibilities are suggested: Those three tunes may have been spliced into the ET, or its date should be revised to 15 November.

The ET is issued on cassette, RADY 2698.

9 December 1943, New York (ref: page 149)

Among the more welcome post-Legacy releases is the Vintage Jazz Classics CD, VJC 1001-2, which makes available to the public alternate takes of some of Benny's V-Discs. In large measure the alternates are listed in Legacy as, "UNISSUED - acetate."

To list the issued V-Disc and its alternates in what is believed to have been their order-of-performance, the 9 December 1943 session is reconstituted here. (As stated herein earlier, the Associated Recording acetate of **Henderson Stomp** is the final complete take of that tune.) Note that Benny's spoken introduction, which begins the CD, precedes **Dinah** on the V-Disc; **Henderson Stomp** is the first track of the CD.

BENNY GOODMAN AND HIS ORCHESTRA   **9 December 1943, New York**

Personnel as per Legacy.

- 0 - alt take	**CD:** VJC 1001-2
XP 33399-1 (VP 407)	VD 159 B, et al, plus **CD:** VJC 1001-2
	Dinah - voc Benny Goodman
-0 - alt take	**CD:** VJC 1001-2
-0 - bkdn	**CD:** VJC 1001-2
XP 33400-1 (VP 408)	VD 159 A, et al, plus **CD:** VJC 1001-2
- 0 - bkdn	**CD:** VJC 1001-2
- 0 - alt take	**CD:** VJC 1001-2
	Henderson Stomp
- 0 - take 1	**CD:** VJC 1001-2
- 0 - take 2	**CD:** VJC 1001-2
	'Way Down Yonder In New Orleans (arr EdSau)

BENNY GOODMAN, GENE KRUPA AND JESS STACEY (SIC)   **same date**

Personnel as per Legacy.

- O - alt take   **CD:** VJC 1001-2
XP 33400-1 (VP 408)   VD 159 A, et al, plus **CD:** VJC 1001-2
                               Limehouse Blues

    V-Disc 159 A/B is also on LP, DAN(J) 5022. V-Disc 159 A, **Henderson Stomp,** is also on LP, SWH 46.

15 December 1943, Annapolis, MD (ref: page 150)
    Al Spieldock's amusing recollection almost guarantees that Gene Krupa was in the band at the U.S. Naval Academy on 15 December. Al tells this tale, recounted to Gil Sandler:

I was playing drums in the band at the Club 21. It was across the street from what used to be the Lord Baltimore Hotel. A guy comes in and tells me Benny Goodman wanted to see me. I knew Goodman was in town, getting ready for a week's stand at the Hippodrome. This guy says, "Goodman wants you to sit in with his band for the week."
    I said, "What happened to Krupa?," and he said, "Nobody knows. He had a fight with Goodman and walked out. Goodman has no idea where in Baltimore Krupa is. So Goodman wants you." I knew the Goodman arrangements well. I had sat in with him before, and I was married to one of his vocalists, Helen Forrest. So, anyway, I went over to the Hipp.
    The curtain went up and we were into "Let's Dance," and in no time at all I was doing the long drum lead-in to "Sing, Sing, Sing." If the audience knew it wasn't Krupa playing that night, it never let on. It cheered and clapped and hollered like it always did for those Goodman numbers. We did "One O'Clock Jump," "Stompin' At The Savoy," "These Foolish Things," "I Let A Song Go Out Of My Heart," "Avalon." We did it all. We knocked them out. I was doing all that Krupa stuff. Nobody seemed to notice that Krupa himself wasn't playing. They thought I was Krupa! Matter of fact, after the show a couple of kids came up to me and begged me to sign autographs. I did. I signed, "Gene Krupa."

    The engagement at the Hippodrome began on 16 December. Thus if Benny didn't know "where in Baltimore" Gene was on the day after the Annapolis gig, Gene must have played for the Navy the day before.
    Buttressing this assignment is Sid Weiss's interview with James Lincoln Collier, **Benny Goodman and the Swing Era** (Oxford University Press), pages 308, 309, wherein Sid specifically links Gene with Annapolis, ecstatically so.

Mid-January 1944, Hollywood (ref: page 150)
    In an earlier book, the author credited AFRS Command Performance 155's **Rachel's Dream** to the 18 January 1944 Esquire concert. He corrected that in Legacy to this date. But he neglected to revise the parenthetical LP credits. Therefore, at least the LPs AC 27 and SB 155 should also have been reassigned to the Esquire bash. (The other LPs are no longer at hand, but probably some of them should also be reassigned.) The LP, SWH 46, IS a dub of AFRS 155.
    Note, too, that the LP, SWH 46, includes a track of **I've Found A New Baby,** a dub of AFRS 208 - Part 1, also mid-January 1944.

18 January 1944, Hollywood (ref: page 150)

As noted above, the LPs AC 27 and SB 155—and likely others, except SWH 46—should be credited to this broadcast, via the Blue Network of NBC. Add to the revised credits the CD set, EPM(Fr) 672. The broadcast was sponsored by Coca Cola, was the 416th in its "Spotlight Band" series.

"SWEET AND LOW-DOWN," February 1944, Hollywood (ref: pages 150, 151)

Typo: The male lead is James CaRdwell, not "CaLdwell." And note the hyphenated "Low-Down," so spelled on a 16 mm print of the film.

Possibly only collector Ken Crawford has a 16mm print, but now all who want a videotape of the film need only duplicate it from the American Movie Classics cable network's telecast, first shown in January 1992.

V-Disc 779 A, **Ten Days With Baby/Rachel's Dream,** is also on the CD, VJC 1001-2, and on the LP, DAN 5022.

12 June 1944, New York (ref: page 152)

All The Cats Join In and **After You've Gone** are also on the LP, EMI 155-1563. **After You've Gone** is also on the LPs, CAP T441 and MOSAIC (set) MQ6-148; and on CD, MOSAIC (set) MD4-148. Delete Legacy listing, CAP T409.

For more information in reference to MOSAIC's relationship with Capitol, see herein, beginning under date of "28 January 1947, Hollywood,"

31 July 1944, New York (ref: pages 152, 153)

All tunes from this date are also on the LP, SG 8016. **After You've Gone** is also on the LP, PHON 7661, and the CD, PHON 7660. **Goodbye Sue** is also on the LP, DAN 5022. **There'll Be A Jubilee** is also on the LP, SB 142.

25 September 1944, New York (ref: page 153)

V-Disc 366 A, **Sweet Georgia Brown/The Sheik Of Araby,** is also on the CD, VJC 1001-2, and on the LP, DAN 5022.

11 October 1944, New York (ref: page 153)

The CD, VJC 1001-2, adds materially to this session:

(THE) BENNY GOODMAN QUINTET   **11 October 1944, New York**

Personnel as per Legacy.

- 0 - alt take	**CD:** VJC 1001-2
D4-TC-446-1A (VP 944)	VD 344 A, et al, plus **CD:** VJC 1001-2
	Untitled (later, "Slipped Disc")
- 0 - alt take	**CD:** VJC 1001-2
D4-TC-447-1 (VP 945)	VD 394 A, et al, plus **CD:** VJC 1001-2
	Rose Room

11 October 1944, continued

11 October 1944, continued

- O - alt take   **CD:** VJC 1001-2
- O - alt take   **CD:** VJC 1001-2
D5-TC-199-1C (VP 1245) VD 446 A, et al, plus **CD:** VJC 1001-2
                                        Just One Of Those Things

17 October 1944, New York (ref: page 153)

V-Disc 446 A, **Rachel's Dream;** and V-Disc 475 A, **Let's Fall In Love,** are both issued on the CD, VJC 1001-2, which also includes a very brief false start preceding **Rachel's Dream.** The "unissued alternate take" of **Rachel's Dream,** listed in Legacy on advice of the owner of the acetates from which the CD, VJC 1001-2, was transferred, proved to be the take on V-Disc 446 A.

16 November 1944, New York (ref: page 154)

Multi-format CO 44437 adds a previously unlisted recording of matrix CO 33816, **Ev'ry Time We Say Goodbye,** to which it assigns take 2. (The 1995 CD release, CO 66198, also includes this take 2, but erroneously credits it as, take "1.") Matrix CO 33816 now consists of:

BENNY GOODMAN QUINTET   **16 November 1944, New York**

Personnel as per Legacy.

CO 33816   **LP:** PHON 7648. **CD:** PHON 8824
CO 33816-1   CO 36767, et al
CO 33816-2   **LP, Cas, CD:** CO 44437. **CD:** CO 66198
                    Ev'ry Time We Say Goodbye - voc Peggy Mann

From this session, CO 44437 also includes: matrix CO 33817-1, **After You've Gone,** first issued on ET, AFRS BML P-307; and unnumbered matrix CO 33818, **Only Another Boy And Girl,** first issued on the LPs, PHON 7648 and BlD T-1002.

CO 44437's liner notes assert that no matrix was assigned to this date's **Only Another Boy And Girl.** This claim is at odds with data gained from Columbia's files many years ago, and with information that accompanied the author's master tapes of this session.

21 December 1944, New York (ref: page 154)

Careless omission in Legacy: The first-listed, unnumbered take of matrix CO 34031, **Only Another Boy And Girl,** is performed by the TRIO—Benny, Teddy Wilson, Morey Feld—not by the Quintet. This take, with vocal by Jane Harvey, remains Unissued as of December 1995.

From this 21 December 1944 session, CO 44437 also includes: matrix CO 34030-1A, **Rachel's Dream,** first issued on the LP, PHON 7648; and matrix CO 34031-2, **Only Another Boy And Girl,** first issued on the 78, CO 36767.

"Prob. December 1944," New York (ref: page 155)

The CD, MC #117, "Hollywood Stars Go To War," suggests a broadcast date of 30

October 1944 for the Quartet's **After You've Gone.** Absent evidence to the contrary, the author accepts this revision.

17 January 1945, N.O., L.A., N.Y. (ref: page 155)
Correct catalog number for the LP's track of **Things Ain't What They Used To Be** is SA 6925, not "6924." Same performance is also on the LP, JSFr 67415.

4 February 1945, New York (ref: pages 155, 156, 318)
The first complete (unnumbered) take of matrix CO 33817, this session, **After You've Gone,** as first issued on the LPs, BID T-1002 and PHON 7648 (3rd track, Side B), is also released on multi-format CO 44292. CO 44292's liner notes designate this take as, 4.

As noted in the Addenda to Legacy, late access to Columbia safety recordings substantially engrossed arrays in the text for certain matrices cut during the years 1945 and 1946. Some of these supplemental takes have now been issued; to list these releases in their order-of-performance, affected matrices will be reconstituted in full herein. These new listings should be substituted for the arrays in Legacy's text.

The first of these revisions is:

BENNY GOODMAN SEXTET   **4 February 1945, New York**

Personnel as per Legacy.

CO 34263	UNISSUED - Tape
CO 34263	UNISSUED - Tape
CO 34263	**7" LP:** PHON XmasMix 1989
CO 34263	UNISSUED - Tape
CO 34263	**LP:** PHON 7661. **CD:** PHON 7660, PHON 8824
CO 34263	**LP:** BID T-1002
CO 34263-2	**ET:** AFRS Basic Music Library P384, et al. **CD:** PHON 8824
CO 34263	**LP:** BID T-1011
CO 34263-bkdn	**LP:** BID T-1011
CO 34263-1	CO 36817, et al., plus: **LP, Cas, CD:** CO 44292
	Slipped Disc

(Notes-long breakdowns preceding and following the release on PHON Xmas-Mix 1989 are too brief to warrant inclusion.)

CO 34264	**CD:** PHON 8824
CO 34264-1	CO 36817, et al
	Oomph Fah Fah

CO 34265-bkdn	UNISSUED - Tape
CO 34265	UNISSUED - Tape
CO 34265	UNISSUED - Tape
CO 34265-bkdn	UNISSUED - Tape
CO 34265-1	CO 36923, et al
CO 34265-bkdn	UNISSUED - Tape
CO 34265-2	CoBr 30-1276, et al. **CD:** PHON 8824
	She's Funny That Way - voc Jane Harvey

(The first listed breakdown, and the first listed complete take, are the additions to the display in Legacy.)

The SEXTET recording of matrix CO 34266, **Body And Soul**, as first issued on the LPs, PHON 7648 and BlD T-1004, is also released on multi-format CO 44437. CO 44437's liner notes designate this take as, R1. In 1993, this same take was also reissued on the CD, PHON 8824.

15 March 1945, Camp Kilmer, NJ (ref: page 157)
Add the LP, JS AA510, to the air check, **Frenesi;** delete the LP, JS AA510, from the air check, **Slipped Disc.**

17 March 1945, New York (ref: pages 158, 318)
Although none of the supplemental takes from the Columbia "safeties" has been issued as of this writing, it is now advisable to display them in their order-of-performance, in anticipation of eventual release. These listings should be substituted for their counterparts in Legacy:

BENNY GOODMAN AND HIS ORCHESTRA   **17 March 1945, New York**

Personnel as per Legacy.

CO 34474	UNISSUED - Tape
CO 34474	UNISSUED - Tape
CO 34474	UNISSUED - Tape
CO 34474	UNISSUED - Tape
CO 34474-bkdn	UNISSUED - Tape
CO 34474-1	**LP:** PHON 7650. **CD:** PHON 8824
CO 34474-2	Test Pressing
CO 34474	UNISSUED - Tape

Two Little Fishes And Five Loaves Of Bread - voc Jane Harvey

CO 34475	UNISSUED - Tape
CO 34475-bkdn	UNISSUED - Tape
CO 34475-bkdn	UNISSUED - Tape
CO 34475	UNISSUED - Tape
CO 34475	UNISSUED - Tape
CO 34475-bkdn	UNISSUED - Tape
CO 34475-1	VD 535 B, et al

Clarinade

Negating the assertion in the Addenda (page 318) that additional takes of matrix CO 34477, **Love Walked In,** were extant, audition of the Columbia "safeties" reveals that they are not from this 17 March 1945 session. Further, their availability to the author proves them to be either duplicates from this session, or from the session of 27 April 1945, and that they are fully listed in Legacy's text.

Unlisted in Legacy, however, is a ballad that most likely was recorded 17 March 1945. The Columbia safety recording positions it after **Clarinade,** and does not assign it a matrix. It should be added to the revised display:

BENNY GOODMAN AND HIS ORCHESTRA   **17 March 1945, New York**

Personnel as per Legacy.

- 0 -   UNISSUED - Tape
                                    As Long As We Still Believe - voc Bob Hayden (arr Alec Wilder)

Another unlisted, undated ballad is on a second set of safeties, also intermixed with takes of 17 March 1945's **Clarinade.** It's a flawed take (the vocalist comes in late) of the big band's **Ain't Misbehavin',** which Benny will record for Columbia on 16 May 1945, with Kay Penton on vocal. But this vocalist doesn't quite sound like Kay, nor like either of her successors, Dottie Reid and Liza Morrow. Could she be Jane Harvey? If so, then this take, for which no matrix is given, may indeed have been recorded during this 17 March 1945 session.

All things considered, however, this discovery is assigned herein to 16 May 1945, q.v. It may be the unconfirmed take cited in Legacy's Addenda, page 318.

Spring 1945, New York

According to the 23 June 1945 edition of **The Billboard,** Benny's band had already been filmed for a sequence in a projected Office of War Information release. Datelined 18 June, the account also cites contributions by Count Basie's orchestra, and by small groups headed respectively by Art Hodes and Max Kaminsky, as being "in the can." John Hammond, then serving in the U.S. Army, is on leave to act as technical advisor.

Associates of the author who specialize in jazz movies have no knowledge of this OWI short subject.

27 April 1945, New York (ref: page 158)

Correction: Columbia album P5-15536's take 1 of matrix CO 34645, **June Is Bustin' Out All Over,** is the second take in Legacy's array. It is NOT the same as the take on the AFRS ET, BML P-385, whose "take 1" number should now be deleted.

7 May 1945, New York (ref: pages 159, 318)

Both matrices recorded this date are affected by recently reviewed Columbia safeties. Each is listed below in its order-of-performance. Both arrays should be substituted in their entireties for those in Legacy.

BENNY GOODMAN SEXTET   **7 May 1945, New York**

Personnel as per Legacy.

CO 34030	**LP:** TL STL J05
CO 34030-bkdn	UNISSUED - Tape
CO 34030	UNISSUED - Tape (this is the added take)
CO 34030-3A	**LP:** PHON 7650. **CD:** PHON 8824
CO 34030-4	CO 36925, et al, plus: **LP, Cas, CD:** CO 44292
	Rachel's Dream
CO 34673	UNISSUED - Tape
CO 34673	UNISSUED - Tape
CO 34673	**7" LP:** PHON XmasMix 1988. **CD:** PHON 8825
CO 34673-bkdns	UNISSUED - Tape (three consecutive aborted attempts)
CO 34673-2	**LP:** BID T-1002, plus: **LP, Cas, CD:** CO 44292
CO 34673-1	CO 36924, et al
	Just One Of Those Things

(Note that the safeties reverse the order-of-performance of takes 1 and 2, matrix CO 34673, from that listed in Legacy.)

Take 4, matrix CO 34030, **Rachel's Dream;** and take 1, matrix CO 34673, **Just One Of Those Things,** are also on the AFRS ET, Music Transcription Library P-S-49.

16 May 1945, New York (ref: page 159)

Legacy (page 158) speculates that Benny's efforts to record **June Is Bustin' Out All Over** satisfactorily on 27 April 1945 was ". . . likely the most attempts Benny ever made to record one tune at one session." Its 14 total tries was tops until recently discovered "safeties" produced a new champion: **Clarinade,** 16 May 1945, a total of 20, count 'em, assorted complete takes and breakdowns.

For the most part, **June Is Bustin' Out All Over's** multiple takes weren't caused by Benny's mistakes. But **Clarinade's** a different case; more often than not, he's at fault. Take after take he fails to execute the written score, one that permits little leeway for improvisation. One recalls **Clarinet A La King,** another tightly structured arrangement, that took him three sessions in 1941 "to get it right." And one wonders why it was that confining jazz charts troubled him so much more than did wholly delimiting classical compositions.

In any event, **Clarinade** here, and its seven takes recorded 17 March 1945, attest to Benny's iron-willed perseverance, if nothing more. Substitute in its entirety this listing for that in Legacy:

BENNY GOODMAN AND HIS ORCHESTRA   **16 May 1945, New York**

Personnel as per Legacy.

CO 34475	UNISSUED - Tape
CO 34475	UNISSUED - Tape
CO 34475-bkdns	UNISSUED - Tape (5 consecutive aborted attempts)
CO 34475	UNISSUED - Tape
CO 34475-bkdn	UNISSUED - Tape
CO 34475	UNISSUED - Tape
CO 34475	UNISSUED - Tape
CO 34475-bkdn	UNISSUED - Tape
CO 34475	UNISSUED - Tape
CO 34475-bkdns	UNISSUED - Tape (2 consecutive aborted attempts)
CO 34475	UNISSUED - Tape
CO 34475-bkdns	UNISSUED - Tape (2 consecutive aborted attempts)
CO 34475-3	**LP:** PHON 7650, plus: **LP, Cas, CD:** CO 44158. **CD:** PHON 8825
CO 34475-4	CO 36823, et al
	Clarinade

(CO 44158's liner notes falsely claim its take 3 to be a first issue. Not so; it's the same take released years before on LP, PHON 7650.)

Take 4, matrix CO 34475, **Clarinade,** is also on ET, AFRS Outpost Concert Series No. 30, Music Of The Jazz Bands 60, Hit Tunes Of 1945 (mx 17-3069).

ADD to the respective arrays in Legacy, each as the first take in order-of-performance, another take of **June Is Bustin' Out All Over,** and our iffy take of **Ain't Misbehavin':**

BENNY GOODMAN AND HIS ORCHESTRA   **same session—16 May 1945, New York**

Personnel as per Legacy.

CO 34645-3	UNISSUED - Tape
	June Is Bustin' Out All Over - voc Kay Penton
CO 34713	UNISSUED - Tape
	Ain't Misbehavin' - voc Kay Penton

May/June 1945, New York (ref: page 160)

Midway in the left-hand column, following **Air Mail Special,** which begins this listing: **Oomph Fah Fah** is issued on the LP, VELP 1, inadvertently omitted from Legacy. Liner notes date this broadcast as 2 June 1945.

18 June 1945, New York (ref: pages 161, 318)

One of the unissued takes of matrix CO 35010, **It's Only A Paper Moon** (per page 318), was released in 1994 on the CD, PHON 8825. Substitute the listing below in its entirety for the array in Legacy, to position the new release in its correct order-of-recording:

BENNY GOODMAN AND HIS ORCHESTRA   **18 June 1945, New York**

Personnel as per Legacy.

CO 35010	UNISSUED - Tape
CO 35010	UNISSUED - Tape
CO 35010-bkdn	UNISSUED - Tape
CO 35010	UNISSUED - Tape
CO 35010	UNISSUED - Tape
CO 35010	**CD:** PHON 8825
CO 35010	UNISSUED - Tape
CO 35010-1	**ET:** AFRS BML P384, et al
CO 35010-2	CO 36843, et al
	It's Only A Paper Moon - voc Dottie Reid

Take 1, matrix CO 35012, **How Little We Know,** is now issued in the Book-Of-The-Month Club album, "Hoagy Carmichael—From Star Dust To Ole Buttermilk Sky," BOM 61-5450. Prior to this release, take 1 was extant only on a test pressing.

29 August 1945, New York (ref: pages 161, 318)
    The several Columbia "safeties" from this session necessitate massive revision to Legacy's listings. Every matrix is affected; several post-publication releases are now incorporated in their order-of-performance; and a hitherto unknown recording is disclosed. This session is reconstituted in its entirety:

BENNY GOODMAN AND HIS ORCHESTRA   **29 August 1945, New York**

Personnel as per Legacy.

CO 35141	UNISSUED - Tape)
CO 35141	UNISSUED - Tape)
CO 35141-bkdn	UNISSUED - Tape) - these are the added takes
CO 35141-bkdn	UNISSUED - Tape)
CO 35141	UNISSUED - Tape
CO 35141	**LP:** PHON 7652. **CD:** PHON 8825
CO 35141-bkdn	UNISSUED - Tape
CO 35141-1A	PaE R3000, et al
	Just You, Just Me

Take 1A, matrix CO 35141, **Just You, Just Me,** immediately above, is the first track on the third "safety" in this set. The second track is a recording of Mel Powell and Ray McKinley's **My Guy's Come Back,** with vocal. The third track on this disc is the initial recording of **Baby, Won't You Please Come Home,** a breakdown. Thus, the juxtaposition of these three tracks almost guarantees that the middle one is from this session.
    The vocalist, however, is unidentifiable. She is certainly not Liza Morrow, whose recordings of **My Guy's Come Back,** 12 September 1945, clearly attest. She doesn't sound a bit like Liza Morrow's predecessor, Dottie Reid; although it's not known when Dottie left the band, note that there are no other recordings with vocals on this session. And no proximate air checks offer a clue to this vocalist's identity.

29 August 1945, continued

29 August 1945, continued

At a guess, this first extant recording of the tune was a trial, both of the arrangement and the vocalist.

BENNY GOODMAN AND HIS ORCHESTRA   same session

Instrumental personnel as per Legacy. Unknown vocalist.

- O -	UNISSUED - Tape
	My Guy's Come Back - voc, unknown

BENNY GOODMAN AND HIS ORCHESTRA   same session

Personnel as per Legacy.

CO 35142-bkdn	UNISSUED - Tape
CO 35142	UNISSUED - Tape
CO 35142	**LP:** PHON 7661. **CD:** PHON 7660, PHON 8825
CO 35142-2B	**LP:** PHON 7652. **CD:** PHON 8825
CO 35142-1	**7" 33-1/3:** CO Bonus Record ZLP 13906, et al
	Baby, Won't You Please Come Home

BENNY GOODMAN SEXTET   same session

Personnel as per Legacy.

CO 35143	**7" 33-1/3:** PHON MX EPH 84. **CD:** PHON MIX 1991, PHON 8825
CO 35143	UNISSUED - Tape
CO 35143-bkdn	UNISSUED - Tape
CO 35143-bkdn	UNISSUED - Tape
CO 35143	UNISSUED - Tape
CO 35143-2	**LP:** PHON LV-50, et al, plus **CD:** PHON 8825
CO 35143-bkdn	UNISSUED - Tape
CO 35143-1	CO 36922, et al
	Tiger Rag

(Note reversal of takes 1 and 2 to correct order-of-performance, from the Legacy array; and note correction of typo for the catalog number of the PHON 7" LP. All takes credited, "UNISSUED - Tape," are previously unlisted recordings.)

CO 35144	UNISSUED - Tape
CO 35144	**EP:** PHON MIX 1986. **LP:** PHON 7661. **CD:** PHON 8825
CO 35144-bkdn	UNISSUED - Tape
CO 35144	**CD:** PHON 9105
CO 35144-2A	**LP:** BID T-1004, PHON 7652. **CD:** PHON 8825
CO 35144-bkdn	UNISSUED - Tape
CO 35144-1	CO 36925, et al
	Shine

(As for "Tiger Rag," note reversal of takes 1 and 2A. All takes except 1 and 2A are previously unlisted. The CD, PHON 9105, is a private issue.)

12 September 1945, New York (ref: pages 161, 162, 318)

Retraction: Braced by any number of collectors, the author recants his linking "Oranges And Lemons" to **My Guy's Come Back,** in print since **BG-Off The Record,** 1958. Must have been all that 140-proof Calvados with Mel and Ray McKinley, Paris, May 1945; stuff burned with a blue flame.

The supplemental breakdown for the aforementioned **My Guy's Come Back** (mx CO 35190, Legacy, page 318) is inconsequential, may be ignored. One complete and two breakdown supplemental takes for matrix CO 35191, **That's All That Matters To Me,** are listed below in their order-of-performance:

BENNY GOODMAN AND HIS ORCHESTRA   **12 September 1945, New York**

Personnel as per Legacy.

CO 35191	UNISSUED - Tape
CO 35191-bkdn	UNISSUED - Tape
CO 35191-1A	**LP:** NOST 1004
CO 35191-bkdn	UNISSUED - Tape
CO 35191-2	**LP:** PHON 7652. **CD:** PHON 8825
	That's All That Matters To Me - voc Liza Morrow

"History In Sound 1941," a release for take 2, that darned **My Guy's Come Back,** is an LP, a specification omitted in Legacy.

18 September 1945, New York (ref: page 162)

Not cited in Legacy's Addenda are supplemental takes for the two Sextet tunes recorded this date. Their discovery on still more Columbia "safeties" is a delightful surprise, for all of the complete takes, and even some of the longer breakdowns, are quite good. Not that Benny's choices for contemporary release are perhaps not the best versions, but it's a close call. Substitute these revisions in their entireties for the arrays in Legacy:

BENNY GOODMAN SEXTET   **18 September 1945, New York**

Personnel as per Legacy.

CO 35206	UNISSUED - Tape
CO 35206	UNISSUED - Tape
CO 35206	UNISSUED - Tape
CO 35206-bkdn	UNISSUED - Tape
CO 35206-bkdn	UNISSUED - Tape
CO 35206	UNISSUED - Tape
CO 35206	**7" 33-1/3:** PHON MX EPH85. **EP:** PHON BGPH86. **CD:** PHON 8825
CO 35206-1	CO 36922, et al
	Ain't Misbehavin'

(All of the supplemental takes precede the PHON issues.)

18 September 1945, continued

18 September 1945, continued

CO 35207	UNISSUED - Tape
CO 35207-bkdn	UNISSUED - Tape
CO 35207	UNISSUED - Tape
CO 35207	**7" 33-1/3:** PHON EPH87. **CD:** PHON 8825
CO 35207-bkdn	UNISSUED - Tape
CO 35207-bkdn	UNISSUED - Tape
CO 35207-bkdn	UNISSUED - Tape
CO 35207-2	CO 36923, et al
CO 35207-1	**LP:** PHON 7652. **CD:** PHON 8825
CO 35207-bkdn	UNISSUED - Tape
CO 35207-bkdn	UNISSUED - Tape
	I Got Rhythm

(Note the reversal of takes 1 and 2, from the listing in Legacy. Except takes 1 and 2, all of the other takes are supplemental.)

The last track on the "safeties" for this session is take 1, matrix XCO 35208, as issued on CO 55038, et al. It may be that the final two breakdowns listed above for matrix CO 35207 were actually the beginnings of this longer version of **I Got Rhythm.** But their brevity doesn't permit that assumption.

Note, too, that CO 44292's liner notes err in citing take 2 for its track of matrix XCO 35208. It's take 1, as issued on CO 55038, et al.

19 September 1945, New York (ref: pages 162, 318)

Further review of the Columbia "safeties" adds a fourth unissued take for matrix CO 35210, **Give Me The Simple Life.** Revise both matrices as follows:

BENNY GOODMAN AND HIS ORCHESTRA   **19 September 1945, New York**

Personnel as per Legacy.

CO 35209	UNISSUED - Tape
CO 35209	UNISSUED - Tape
CO 35209	UNISSUED - Tape
CO 35209-1B	VD 574 A, et al
CO 35209-2A	**LP:** NOST 1004, et al. **CD:** PHON 8825
	Fishin' For The Moon - voc Liza Morrow

CO 35210-bkdn	UNISSUED - Tape
CO 35210	UNISSUED - Tape
CO 35210	UNISSUED - Tape
CO 35210	UNISSUED - Tape
CO 35210-bkdn	UNISSUED - Tape
CO 35210	UNISSUED - Tape
CO 35210-?	VD 585 A, et al
	Give Me The Simple Life - voc Liza Morrow

24 September 1945, New York (ref: pages 162, 163, 318)

A souvenir CD, PHON XMCD 93, includes the final Sextet recording of matrix CO 35234, **Liza,** initially released on the LP, BlD T-1012. It immediately precedes the take -1 recording by the Quintet, in Legacy's array.

In 1988 a multi-format Columbia release included a previously unknown recording by the Sextet. (A second take of this recording is believed to exist, but the author does not have a copy.) Neither matrix nor title was assigned to it; Columbia named it arbitrarily. Nor is its order-of-performance known; at a guess, position it after **China Boy** in Legacy's listing.

BENNY GOODMAN SEXTET   24 September 1945, New York

Personnel as per Legacy.

- 0 - ?	? UNISSUED ?
- 0 -	**LP, Cas, CD:** CO 44292
	My Daddy Rocks Me

Supplemental takes for the orchestral recordings this session (Legacy, page 318) are incorporated in order-of-performance:

BENNY GOODMAN AND HIS ORCHESTRA   same session

Personnel as per Legacy.

- 0 -	UNISSUED - Tape
- 0 -bkdn	UNISSUED - Tape
- 0 -	UNISSUED - Tape
	King Porter Stomp
CO 35237	UNISSUED - Tape
CO 35237	UNISSUED - Tape
CO 35237	UNISSUED - Tape
CO 35237-bkdn	UNISSUED - Tape
CO 35237-1	**LP:** NOST 1004
CO 35237-2	**LP:** PHON 7652. **CD:** PHON 8825
	Lucky (later, "You're Right—I'm Wrong")

"17 October 1945"

Released in 1994, HINDSIGHT CD 254 claims its first two tracks were recorded for AFRS on this date. Not so. **After You've Gone** was recorded for Columbia, matrix CO 33817-1, on 16 November 1944 (Legacy, page 154). **Body And Soul** was also recorded for Columbia, matrix CO 34266, fourth take by the Trio, on 4 February 1945 (Legacy, page 156). Nor, as the CD claims, are its remaining tracks "previously unissued."

20 November 1945, New York (ref: pages 163, 319)

Two of the three supplemental breakdowns listed in Legacy (page 319) for matrix CO 35210, **Give Me The Simple Life,** are merely false starts and may be ignored. Thus, the revised array, in its entirety, becomes:

BENNY GOODMAN AND HIS ORCHESTRA   **20 November 1945, New York**

Personnel as per Legacy.

CO 35210	UNISSUED - Tape
CO 35210	UNISSUED - Tape
CO 35210	UNISSUED - Tape
CO 35210	UNISSUED - Tape
CO 35210-bkdn	UNISSUED - Tape
CO 35210	UNISSUED - Tape
CO 35210-4	**LP:** CO alb P6-14538, et al. **CD:** PHON 8825
CO 35210-3	CO 36908, et al
	Give Me The Simple Life - voc Liza Morrow

(Note the reversal of takes 3 and 4 from the listing in Legacy.)

8 December 1945, New York (ref: page 164)
     Somebody Loves Me from this broadcast is also issued on the 7" 33-1/3 LP, PHON MIX 1990.
     Some speculation has it that this broadcast was pre-recorded in the Schirmer Studios on 4 December 1945. No confirmation of this possibility has been proffered as of this writing.

19 December 1945, New York (ref: pages 164, 319)
     A supplemental take of matrix CO 35523, **Rattle And Roll,** has been released, but the supplemental takes of matrix CO 35237, **Lucky,** from this session remain unissued. In order-of-performance, these matrices now are:

BENNY GOODMAN AND HIS ORCHESTRA   **19 December 1945, New York**

Personnel as per Legacy.

CO 35237	UNISSUED - Tape (see parenthetical note)
CO 35237	UNISSUED - Tape
CO 35237	UNISSUED - Tape
CO 35237-3	**LP:** VELP 1, et al. **CD:** PHON 8825
CO 35237-4	CoE DB2443, et al
	Lucky (as **You're Right - I'm Wrong** on PE 10)
CO 35523-bkdn	UNISSUED - Tape
CO 35523	UNISSUED - Tape
CO 35523	**LP:** PHON 7661. **CD:** PHON 7660, PHON 8825
CO 35523-1	CO 36988, et al
	Rattle And Roll

(The first unissued take of **Lucky**, above, may be from the 20 November 1945 session. Its position on the "safeties" suggests this possibility.)

25 December 1945, New York (ref: page 165)
     "Johnny Presents" is now confirmed as the program source of this air check. And a second performance by the Trio on this broadcast is now known to be extant: **Slipped Disc.**

14 January 1946, Culver City, CA (ref: page 166)
 Body And Soul is included in the LP, GOJ 1017.

26-29 January 1946, Culver City, CA (ref: page 167)
 Oh, Baby!, from the ET, AFRS Magic Carpet No. 220; and **Give Me The Simple Life**, from the ET, AFRS Magic Carpet No. 225, are both on the LP, JS 508.

27 January 1946, Culver City, CA (ref: page 167)
 The bulk of AFRS One Night Stand No. 856 is issued on an Italian CD, JAZZ & JAZZ No. 608.

8 March 1946, New York (ref: page 168)
 The "UNISSUED - CO Ref" take of matrix CO 35952, **Don't Be A Baby, Baby,** is on an unlabeled 12-inch test LP, as the third track on the disc's Side 2. The LP was produced by Phontastic, with the thought that it might be released; but it never was. There are eight other tracks on the LP; when the LP was made, some of them were then also unissued. But over time these were released and all of them are listed in Legacy, credited to the several public and private issues.

14 May 1946, New York (ref: pages 169, 319)
 Correction: Reassign credits for the LP, FR Series, from both takes 1, matrices XCO 36286 and XCO 36287, to both takes 2, same matrices, **Oh, Baby!**, Parts 1 and 2.

 Below are revised arrays for matrices CO 36288, **Blue Skies,** and CO 36289, **I Ain't Mad At Nobody.** In 1995, Columbia released a previously-unknown take of **Blue Skies,** mistakenly identified as take "1," which properly belongs to the original 78 rpm issue. And note that there are now four supplemental complete recordings of matrix CO 36289, not the three cited in Legacy (page 319).

BENNY GOODMAN AND HIS ORCHESTRA   **14 May 1946, New York**

Personnel as per Legacy.

CO 36288-"1"	**CD:** CO 66198
CO 36288	UNISSUED - Tape
CO 36288-bkdn	UNISSUED - Tape
CO 36288	UNISSUED - Tape
CO 36288	UNISSUED - Tape
CO 36288-1	CO 37053, et al
	Blue Skies - voc Art Lund
CO 36289	UNISSUED - Tape
CO 36289-bkdns	UNISSUED - Tape (3 consecutive aborted attempts)
CO 36289	UNISSUED - Tape
CO 36289	UNISSUED - Tape
CO 36289	UNISSUED - Tape
CO 36289-1	**EP:** CoE SEG7524, et al. **CD:** PHON 8825
	I Ain't Mad At Nobody - voc Johnny White

Following the final track of **I Ain't Mad At Nobody** on the source Columbia "safety" is a one-minute, 23-second burlesque rendition of **Whispering Grass.** A male vocalist, in falsetto voice reminiscent of Jerry Colonna's, parodies this treacly ballad. He is accompanied by a pianist who could be Mel Powell. Faintly, at the end of this track, someone—possibly Benny—says something like, "Come on, we've got one more . . .".

Is it Mel and one of the other Goodman sidemen having fun after a long day in the studio? Probably, but certainly not positively.

Broadcast, 5 June 1946, New York (ref: page 170)
ABC was the network of origin of this broadcast.

ET, 5 June 1946, New York (ref: page 170)
I've Got The Sun In The Morning, from the ET, AFRS One Night Stand No. 1024, is also on the LP, SWH 46.

12 June 1946, New York (ref: page 171)
Love Doesn't Grow On Trees is also on the LP, SB 156.
The AFRS ET, One Night Stand No. 1046, is on cassette, RADY 3155.

8 July 1946, New York (ref: page 172)
The LP, SG 8016, adds **Blues In The News** by the Sextet, with vocal by Johnny Mercer, to the listing in Legacy. The tune was on the broadcast, but it is not on the AFRS ET. SG 8016 omits **Dizzy Fingers.**

18 July 1946, New York (ref: page 172)
Multi-format CO 44158's liner notes claim its track of take 1, matrix CO 36659, **Fly By Night,** to be "previously unissued." Not so; five years earlier, it was released on LP, PHON 7654, and later on CD, PHON 8825.

7 August 1946, New York (ref: pages 173, 319)
Dropouts caused by faulty equipment mar the first of the supplemental takes of matrix CO 36736, **A Kiss In The Night.** But the gear was running properly for the last of the supplemental takes, recorded Benny's wry comment, "Think that'll sell records?", when the take was finished. In its entirety the revised array is:

BENNY GOODMAN AND HIS ORCHESTRA   **7 August 1946, New York**

Personnel as per Legacy.

CO 36736	UNISSUED - Tape (dropouts)
CO 36736-bkdn	UNISSUED - Tape
CO 36736-bkdn	UNISSUED - Tape
CO 36736	UNISSUED - Tape (comment)
CO 36736-1	Co 37149, et al
	A Kiss In The Night - voc Art Lund

26 August 1946, New York (ref: page 174)

The LP, MAGIC 23, contains excerpts from this AFRS Program #9 ET.

29 August 1946, New York (ref: page 174)

Unreported when Legacy's Addenda was written are several "safeties" that offer sup-plemental takes for certain matrices from the studio sessions of 29 August, 15 October, and 22 October, all 1946. The first take of the only affected matrix from this session is quite in-teresting: Marked by the producer "too long" (running time, 4:15), Benny and Johnny White play a duet after the intro. Here is the new array in its entirety:

BENNY GOODMAN AND HIS ORCHESTRA   **29 August 1946, New York**

Personnel as per Legacy, including Johnny White, vib, first take.

CO 36738	UNISSUED - Tape
CO 36738	UNISSUED - Tape
CO 36738-bkdn	UNISSUED - Tape
CO 36738	UNISSUED - Tape
CO 36738	UNISSUED - Tape
CO 36738-3	CO 37091, et al

Put That Kiss Back Where You Found It - voc Art Lund

27 September 1946, Culver City, CA (ref: page 175)

The first two tunes on this broadcast are on the LP, SB 156, not 154.

15 October 1946, Los Angeles (ref: page 176)

Supplemental takes for two of the three matrices recorded this date are on Columbia "safeties." Their complete new arrays are:

BENNY GOODMAN AND HIS ORCHESTRA   **15 October 1946, Los Angeles**

Personnel as per Legacy.

HCO 2083	UNISSUED - Tape
HCO 2083-bkdn	UNISSUED - Tape
HCO 2083-bkdn	UNISSUED - Tape
HCO 2083	UNISSUED - Tape
HCO 2083-1	CO 37207, et al

Hora Staccato

HCO 2085-bkdn	UNISSUED - Tape
HCO 2085	UNISSUED - Tape
HCO 2085-2	CoAu DO3129, et al
HCO 2085-1	UNISSUED - Test Pressing

That's The Beginning Of The End - voc Eve Young

(Note the reversal of takes 1 and 2, above, from the listing in Legacy.)

22 October 1946, Los Angeles (ref: page 177)

The Columbia "safeties" provide one additional supplemental take for a recording by the full orchestra, and several for a Sextet side. One of the latter was issued by Columbia in 1988. These are the revised arrays for both matrices, both in order-of-performance:

BENNY GOODMAN AND HIS ORCHESTRA   **22 October 1946, Los Angeles**

Personnel as per Legacy.

HCO 2110	UNISSUED - Tape
HCO 2110-2	CO 37207, et al
	Man Here Plays Fine Piano - voc Eve Young

BENNY GOODMAN SEXTET   **same session**

Personnel as per Legacy.

HCO 2112	UNISSUED - Tape
HCO 2112-bkdn	UNISSUED - Tape
HCO 2112-2	**LP, Cas, CD:** CO 44292
HCO 2112-1	CoC 1025, et al
	I'll Always Be In Love With You

28 October, 1 November 1946, New York (ref: page 177)

Dick "Kohler" is not the vocalist on the 28 October Benny Goodman Show; his identity is unknown. But Dick CULVER (Ott) is the male vocalist on the 1 November One Night Stand.

Dick accompanied his father-in-law, composer/band leader Terry Shand, to Hollywood in midyear 1945. There he cut a demo that soon brought him offers from Jimmy Dorsey and Benny Goodman. Dick chose Jimmy because the Dorsey band featured its vocalists more than Benny's did. He remained with JD until the end of 1945, and eventually went to New York to seek stage work as a single. Benny, in need of a vocalist because of Art Lund's departure, renewed his offer, and Dick accepted. But not for long; when he got his first week's pay—$150, half of what Dorsey had paid him—he quit and began a lengthy and successful career in radio, the stage, and the movies.

16 December 1946, Hollywood (ref: page 179)

The Sextet's **Where Or When** is on the LP, SB 155, not SB 156.

28 January 1947, "Hollywood" (ref: page 181)

A 1995 Capitol release, CD 32086, "Benny Goodman—Undercurrent Blues," spans Benny's dalliance with bop from January 1947 through October 1949. Five of its 15 tracks are by small groups, duplicating those in the comprehensive MOSAIC album, LP: MQ6-148/CD: MD4-148, upcoming. Six of 10 recordings by the orchestra have been available on earlier issues, and are not detailed herein; but note that its track of **Lonely Moments** is the alternate take (now designated as -5) originally on the LP, EMIFr 1551563. The four remaining big band sides are first-issues from the sessions of 12 April 1949 and 5 July 1949, q.v.

Delete the EP, CAP EAP 1-409, from the credits for **Lonely Moments,** take 4L-1.

The initial waxing of **Moon-Faced, Starry Eyed**, matrix 1611, is issued on the LP, Blu-Disc T-1016. For the remake of the same tune, matrix 1619-4R, CAP 376, see the succeeding entry for a change in date.

When recorded, Capitol titled matrix 1612, "Whistler's Blues."

The correct location of the recording studio is Los Angeles, not "Hollywood." For an explanation of this revision, see the next entry.

"28 January 1947, Hollywood" (ref: page 181)

In the mid-1950s, Capitol producer Bill Miller supplied details of his company's Goodman recordings for inclusion in **BG-Off The Record**. Later correspondence from him augmented those details for publication in **BG-On The Record.** Finally, Capitol producer Dave Cavanaugh provided "full particulars," and these are arrayed in **. . . Legacy.** Dave assured the author that now at last all of Benny's CAP recordings were accounted for, and in correct detail.

Unhappily, this has proven not to be true. Access to Capitol's "Recording Records" for the years 1947 through 1955, made available to Mosaic's Scott Wenzel and Mike Cuscuna, revises and adds materially to prior listings. In some instances, only studio locales need be changed, or take numbers appended. In others, changes are substantial.

Among other things, the "Records" reveal that all of Benny's 1947 California CAP recordings were cut in the studios of Radio Recorders, Los Angeles. This change in locale is noted herein. His 1949 California CAP recordings were made in Capitol's own studios; although technically Los Angeles can be considered the locale for them, Hollywood is given as Capitol's address on its labels, and this designation is unchanged.

The "Records" show that Benny's royalties were to be shared with Peggy Lee and Harry James, for those sides in which they participated; and that Benny was due "No Pay" for certain re-makes, and no compensation for "N.G." ("no good") recordings. Save for mention of Peggy, Harry and Fred Astaire, the "Records" are absent personnel, even instrumentation. Mosaic's 1993 release, "The Complete Capitol Small Group Recordings of Benny Goodman, 1944–1955," gives details for its tracks. Similar detail for some big band sides, in main those not previously listed, and for one unissued Quintet recording, has been obtained from AFofM sources.

The initial revision to Legacy's CAP arrays is re-make matrix 1619; the "Records" specify a 30 January 1947 date. And note correction of Legacy's careless error: Johnny Mercer, not Matt Dennis, is the vocalist.

Thus, DELETE matrix 1619-4R from the 28 January session, then enter:

BENNY GOODMAN AND HIS ORCHESTRA   **30 January 1947, Los Angeles**

Personnel as per Legacy, 28 January, except: Mannie Klein, tpt, for Wendt; Ed Kusby and Tommy Pederson, tbn, for Ballard and Schaefer; Gus Bivona, as, for Herfurt; Lou Fromm, d, for Weiss; and Johnny Mercer, voc, for Dennis.

1619-4R   CAP 376
        Moon-Faced, Starry-Eyed - voc Johnny Mercer

12 February 1947, "Hollywood" (ref: page 182)

The first previously unissued track in Mosaic's 6-LP/4-CD set is the alternate take of **Sweet Lorraine** that a few collectors had on tape. Because CAP's recording data, and now Mosaic's discography, append take numbers, this session is detailed in its entirety.

Correct the locale to Los Angeles.

BENNY GOODMAN QUINTET   **12 February 1947, Los Angeles**

Personnel as per Legacy.

1631-6   CAP 15768 et al, plus: **LP: MOSAIC MQ6-148. CD: MOSAIC MD4-148**
                Sweet Georgia Brown

1632-4   **LP:** CAP H479 et al, plus MOSAIC sets as above
                I'll Always Be In Love With You

1633-1   **LP:** CAP H441 et al, plus MOSAIC sets as above
1633-2(R)   **LP:** MOSAIC MQ6-148. **CD:** MOSAIC MD4-148
                Sweet Lorraine

1634-3   **LP:** CAP H479 et al, plus MOSAIC sets as above
                St. Louis Blues

19 February 1947, "Hollywood" (ref: page 182)

Matrices 1658, **I Know That You Know,** and 1659, **I Can't Get Started,** are also on LP, MOSAIC MQ6-148, and CD, MOSAIC MD4-148.

Take numbers for matrices 1656 and 1657, which remain unissued, are both, -2. Take number for matrix 1659 is, -4.

Again, note change in recording locale to Los Angeles.

27 February 1947, prob. Los Angeles

Benny's 19 February recordings were cut on Capitol's—not Benny's—538th session. He next is listed on the 542nd session, but details are sparse; the studio's locale is not given, and Fred Astaire's participation is not specified. However, since Capitol apparently was utilizing Radio Recorders' studios exclusively at this time, Los Angeles is postulated as the locale.

BENNY GOODMAN QUINTET with FRED ASTAIRE   **27 February 1947, Los Angeles**

Benny Goodman, clt; Ernie Felice, acc; Jess Stacy, p; Harry Babasin, b; Nick Fatool, d. Fred Astaire, voc and/or tap dancing.

1670-6   UNISSUED
                The Astaire - with Fred Astaire

5 March 1947, prob. Los Angeles

Equally meager are details for the follow-on session No. 548. But for obvious reasons, this one can be fleshed out with more assurance:

BENNY GOODMAN and NADIA REISENBERG   5 March 1947, Los Angeles

Benny Goodman, clt; Nadia Reisenberg, p.

1694-2   UNISSUED
                **Grand Duo Concertante for Piano and Clarinet, Opus 48, in E-Flat Major
                (von Weber). First Movement.**

1695-2   UNISSUED
                **Grand Duo Concertante for Piano and Clarinet, Opus 48, in E-Flat Major
                (von Weber). First Movement.**

1696-2   UNISSUED
                **Grand Duo Concertante for Piano and Clarinet, Opus 48, in E-Flat Major
                (von Weber). Second Movement.**

1697-1   UNISSUED
                **Grand Duo Concertante for Piano and Clarinet, Opus 48, in E-Flat Major
                (von Weber). Second Movement.**

7 March 1947, "Hollywood" (ref: page 183)

Both sides this date are also issued on LP and CD, Mosaic MQ6-148, and MD4-148 respectively. Also, change studio locale to Los Angeles.

28 March 1947, Los Angeles

Note that all three recordings from this previously unlisted session were later re-made and released; and that Peggy Lee splits the royalties with Benny for her side. To differentiate between two well known tunes both titled, **I Never Knew,** the parenthetical (**I Could Love Anybody**) is appended here to specify the one written by Tom Pitts, Ray Egan and Roy Marsh.

BENNY GOODMAN SEXTET / QUARTET   28 March 1947, Los Angeles

Benny Goodman, clt; Ernie Felice, acc; Tommy Todd, p; Dave Barbour, g; Harry Babasin, b; Tommy Romersa, d. Peggy Lee, voc.

1800-6   **LP:** MOSAIC MQ6-148. **CD:** MOSAIC MD4-148
                The Bannister Slide

1801-5   **LP:** MOSAIC MQ6-148. **CD:** MOSAIC MD4-148
                Eight, Nine And Ten - voc Peggy Lee

omit acc, g

1802-3   **LP:** MOSAIC MQ6-148. **CD:** MOSAIC MD4-148
                I Never Knew (I Could Love Anybody)

"6 April 1947, Hollywood" (ref: pages 183, 184)

Per Capitol's "Recording Records," change the date of this session from Legacy's 6 April to **16** April 1947, and the recording locale to Los Angeles. Also, append take -2 to both matrices 1842 and 1844. Note that **I Never Knew** here is again the Pitts-Egan-Marsh composition.

All four sides this date are also issued on LP and CD, Mosaic MQ6-148 and MD4-148, respectively.

Correct the catalog number of the SW LP for matrix 1844 from "1346" to 1364, an undetected typo in Legacy.

17 April 1947, "Hollywood" (ref: page 184)

All three sides this date are also issued on LP and CD, Mosaic MQ6-148 and MD4-148, respectively. Revise the recording locale to Los Angeles.

23 April 1947, "Hollywood" (ref: page 184)

Both sides this date are also issued on LP and CD, Mosaic MQ6-148 and MD4-148, respectively. Correct the studio locale to Los Angeles. Append take -4 to matrix 1859.

24 April 1947, "Hollywood" (ref: page 184)

Change the studio location to Los Angeles.

29 May 1947, "Hollywood" (ref: page 185)

All three sides this date are also issued on LP and CD, Mosaic MQ6-148 and MD4-148, respectively. Change the locale to Los Angeles.

"5 June 1947, Hollywood" (ref: page 186)

Again, the "Recording Records" correct the date of this session from Legacy's 5 June to **3** June 1947, and the studio's location to Los Angeles. Append take -5 to matrix 2023, and take -2 to matrix 2024.

6 June 1947, "Hollywood" (ref: page 186)

All four recordings from this session are also included in the Mosaic album: LP, Mosaic MQ6-148, and CD, Mosaic MD4-148. Append take -2 to matrix 2036. Studio location, Los Angeles.

23 June 1947, Pasadena (ref: page 186)

Delete the credit SWH 17 for **Puttin' On The Ritz.** That tune on this LP is properly attributed to the Sextet performance of 14 April 1947.

11 August 1947, "Hollywood" (ref: page 188)

Both tunes recorded this date are also issued on LP and CD, Mosaic MQ6-148 and MD4-148, respectively. Append take number -3 to both matrices, 2149 and 2150. Make the studio location Los Angeles.

When recorded, matrix 2149 was titled, **Gulliver Travels.** When released it became the familiar, **Hi 'Ya Sophia,** Benny's tribute to one of his three stepdaughters.

25 August 1947, "Hollywood" (ref: page 188)

Capitol's "Recording Records" confirm that **Nagasaki** was the only tune cut this date; take number of its matrix, 2198, is -3. It is also issued on LP and CD, Mosaic MQ6-148 and MD4-148, respectively. Credit the locale to Los Angeles.

12 September 1947, "Hollywood" (ref: page 188)

Append take number -4 to matrix 2247. Change the studio location to Los Angeles. Note that Benny participated in this session, Capitol's No. 680, under a "Special Contract."

22 September 1947, "Hollywood" (ref: page 188)

Both tunes this date are also issued on LP and CD, Mosaic MQ6-148 and MD4-148, respectively. Append take number -3 to matrix 2262; it appears on some copies of CAP 15008. Change the locale to Los Angeles.

23 October 1947, "Hollywood" (ref: page 189)

Capitol's "Recording Records" provide some substantive data for this session, but also raise some questions that are as yet unanswerable. First, let's dispose of the certainties: Append take number -7 to matrix 2370, -2 to matrix 2372, -2 to matrix 2373, and -1 to matrix 2374. And change the recording locale to Los Angeles.

At least some copies of CAP 15020, **Sweet And Lovely,** matrix 2371, bear the take inscription, -3. This is at odds with the -4 take cited in the "Records" for matrix 2371. Whether this discrepancy is merely an error, or whether one or more of the multiple releases of this recording is in fact an alternate take, is unknown to the author.

CAP's sheets then add two previously unknown matrices to this date. As before, there is no indication of personnel, not even instrumentation. The first of the two tunes will be cut later, as we shall see, by Benny's Sextet, and it is noted as a "re-make." But there's also an unsigned, undated big band arrangement of the tune in the Archives at Yale . . .? And we've no clues as to the second tune.

For the time being, then, ADD this fragmentary listing to this session:

BENNY GOODMAN   **23 October 1947, Los Angeles**

Instrumentation unknown; personnel likely derived from Legacy's array for this date. No vocalist(s) cited.

2375-3   UNISSUED
                That's A-Plenty

2376-2   UNISSUED
                Please Be Kind

7 November 1947, New York (ref: page 189)

All six recordings this date are also issued on LP and CD, Mosaic MQ6-148 and MD4-148, respectively. Take numbers are: 1996, -1; 1997, -4; 1998, -3; 1999, -3; 2500, -l; and 2501, -2.

Typo: For matrix 1997, make it CAP 15886, not "15888."

17 November 1947, New York (ref: page 189)

The four sides cut this session are also released on LP and CD, Mosaic MQ6-148 and MD4-148, respectively. Take numbers are: 2517, -6; 2518, -6; 2519, -2; and 2520, -1.

25 November 1947, "Hollywood" (ref: page 190)

Two tunes were recorded in Los Angeles (not Hollywood) this date. Only one is listed in Legacy: **You Turned The Tables On Me.** Its take is unknown, for Capitol shows it as, "?".

The second is a previously unknown recording under matrix 2606, take number again as, "?". The "Recording Records" give no other details. But because a 1946 Mel Powell arrangement for this unissued recording has the same instrumentation as that for **You Turned The Tables On Me**—including flute, French horn—personnel for both sides are most likely the same. Thus, ADD it to the display in Legacy:

BENNY GOODMAN AND HIS ORCHESTRA   **25 November 1947, Los Angeles**

Instrumental personnel as per Legacy. Possible vocal, Emma Lou Welch.

2606-?   UNISSUED
               It's Been So Long - voc Emma Lou Welch ? (arr MP)

The title, **It's Been So Long,** also appears on a separate "Recording Record," matrix and take given as 3585-5, but with no date assigned. Further remarks about this CAP listing are herein, under date of 9 September 1948.

2 December 1947, "Hollywood" (ref: page 190)

Three small group sides recorded this date are also released on LP and CD, Mosaic MQ6-148 and MD4-148, respectively. Take numbers for them are: 2721, -3; 2722, -2; and 2724, -2. (Take number for the "big band" side, matrix 2723, is -2.) Add trombonist Ed Kusby to Legacy's personnel for matrix 2721; he's barely audible.

Mosaic cites **Keep Me In Mind** as unissued, but in fact it was released on the LP, Blu-Disc T-1016, almost eight years earlier. Peggy Lee and Benny split royalties for it and for **For Every Man There's A Woman.**

Mel Powell both composed and arranged **Shirley Steps Out.** Untitled when recorded, Benny named it for one of his three stepdaughters for the release. It's also available on CAP CD 32086.

Change the recording locale to Los Angeles.

9 December 1947, "Hollywood" (ref: page 190)

All three recordings this date are also issued on LP and CD, Mosaic MQ6-148 and MD4-148, respectively. Take numbers are: 2794, -3; 2795, -4; and 2796, -3. (Last matrix is the remake of matrix 2375, **That's A-Plenty,** referred to herein under date of 23 October 1947.)

Note that **I'm In A Crying Mood** was first released on the LP, Blu-Disc T-1016. Contrary to an opinion in Legacy, it was arranged by Henderson. An unsigned, uncredited arrangement of **High Falutin'** is at Yale, but the Archives have only a big band chart for **That's A-Plenty,** also unsigned.

Studio location is Los Angeles.

11 December 1947, "Hollywood" (ref: page 190)

Because a previously unknown take of one of the three tunes recorded this session is now available, the display below should be substituted in its entirety for Legacy's listing. Note the change in recording locale, appended take numbers, and correct arranger credits. And, in deference to Mosaic's liner notes, include Allan Reuss in all three matrices.

BENNY GOODMAN SEPTET   **11 December 1947, Los Angeles**

Personnel as per Legacy Septet.

2830-2   CAP 15766, et al, plus **LP:** Mosaic MQ6-148. **CD:** Mosaic MD4-148
            Henderson Stomp (arr FH)

2831-alt   **LP:** BID T-1016
2831-2   **LP:** Mosaic MQ6-148. **CD:** Mosaic MD4-148
            You Took Advantage Of Me

2832-3   CAP 15768, et al, plus **LP:** Mosaic MQ6-148. **CD:** Mosaic MD4-148
            Behave Yourself - voc Benny Goodman (arr FH)

Even at this late date, **Henderson Stomp** is titled **Notes To You** on CAP's "Recording Records," was retitled when released. This small group arrangement is Fletcher Henderson's; it's in the Archives under his original title. He also wrote the chart for **Behave Yourself;** Ralph Burns's arrangement is for an orchestra. Both are now at Yale. Also there is the manuscript for **You Took Advantage Of Me,** but it's unsigned and uncredited.

23 December 1947, "Hollywood" (ref: page 190)

Take numbers for the four matrices recorded this date—in Los Angeles, not Hollywood—are: 3054, -3; 3055, -1; 3056, -2; -3057, -3.

30 December 1947, "Hollywood" (ref: page 191)

To complete Benny's produce for 1947, let's detail Capitol session No. 924 in its entirety:

BENNY GOODMAN AND HIS ORCHESTRA   **30 December 1947, Los Angeles**

Personnel as per Legacy, 30 December.

3147-4   CAP 15030, et al
            Beyond The Sea (La Mer) (arr PN)

3148-4   **LP:** BID T-1016
            Darn That Dream - voc Emma Lou Welch (arr PN)

BENNY GOODMAN SEXTET (sic)   **same session**

Personnel as per Legacy, 27 December Quintet.

3149-2   CAP 15069, et al, plus **LP:** MOSAIC MQ6-148. **CD:** MOSAIC MD4-148
                The World Is Waiting For The Sunrise

3150-3   **LP:** MOSAIC MQ6-148. **CD:** MOSAIC MD4-148
                The Record Ban Blues - voc Emma Lou Welch

Note that Mosaic's liner notes—not its discography—erroneously add trumpeter Jake Porter to the Quintet. He is not present.

"Click," May/June 1948, Phila. (ref: page 192)

A 1988 CD, PHON 8802, reissues four tracks previously released on DR and SWD LPs, plus some Hasselgard performances with groups other than Benny's. A 1992 CD, DR 183, adds a half-dozen tracks not on its LP, DR 16; three of them are on AFRS One Night Stand 1722. Date assignments given in both CDs are correct; however, DR 183 insists on titling **Indiana** as "Donna Lee" in two instances. "Donna Lee" was the title Mary Lou Williams gave her arrangement of the Hanley/McDonald classic; it's in the Archives at Yale. But Benny always announced it as "Indiana," and so does the announcer on the 5 June 1948 CBS broadcast.

A 1990 Japanese CD, VAVAN MEDIA 20115, combines "Click" and White Plains tracks previously issued on SWD LPs 25-9008 and 25-9016. Digital remastering offers somewhat better sound, but what is noteworthy is this warning on its label: "All rights of the producer and of the owner of the work reproduced reserved. Unauthorized copying, lending, public performance and broadcasting of this work prohibited." What's the Japanese word for chutzpah . . . ?

"Prob. July 1948, New York" (ref: pages 193, 319)

Daunted by working with Benny, who'd given him a hard time on earlier V-Disc sessions, producer Tony Janek invited Bill Savory to participate, "smooth things over." He did; and his notes supply the exact date of these small-group recordings, 20 August 1948.

A 1987 release, the English LP HEP 36 (later re-released on CD), substantially augments the sides recorded at the WOR Guild Theater Playhouse, New York. All of the takes displayed under several headings in Legacy's text and Addenda are from this session. To blend them with those on HEP(E) 36, the session is reconstituted below.

Source acetates lack matrices and takes. Matrices given for the V-Discs are thereon inscribed. Takes assigned by HEP(E) 36's liner notes are arbitrary. The new array suggests a reasonable order-of-performance.

HEP titles the first tune (three tracks) as, **Mary's Idea;** since HEP is the first issue, that title is given here. However, its registered title is **Just An Idea,** per MLWilliams's signed arrangement. (Benny also announces it as **Mary's Idea** on the "Click" broadcasts (page 192), but an M.C. correctly says **Just An Idea.** To avoid confusion in those listings, **Mary's Idea** was used throughout.)

BENNY GOODMAN SEXTET   **20 August 1948, New York**

Benny Goodman, clt; Wardell Gray, ts; Mary Lou Williams, p; Billy Bauer, g; Clyde Lombardi, b; Mel Zelnick, d. Jackie Searle, voc.

- 0 - "take 1"	**LP, CD:** HEP(E) 36
- 0 -bkdn ("take 2")	**LP, CD:** HEP(E) 36
- 0 - "take 3"	**LP, CD:** HEP(E) 36
	Mary's Idea (arr MLW)

- 0 - "take 1"	**LP:** SB 144, HEP(E) 36. **CD:** HEP(E) 36
- 0 - "take 2"	**LP, CD:** HEP(E) 36
	Bye Bye Blues ("Bye Bye Blues Bop" on HEP)

- 0 -	UNISSUED - studio acetate
- 0 -	UNISSUED - studio acetate
J-640-USS-1070	V-Disc 880 A, et al, plus **LP:** TRIB. **CD:** HEP(E) 36
	Benny's Bop (as "Wardell's Riff" on TRIB LP)

- 0	**LP, CD:** HEP(E) 36
	Blue Views (arr Chuck Wayne)

- 0 -	**LP:** SB 144, HEP(E) 36. **CD:** HEP(E) 36
	I Can't Give You Anything But Love, Baby - voc Jackie Searle

BENNY GOODMAN ("SEXTET" - sic) QUARTET   **same session**

Goodman, Williams, Lombardi, Zelnick.

- 0 -bkdn ("take 1")	**LP:** IAJRC 51, HEP(E) 36. **CD:** HEP(E) 36
- 0 - "take 2"	**LP:** SB 144, HEP(E) 36. **CD:** HEP(E) 36
J661-1091	V-Disc 890 B. **LP, CD:** HEP(E) 36
	There's A Small Hotel (arr MLW)

(Other Goodman tracks on HEP(E) 36—3 on the LP, 5 on the CD—are correctly identified in liner notes. And note the above revises the take of SB 144's track of **There's A Small Hotel** from that listed in Legacy.)

9 September 1948, "Hollywood" (ref: page 193)

One of only two tunes on a CAP "Recording Record," **Stealin' Apples** is now certain to have been cut in New York. Thus, change Legacy's locale, and ADD Mosaic LP and CD, MQ6-148 and MD-4-148, respectively, to the credits. Its take is, -3. It's also duplicated on the 1995 release, CAP CD 32086.

It's Been So Long, 3585-3, is the other entry on this sheet. No date is given for it. It may be 25 November 1947's matrix 2606, with a reassigned "release" matrix number. Or it could be a new recording. We may never know.

A photo caption in Mosaic's excellent included booklet has Benny in New York's Paramount in "October 1948." Engagement began 15 December.

10 February 1949, Hollywood (ref: page 195)

Take number for matrix 3958 is, -7; for 3959, -6. Chico O'Farrill arranged **Ma Belle Marguerite.**

Billed as "Direct from the Inaugural Ball," the band, rejoined by Benny, played a one-nighter in the Beardsley Ballroom, Bakersfield, CA, on 13 February.

24 March 1949, Hollywood (ref: page 196)

Take numbers for the first three recordings this date are: 4114, -3; 4115, -2; and 4116, -4. No take number is given for matrix 4117; instead, it is marked, "No Pay - N.G." The tune, **It Isn't Fair,** was eventually released on CAP 860, et al, including a 45 rpm issue, also numbered CAP 860. Since no other "Recording Record" lists a re-make, it is assumed that it is this 24 March 1949 recording that is issued.

? 25 March 1949, Hollywood (ref: page 196)

There is some evidence to support a 30 March broadcast date for this AFRS One Night Stand ET. Delete **Trees** from the parenthetical credits for the LP, SWT 100.

29 March 1949, Hollywood (ref: page 196)

Delete **Fresh Fish** and **Someone Like You** from the parenthetical credits for the LP, DAN 5023.

31 March 1949, Hollywood (ref: page 196)

Take numbers for the matrices this date are: 4126, -4; 4127, -4; 4128, -3; and 4129, -1. For matrix 4129, correct catalog number in Legacy to, CapJap ECJ40001. And in its personnel listing, substitute Irving Goodman, tpt, for Travis; and add Bud Herrman, p, replacing Buddy Greco, on **Don't Worry 'Bout Me.**

12 April 1949, Hollywood (ref: page 197)

This session is revised in its entirety, to take cognizance of a 1995 CD, personnel changes, take numbers and arranger credits; and to add matrix 4199, **Star Dust.** Substitute it for the display in Legacy.

All three issued tracks are identical to the master tapes listed in Legacy. **Lover Man** remains unissued as of December 1995. **Star Dust** may never be released; the "Recording Record" for this date notes that it is "N.G.," and its master may well have been destroyed.

Benny cut his first records with Ben Pollack's band in 1926. An incredible 59 years later, he made his last with his own orchestra. From left: Briedis, Kessler, Harry Goodman, Pollack, Greenberg, Benny Goodman, Harris, Livingston, Miller, Rodin. (Benny Goodman Collection, Yale University Music Library)

Benny's last band in rehearsal, 22 August 1985, RCA Studios, New York. From the top, left to right: Sandke, Cohen, Eckert, Sudhalter; Bert, Finders, Woodman; Schoenberg, Stuckey, Wilson, Peplowski, Bank (behind Benny). Chirillo off-camera, left. With some substitutions, Benny made his last records with this personnel in January 1986. (Photo, Ed Berger)

Absent Johnny "Scat" Davis's fake fourth trumpet, THIS is the band that made "Hollywood Hotel." Possibly because the producer insisted on Davis's presence in the orchestra's scenes, this set is in neither the feature film nor the "Auld Lang Syne" charity promo, suggesting that yet another Goodman sequence was cut from the final print.   (Benny Goodman Collection, Yale University Music Library)

Brown, Auld, Krupa, Neagley, Elman, Crosby and Wilson are all smiles as
Benny makes a point just prior to the 10 April 1953 kickoff of the ill-fated
Goodman/Armstrong tour. For tapes of that first concert, see section on
Savory's air checks.   (Photo courtesy Bob Bierman)

Benny and his "Far East" band in Seattle, 21 November 1956. Martha
Tilton was featured vocalist during the band's West Coast swing, but was
replaced by Dottie Reid when it flew to Thailand on 2 December.
(Benny Goodman Collection, Yale University Music Library)

Laryngitis caused Benny to ask Peanuts Hucko to rehearse this band, prior
to its March 1957 opening in the Waldorf-Astoria. "How come, Benny?
You can listen, without playing yourself." "I know, but I wanna hear how
I sound, and you play more like me than anybody I know." Praise indeed.
(Benny Goodman Collection, Yale University Music Library)

Inspired by this base personnel, Benny played brilliantly for one full year,
his most consistent performance after World War II. Goodman, Norvo,
Sheldon, Harris, Dodgion, Phillips, Freeman, Wyble, Wootten
and Markham, 20 October 1959, Hannover, Germany.
(Benny Goodman Collection, Yale University Music Library)

An enthusiastic audience jammed Leningrad's Winter Stadium in
July 1962 to applaud what has become Benny's most controversial concert
tour. Despite dissension in the ranks, this band produced some excellent,
albeit relatively few, recordings. See text for further comment.
(Benny Goodman Collection, Yale University Music Library)

Three days before "Benny Goodman Day" at the New York World's Fair,
24 August 1964, Red Skelton poses Mrs. Skelton, Benny and daughter
Benjie for his personal film library. Benny had performed in every
world fair since his first, also in New York, 25 years earlier.
(Benny Goodman Collection, Yale University Music Library)

Curious coincidence: The last week in April, especially the 25th of that month, is a recurrent date in Benny's classical career. Here he and the Budapest String Quartet rehearse the Mozart Clarinet Quintet, 25 April 1938. This, his first, was his favorite of all his classical recordings.

Goodman first recorded Morton Gould's "Derivations For Clarinet And Band" in September 1956. Dissatisfied with it, he re-recorded it, with the maestro conducting—on 25 April 1963. Was September simply an unfavorable month? (Photos, Benny Goodman Collection, Yale University Music Library)

Atlantic City's justly famed Steel Pier on a cool Sunday evening, 29 May 1938.
This Memorial Day weekend, and the Easter, Fourth of July and Labor Day
holidays, were prized bookings, awarded to the nation's most popular bands.
(Photo, Princeton Antiques Book Shop, Atlantic City)

Onstage at the Mark Hopkins, San Francisco, June 1940. Ignoring constant pain, Benny was playing exceedingly well, recalls Jerry Jerome, and the band was "really cookin'." Too bad; a month later it broke up when Benny entered the Mayo Clinic for back surgery.   (Photo courtesy Rich Dondiego)

Benny seems dubious—is that the "Ray"?—as somber Gene Krupa and Harry James are prepped for the motion picture *Syncopation* February 1942, Fox-Movietone Studios, New York. See text for comment.   (Photo courtesy Bob Bierman)

Disqualified for service because of a ruptured spinal disk, Benny aided the war effort by touring military bases and selling bonds. Here's the band in Central Park, New York, May 1942. That's Peggy Lee, her upswept hairdo partially obscured by Benny's elbow.   (Photo courtesy Jack Ellsworth)

Possibly in the band solely for this 25 February 1945 Columbia session, trumpeter Sonny Berman is flanked by Badale and Faso. Trummy Young is barely visible, left of Pritchard and Matthew. Bottom: Lombardi, Sachs, Bryan, Shine, Epstein, Benny, Bank.   (Photo courtesy Jack Ellsworth)

Frank Sinatra got his first big break as a solo performer with Benny Goodman at
the Paramount Theater, beginning 30 December 1942. Here he returns the favor,
featuring Benny's Sextet on his "Songs With Sinatra" radio program, 30 January
1946. AFRS recorded the broadcast.
(Benny Goodman Collection, Yale University Music Library)

Longest tenured Goodman male vocalist, handsome Art Lund sang with Benny's
band both before and after his military service in World War II. Note the "ruptured
duck" honorable discharge button in his lapel. Backstage at the Paramount, New
York, 12 March 1946. (Benny Goodman Collection, Yale University Music Library)

"Benny Goodman Day" at radio station WNEW, New York, 24 July 1946.
Surrounding Benny are wife Alice, Cab Calloway, Mannie Sachs,
John Hammond, Art Ford and Martin Block. Benny was a frequent guest
of WNEW, a few short blocks distant from his Manhattan House apartment.
(Benny Goodman Collection, Yale University Music Library)

Benny, Billy Bauer and Wardell Gray, 2 July 1948, White Plains, NY. Benny
bankrolled eight weekend dates at the Westchester County Center, cancelled
early when traditional fans stayed away from his excursion into "bop ." Critics
applauded it.   (Photo, Popsie)

Opening night at the London Palladium, 18 July 1949. Denied use of
U.S. musicians by a British union, Benny's backed by Herkie Styles and
The Skyrockets. That's a young Toots Theilmanns playing the harmonica.
(Benny Goodman Collection, Yale University Music Library)

Vital to Benny's early success and enduring fame, Helen Ward, Fletcher
Henderson and John Hammond celebrate release of Columbia's
"Jazz Concert No. 2" album, 22 October 1952, New York. And add
Bill Savory, also present, for it was he who supplied those marvelous
live performances.   (Photo, Herman Leonard)

Missing the 25th by three days, Benny rehearses George Balanchine's
"Clarinade" on 28 April 1963, for the next evening's premiere performance at
Lincoln Center. From left: Balanchine, Muriel Zuckerman, Benny, Morton Gould.

Benny and Igor Stravinsky record the maestro's "Ebony Concerto,"
25 April 1965, unique among all of Goodman's classical efforts
on wax: The "Andante" movement was taped after Benny left
the studio, and Charles Russo played its clarinet soli.
(Photos, Benny Goodman Collection, Yale University Music Library)

Hank Jones, Slam Stewart, Benny, Bucky Pizzarelli, Ronnie Bedford, Urbie Green, Mel Davis and Zoot Sims rehearse in the Nanuet Star Theater, whose acoustics are conducive to excellent, if unauthorized, audience recordings. 16 May 1975.   (Photo, Jack Bradley)

Because of their close friendship, Jack Ellsworth (with wife Dot, left) got a $1,500 discount from Benny's usual fee for this 13 April 1973 "Skills Unlimited" charity affair. A tape of the event is extant.   (Photo, Jim Mooney)

Late in life, Benny relished private classical duets with his friend, fishing companion and attorney, Bill Hyland, now co-executor of his estate. Was Benny helpful or critical? "Both."   (Photo, the Goodman Estate)

No, that's not Phil Spitalny and his All-Girl Orchestra. Benny is welcomed
onstage for a Sunday afternoon concert as soloist with the Elgin Symphony
Orchestra, 21 November 1976, Hemmens Auditorium, Elgin, Illinois.
(Photo, Jim Kutina)

BENNY GOODMAN AND HIS ORCHESTRA   **12 April 1949, Hollywood**

Personnel as per this text, 31 March 1949, except: Sigmund "Ziggy" Schatz, tpt, replaces Irving Goodman; and Bob Dawes, bar, replaces Molinelli. Bud Herrman, p, is listed as also present.

4195-2	**CD:** CAP 32086 **Bop Hop** (arr Chico O'Farrill)
4196-2	**CD:** CAP 32086 **Trees**
4197	UNISSUED - Tape **Lover Man** (arr Mel Powell)
4198-3	**CD:** CAP 32086 **Dreazag**
4199	UNISSUED (master marked "N.G.") **Star Dust**

(Note that neither Lincoln Center nor Yale has arrangements for **Trees** and **Dreazag**. **Star Dust** is likely Fletcher Henderson's 24 January 1946 update of his 1935 chart.)

14 April 1949, Hollywood (ref: page 197)

All four tunes recorded this date are also on LP and CD, Mosaic MQ6-148 and MD4-148, respectively. Take numbers are: matrix 4203, -5; 4204, -3; 4205, -3; and 4206, -2. **There's A Small Hotel** is also issued on the ET, AFRS Music Transcription Library No. P-2-49. Additionally, **Bedlam, Oo-Bla-Dee,** and **Blue Lou** are on CAP CD 32086.

5 July 1949, Hollywood

Refuting a statement in Legacy—"At the end of June Benny gave the orchestra a six-week vacation . . . "—the "Recording Records" reveal a hitherto unknown Goodman recording session, Capitol's No. 1283. Only one recording from this date has been issued, and there's a minor discrepancy as to it: Per its tape, **Fiesta Time** is announced as, "take 3," while its "Recording Record" lists, "-4." We'll go with the former.

BENNY GOODMAN AND HIS ORCHESTRA   **5 July 1949, Hollywood**

Personnel as per this text, 12 April 1949, except: There is some evidence that neither Eddie Bert nor Clyde Lombardi was present, and no replacements for them are noted.

4255-3   **CD:** CAP 32086
           Fiesta Time (arr Chico O'Farrill)

4256-4   UNISSUED
           Don't Worry 'Bout Me - prob. voc Buddy Greco

4257-2   UNISSUED
           Brother Bill - prob. voc Buddy Greco, chorus

4258-2   UNISSUED
           Goodnight My Love - voc ?

(There are no known extant arrangements for the three unissued sides, except possibly an undated "revised" chart for Jimmy Mundy's **Goodnight My Love** at Yale.)

18 September 1949/"15 October 1949," New York (ref: page 198)
    Contrary to all prior advice and intelligence, the "Recording Records" revise Legacy's 15 October 1949 date to 18 September 1949 for Capitol session No. 1292. To this juncture revised dating has been accepted, but one wonders. . . . Takes are: matrix 4288, -6; 4289, -3; 4290, -4; and 4291, -3.

Roxy engagement, September 1949, New York (ref: page 198)
    Make that Bob DAWES, not Davies.

27 October 1949, New York (ref: page 198)
    The "Recording Records" state that Benny got "No Pay" for the re-makes of **Brother Bill** and **Spin A Record,** both released from this session. Takes for all four sides are: matrix 4304, -4; 4305, -3; 4306, -3; and 4307, -4. The sheets do not cite a recording of **Get Yourself Another Fool,** although Chico O'Farrill's arrangement of it is at Yale. Conversely, there's none for the issued, **I Had Someone Else Before I Had You.** Is it possible they're one and the same tune, retitled for some reason. . . ?
    For matrix 4305, correct credit to, CapJap ECJ40001.

BENNY GOODMAN, 1950–1995

24 April 1950, Stockholm (ref: page 199)

Inadvertent omission: **(I Would Do) Anything For You,** by the full group with vocal by Nancy Reed, follows **Star Dust.**

Absent six renditions and the closing theme, this concert is on the Swedish CD, SWEDISH JAZZ RADIO (SJR) 101. Excellent audio quality.

Ed Shaughnessy, a key sideman with Doc Severinson's fine orchestra on Johnny Carson's defunct NBC-TV "The Tonight Show," says it is he, not Sonny Igoe, in Legacy's photo of the group that includes Roy Eldridge, Zoot Sims, et al: "In those years, we ALL looked alike!" Sorry, Ed; to these old eyes, nothing looks like it once did.

Ed remembers this Stockholm concert—and indeed, the entire tour—with great clarity and relish: "Playing with 'The King' was in a class by itself." Then but 21 years of age, he admits he was very apprehensive about joining Benny. He sought advice from some of Benny's former sidemen, got this from Lionel Hampton: "When Benny starts to come on strong to you, beat him to it, come on strong to him. That'll cool him right down." Did it work? "Did it ever! One day I was late for a rehearsal, all the guys were there, and I could see 'The Ray' starting to come on. So I said, 'Well, what're we all standing around for? Let's play.' Benny just looked at me, kind of wide-eyed, then turned to the guys and said, 'Yeah, he's right, let's get started.' After that, I never had any trouble at all."

And this: "One time, I either cracked or lost a cymbal, I forget which, and somebody promised to give me another, a new Italian cymbal. But it was delivered to Benny, not to me. So he called me over, said, 'Ed, I got a cymbal for you,' and he tried to sell it to me! I was dumbstruck, but finally he said, 'Just kiddin', Ed,' and he gave it to me." Oh. . .?

Now in his mid-sixties, Ed says, anent the author's comment in Legacy, "I finally learned to play two bass drums." And he has: his facility with all of his kit, with Severinson on TV, in concert and on record; and with his own small groups, in person and on record, is outstanding.

13 May 1950, Lausanne, Switzerland

Although the author has not heard them, he is informed that good audio quality tapes of a concert in the Palais de Beaulieu, Lausanne, Switzerland, are extant:

PALAIS DE BEAULIEU CONCERT   *13 May 1950, Lausanne*

Personnel as per Legacy, 24 April 1950.

Theme
After You've Gone - QUARTET
Body And Soul - QUARTET
Just One Of Those Things - QUARTET
(Lover - Hyman p solo
The World Is Waiting For The Sunrise - QUARTET
(Rockin' Chair - Eldridge w/rhythm - NO BG

(I Would Do) Anything For You - voc Nancy Reed
I Can't Give You Anything But Love, Baby - voc Nancy Reed
'Deed I Do - voc Nancy Reed
Air Mail Special
That's A-Plenty
Stompin' At The Savoy (n/c)
Rose Room - QUARTET
Let Me Off Uptown - voc Nancy Reed, Roy Eldridge
(Star Dust - Theilmanns, hca, w/rhythm - NO BG
(All The Things You Are - Sims w/rhythm - NO BG
(Hi Ho Trailus) Boot Whip - voc Roy Eldridge
Undecided
Flying Home

Note: Information supplied cites "Let's Dance" as the opening theme. That may be incorrect; during this tour, Benny was playing "Stompin' At The Savoy" to begin each concert.

24 November 1950, New York (ref: page 201)
Multi-format Columbia and CBSFr releases include two previously-unissued takes from this Sextet session. ADD them to the display in Legacy:

BENNY GOODMAN SEXTET   **24 November 1950, New York**

Personnel as per Legacy.

CO 44674-2   **LP, Cas, CD:** CO 40379, CBSFr 450.111, CBSFr 450.979
                           Lullaby Of The Leaves

CO 44677-2   **LP, Cas, CD:** CO 40379, CBSFr 450.111
                           Temptation Rag

"Benny Goodman Music Festival," New York (ref: page 203)
Another two-sided 12-inch LP in the "Benny Goodman Music Festival" WNEW-BMI series has been discovered. It bears matrices "BG 107" and "BG 108"; its seven tracks embrace Programs 14 through 20, inclusive.
Together with the LP discussed in Legacy, this addition points to an as yet undiscovered LP, "BG 105 / BG 106," which would include the Programs 8 through 13, inclusive.
Further, if Benny's "Festival" ran for the standard 26 weeks, another LP in the series should be "BG 109 / BG 110," for Programs 21 through 26, inclusive.

29 April 1951, New York (ref: page 203)
Error: Delete the LP, HA HL7225, from credits for matrix CO 45677, **King Porter Stomp.** (Legacy typo has it as "7255," compounding the error.)

Hollywood Bowl Concert (ref: page 203)
Recently discovered, a set of thirteen 16-inch transcriptions confirms speculation in Legacy, last paragraph, page 203: The concert took place on 15 September 1951, and NBC did record it for AFRS. However, the ETs are not the usual AFRS vinyl or shellac pressings;

they are acetates, and they are absent inscribed or printed matrix, series, or program numbers. An AFRS label is affixed to each disc, carrying the title, "PERSONAL PRESENTATION COPY." Typed on each label is, "HOLLYWOOD BOWL CONCERT, Saturday, September 15" and a sequential Part number.

The title, "PERSONAL PRESENTATION COPY," strongly suggests that these acetates were intended to be given to the featured performers on the concert. To date, no AFRS pressings of the concert have been reported.

Benny's contribution is on Part No. 11. Bob Hope introduces him, and Benny plays three of his extended arrangements with Johnny Green's augmented orchestra.

HOLLYWOOD BOWL CONCERT   15 September 1951, Hollywood

Benny Goodman, clt, with Johnny Green and his Orchestra.

- 0 -   **Acetate ET:** AFRS Personal Presentation Copy, Part 11
                          The Man I Love
                          I Only Have Eyes For You
                          Dizzy Fingers

(Available on CD, VJC 1034.)

26 September 1951, New York (ref: page 204)

Typographical error: Initial issue of matrix CO 47080, **When Buddha Smiles,** is the LP, PB 1957 (the year of the release), not "31957."

A clandestine tape, labeled "NOSTALGIA," contains what may be the totality of the recordings of matrix CO 47082, **You Can't Pull The Wool Over My Eyes,** from this session. Order-of-performance is derived from comments made by producer Teo Macero, audible on the tape. Substitute the following for the array in Legacy:

BENNY GOODMAN AND HIS ORCHESTRA   26 September 1951, New York

Personnel as per Legacy.

CO 47082   CO Ref. "Nostalgia" tape
CO 47082-1   "Nostalgia" tape
CO 47082-bkdns   "Nostalgia" tape (3 consecutive aborted attempts)
                      You Can't Pull The Wool Over My Eyes - voc Nancy Reed

(Macero announces "take 1" following the first complete rendition, the version on the Columbia Reference Recording.)

5 March 1952, Los Angeles (ref: page 205)

Delete the LP, CO 21064, from the issue credits for matrices RHCO 10141-1A and 10142-1A, **Lover Come Back To Me** and **If I Had You,** respectively. Delete the album, CO P4M-5678, from the issue credits for matrix RHCO 10141-1A, **Lover Come Back To Me.**

29 & 30 July 1952, New York (ref: page 205)

Reissues of all seven previously-released matrices from these two consecutive Sextet sessions are included in multi-format CO 40379 and CBSFr 450.111. Each take is now designated -1 by Columbia. Matrices CO 48136, 48137 and 48140 remain unissued as of this writing.

Of greater interest than those reissues is the discovery of two previously unknown sides from the 30 July session, both on a 16-inch Columbia Reference transcription. ADD them to the display in Legacy:

BENNY GOODMAN SEXTET   **30 July 1952, New York**

CO 48135-alt   UNISSUED - Co Ref - ET
                                Under A Blanket of Blue

CO 48137   UNISSUED - Co Ref - ET
                                Four Or Five Times - voc Benny Goodman

20 August 1952, Chicago (ref: page 206)
    The LP, JAZ 36, is absent both themes.

22 October 1952, New York (ref: page 206)
    Multi-format CO 40379 and CBSFr 450.111 assign take -1R to matrix CO 48136-R, and take -2R to matrix CO 48137-R(2), both from this makeup session. Both takes were first issued on the EP, CO B1845. The relatively scarce take -R(1), matrix CO 48137, **Four Or Five Times,** was unfortunately not included in the Columbia and French CBS releases.

25 January 1953, New York (ref: page 207)
    The 1990 PBS telecast of the "John Hammond" special in its "American Masters" se-ries includes a brief excerpt of the Trio's **The World Is Waiting For The Sunrise** from this date's "Omnibus" telecast.

23 February 1953, New York (ref: page 207)
    A take -1A copy of matrix CO 48875, **What A Little Moonlight Can Do,** on an orig-inal-issue 78, CO 39976, is reportedly in the collection of a reliable correspondent. (The author has not examined this record.) This would seem to increase the possibility that it may also be on PhilAu B21051H.

4 March 1953, New York (ref: page 207)
    Present this date to position the instruments and microphones to Benny's satisfac-tion, Bill Savory explains why matrix CO 48915, **It's Been So Long,** is unissued and is likely to remain so. "This was an all-Henderson session, so Benny put up Fletcher's new arrangement. It's much different than David Rose's, and Helen (Ward), especially, had trouble with it. After a couple of takes were aborted, I said to him, 'Really, Benny, Rose's original arrangement is much better than this one.' He didn't hesitate a minute: 'You know, you're right,' and with that he told everybody to put Fletcher's chart aside."
    Bill kept "one of the longer" aborted takes as a souvenir.

Spring 1953, Benny Goodman Tour (ref: page 207)

It is now confirmed that Benny is not on any of the tapes referred to in Legacy's penultimate paragraph, page 207. Benny had left the tour before the sideman (who prefers anonymity) felt "comfortable" in recording the concerts. (But see separate section on Bill Savory's air checks.)

The author has one of the tapes: 20 May 1953, Union Theater, Madison, WI. Its sound quality varies, but both the Armstrong and "Goodman" segments offer some very good audio tracks. Georgie Auld and Gene Krupa share announcing duties for the big band's portion. At its end, Gene and Cozy Cole, from Louis's group, trade drum soli. (They were partners in a drum studio in Manhattan, remember?) Then Louis and his full group join the "Goodman" band for the closer, **When The Saints Go Marching In.**

If Benny had not already quit the tour for "medical reasons," that grand finale might have made him ill.

13 January 1954, New York

Benny began the second of his two Capitol contracts with a previously unknown session this date. The "Recording Records" are devoid of details, but because of Benny's known whereabouts, we assume New York was the locale. Note that for all of 1954 and 1955, the "Records" are absent take numbers. And for 1954, they insert a comma in each matrix number, as shown below:

BENNY GOODMAN AND HIS ORCHESTRA   **13 January 1954, New York**

Instrumentation, personnel unknown. No vocals cited.

20,310	UNISSUED	**(I Would Do) Anything For You**
20,311	UNISSUED	**The Dixieland Band**
20,312	UNISSUED	**Lullaby In Rhythm**

28 January 1954, New York (ref: page 208)

Long ago advice from Capitol, and now its "Recording Records," both title matrix 20,334 as, **Everything I Have (or, I've Got) Is Yours,** the listing in Legacy. All three are wrong; the tune is Rodgers and Hart's, **Ev'rything I've Got (Belongs To You).**

All four matrices recorded this date are also released on LP and CD, Mosaic MQ6-148 and MD4-148, respectively. Takes are, per Mosaic's determination: matrix 20,333, -5; 20,334, -6; 20,335, -2; and 20,336, -3. But Mosaic's claim that **Ev'rything I've Got (Belongs To You), But Not For Me,** and **Margie** were "unissued" is incorrect; all are on the LP issued in late 1986, BluDisc T-1016.

29 January 1954, New York

For the last time, the "Recording Records" list a Goodman session (No. 5084) that is not in Legacy:

BENNY GOODMAN AND HIS ORCHESTRA   **29 January 1954, New York**

Instrumentation, personnel unknown. No vocals cited.

20,337   UNISSUED
                          Stealin' Apples

20,338   UNISSUED
                          If I Could Be With You (One Hour Tonight)

20,339   UNISSUED
                          A Smo-o-o-oth One

July 1954, New York (ref: page 208)
    Although Benny's Park Recording Company was not sanctioned by the AFofM until August/September 1955, he began to tape his engagements more than a year prior to the union's OK. Possibly the first of these is his Basin Street stand that opened 13 July 1954. Excerpts from those tapes—specific dates unknown—were issued in 1994 as Volume 9 in the Yale/MusicMasters series:

The Yale University Music Library
BENNY GOODMAN, Volume 9: LIVE AT BASIN STREET, 1954   **July 1954, New York**

Benny Goodman, clt; Charlie Shavers, tpt; Mel Powell, p; Steve Jordan, g; Israel Crosby, b; Morey Feld, d. TRIO: Goodman, Powell, Feld

- 0 -   **CD:** MM 65111-2
                          After You've Gone - TRIO
                          Body And Soul - TRIO
                          Nice Work If You Can Get It - TRIO
                          The World Is Waiting For The Sunrise - TRIO
                          Avalon
                          (**Dark Eyes** - Shavers w/rhythm section - NO BG
                          Don't Be That Way
                          How High The Moon
                          One O'Clock Jump
                          I've Found A New Baby - TRIO
                          On The Sunny Side Of The Street - TRIO
                          Runnin' Wild - TRIO
                          Liza - TRIO
                          Exactly Like You - TRIO
                          Someday, Sweetheart - TRIO
                          China Boy - TRIO
                          (piano interlude - NO BG
                          (**Our Love Is Here To Stay** - Shavers w/rhythm section - NO BG
                          That's A-Plenty

    Volume 9 was released 14 June 1994, on CD only. In future it may be re-released on the JHS & MHS labels, and possibly in other formats.

For further comment in reference to the Yale/MusicMasters series, see under date of 25/26 March 1955, herein.

8 November 1954, New York (ref: page 208)

Matrices 20,528, **Ain't Misbehavin',** and 20,530, **Slipped Disc,** were first issued on the LP, BluDisc T-1016. All four tunes are also released on multi-format CAP 92864, and on LP and CD, Mosaic MQ6-148 and MD4-148, respectively. Takes are: matrix 20,527, -5; 20,528, -6; 20,529, -10; and 20,530, -8. Credit Mel Powell for the arrangement of **Get Happy.**

Not in Legacy's credits are two 10-inch LPs that embrace all of the tunes in Capitol's "B.G. in Hi-Fi" several releases, CAP H1-565 and H2-565. The bootleg CD, JOKER 0240, also dubs the "Hi-Fi" tracks.

9 November 1954, New York (ref: pages 208, 209)

All seven sides from this session are also released on multi-format CAP 92864.

16 November 1954, New York (ref: page 209)

The four tunes recorded this date are also issued on multi-format CAP 92864, and on LP and CD, Mosaic MQ6-148 and MD4-148, respectively. Takes are: matrix 20,547, -4; 20,549, -14; and 20,550, -4. Neither the "Recording Records" nor Mosaic's liner notes gives a take number for matrix 20,548.

Note that multi-format CAP 92864 excises the first few notes of **Rose Room;** the Mosaic releases offer the complete take.

17 November 1954, New York (ref: page 209)

The complete take of matrix 20,552, **(I Would Do) Anything For You,** and the other three sides from this session, are also released on multi-format CAP 92864. The breakdown, and the complete take, of **(I Would Do) Anything For You,** were first issued on the LP, BluDisc T-1016.

25/26 March 1955, New York (ref: page 210)

Yale University chose the Musical Heritage Society, theretofore noted for its classical catalog, as the issuing agency for his tapes that Benny had willed to the Benny Goodman Archives at Yale. He would have approved that choice, for he was pleased with the meticulous care the Society had given its 1985 release of his "Benny Goodman—Private Collection" album (Legacy, pp 210, 211, 219).

Initial releases were only on the Society's MusicMasters (MM) label. Over time, they were reissued on the Society's Jazz Heritage Society (JHS) and Musical Heritage Society (MHS) labels. In 1993, Volumes 1 through 5 in the Yale/MusicMasters series, six CDs in all, were re-released in a box set, MM 65095-2.

Volume 1 in the series was announced at a press conference at the Yale Club, Manhattan, on 16 May 1988. It surveys the full span of Benny's Park Recording Company tapes (1954-1977), plus a January 1986 MusicMasters session. One track only is from the March 1955 Basin Street West engagement.

Volume 2 is devoted solely to that booking. All of its tracks, save two, are first issues: **Stairway To The Stars** and **Body And Soul** are the same performances as those in the Classics Record Library album. (Note that CLRL is the correct abbreviation for that label, not "CRL," a typographical error in Legacy. "CRL" properly identifies the CORAL label.)

Unless otherwise noted, performances arrayed below are by the Octet. In Legacy, tracks by Benny and rhythm are attributed to a Quintet. Review of those tracks, and like ones here, fails to discern Perry Lopez's guitar in any of them. Thus they are attributed to a QUARTET now, an ascription that applies equally to those in the CLRL and HOM albums.

Liner notes for Volumes 1 and 2 date all performances as, 26 March. Aware of Benny's casual attitude toward detailing his tapes, the author suggests either of two dates:

The Yale University Music Library
BENNY GOODMAN, Volume 1   **25/26 March 1955, New York**

Octet personnel as per Legacy. QUARTET: Goodman, Wilson, Hinton, Donaldson.

- 0 -   **StLp:** MM 20142, JHS & MHS 922277. **Cas:** MM 40142, MM 5000-4, JHS & MHS 322277. **CD:** MM 60142, MM 5000-2, JHS & MHS 522277
                  Slipped Disc

(Note that JHS & MHS releases are double albums, combining Volumes 1 and 2, and that they use identical catalog numbers. This practice continues with JHS & MHS releases for Volumes 3 and 4. **Slipped Disc** is also on a promo CD, MM 65099-2.)

The Yale University Music Library
BENNY GOODMAN, Volume 2: LIVE AT BASIN STREET   **same dates**

Personnels as preceding.

- 0 -   **StLp:** MM 20156, JHS & MHS 922277. **Cas:** MM 40156, MM 5006-4, JHS & MHS 322277. **CD:** MM 60156, MM 5006-2, JHS & MHS 522277
                  Let's Dance (theme)
                  Honeysuckle Rose
                  Runnin' Wild - QUARTET
                  Mean To Me - feat. Braff - Octet in coda
                  Memories Of You - QUARTET
                  Stompin' At The Savoy
                  (Blue And Sentimental - feat. Quinichette - Braff & Green in coda - NO BG
                  One O'Clock Jump
                  I Found A New Baby (sic) - QUARTET - also on promo CD, MM 65099-2.
                  (Stairway To The Stars - Green w/rhythm - NO BG - also on CLRL RL7673, et al
                  Body And Soul - QUARTET - also on CLRL RL7673, et al
                  Air Mail Special
                  Nice Work If You Can Get It - QUARTET
                  Sing, Sing, Sing
                  Good-Bye (theme)

March/post-March 1955, New York (ref: pages 210, 211)

Comment below applies equally to March/post-March 1955, New York, and to May 1957, Stamford, page 219, q.v.

MusicMasters classical album, BENNY GOODMAN—PRIVATE COLLECTION, was initially released in 1985. The two-LP set, MM 20103 A/20104 B, embraced four compositions: one by von Weber, one by Beethoven, and two by Brahms. But its companion CD, MM 60103Y, contained only two of those compositions: the von Weber, and but one by Brahms.

Through 1990, the album has been re-issued in three formats, under three labels, and with varied contents. For example, the MM CD 62103Z contains both of the Brahms opuses, while its companion MM CD 62104X contains the von Weber and the Beethoven.

In sum, the reissues are: LP set, MHS 827355; Cassette, MM 40103, MM 40104, MM 5027-4, JHS 42103, MHS 829355; and CD, MM 62103, MM 62104, MM 5027-2, JHS 62103. (This listing supplied by MusicMasters.)

Spring? 1955, Lenox, MA

Reputedly extant is a "superb quality" 90-minute tape of a Goodman engagement at the Berkshire Festival, Tanglewood, Lenox, MA, date and other details unspecified. The author had found no notice of such a concert in Benny's files.

27 June 1955, Hollywood (ref: page 211)

During his appearance this date on Steve Allen's "Tonight Show," Gene Krupa remarks that he's been in Hollywood for "about two weeks." Allen says he understands the music sounds great, asks what's been recorded so far. Gene replies: "Well, we've made **Down South Camp Meeting,** we've made **Don't Be That Way, Sing, Sing, Sing, Memories Of You,** all the old tunes, you know." Later, Allen says he'd heard some of the records "just today, because I have to learn the fingering."

These statements advance the August date Decca supplied the author for at least some of its "The Benny Goodman Story" releases by almost two months. Revise the date to, Summer 1955.

"The Benny Goodman Story," Summer 1955, Hollywood (ref: page 212)

Individual matrices for the Decca releases are numbered 89016 through 89036, inclusive (matrices cited in Legacy are for the LP pressings). Note that Decca set DXB188 includes all 21 tracks.

"The Benny Goodman Story," Summer 1955, Hollywood (ref. page 319)

For this work, Fred Cohen, proprietor of Manhattan's Jazz Record Center, made his U-I LPs and acetates available for comprehensive evaluation. Details follow; approx. running times are in minutes:seconds.

Mozart Concerto (unique to LP 1106)
Same as film, except :40 longer. No DE release.

Stompin' At The Savoy (LP 1106, acetate)
Same take in film, DE release, U-I LP, acetate, but: **Film** (1:42) omits 1st clt solo, 2nd tbn solo, ts solo.
DE release (2:34) omits ts solo, portion of 1st tbn solo.
U-I LP, acetate (3:06), ostensibly complete. Soli sequence: clt-tbn-ts-tbn-clt.

"Dixieland One-Step" (LP 1107, acetate)

Mistitled on both LP and acetate, this is NOT the Goodman/Ory performance in the film's riverboat sequence. It is **Sensation Rag,** from the film's Carnegie sequence. Identical take in film, U-I LP, acetate. No DE release.

Note that Sims does not participate; revise the "Octet" listing to Septet—Goodman, Clayton, Green, rhythm section.

No Name Blues (unique to acetate)

No counterpart in film or on DE. A relaxed Quartet enjoying themselves for 6:04.

"Main Title Music" (unique to acetate)

Flowery, brief (:46) intro to **Don't Be That Way.** No counterpart in film or on DE.

And a complex revision, involving the (now) four versions of **Sing, Sing, Sing:**

Film (5:32): Goodman's, James's soli complete, identical to DE release, 45 U-I 78189 (page 212), U-I LP 1108, acetate. Much tom-tom soli excised. All Sims's ts soli omitted. BUT: in the film, Krupa plays snare-tom-cymbal triplets in coda, not audible in the three extant discs cited above and next:

DE release (8:09): First Sims ts solo included. Opening eight bars of Sims's 2nd solo are excised.

45 U-I 78189 (7:46): First Sims ts solo omitted. Second Sims ts solo complete.

U-I LP 1108, acetate (8:23): Both Sims's ts soli included and complete. Likely the full recording of the version on DE, U-I 78189. Bear in mind that the film's coda apparently is from a different take.

Many tunes on the U-I LPs, 1106, 1107 and 1108, are also on the seven acetates, and they are identical to each other. All of these tunes are also the same takes as on the DE release.

8 September 1955, New York (ref: pages 213, 319)

Inspired experimentation discovered that tapes from this date had been recorded in an unusual three-track mode, one for vocals. Remastering brought the otherwise inaudible voices to the fore, and also salvaged four tunes not listed in Legacy. Among them is a warmup **On The Alamo,** akin to the "Ad Lib Blues" that began the 28 October 1940 Columbia session. Since Benny does not participate, it's not detailed below.

As of this writing, a spliced take included in Volume 1 of the Yale/MusicMasters series is the sole issue. Further releases are anticipated in future.

Substitute the revised display below for Legacy's listing/addendum:

THE BENNY GOODMAN SEPTET   **8 September 1955, New York**

Personnel as per Legacy.

- 0 - take 1	UNISSUED - Tape
- 0 - take 2	UNISSUED - Tape
- 0 -	UNISSUED - Tape (two consecutive rehearsals, coda)
	Oh, By Jingo! - voc Art Lund, Nancy Reed (arr Al Cohn)
- 0 - take 1	UNISSUED - Tape
- 0 - take 2	UNISSUED - Tape
	Easy To Love - voc Art Lund (arr Al Cohn)

8 September 1955, continued

8 September 1955, continued

- 0 - take 1	UNISSUED - Tape
- 0 - take 2	UNISSUED - Tape
- 0 - S	**StLP:** MM 20142, JHS & MHS 922277. **Cas:** MM 40142, MM 5000-4, JHS & MHS 322277. **CD:** MM 60142, MM 5000-2, JHS & MHS 522277
	Soft Lights And Sweet Music

(Splice consists of: Take 2, intro thru Green's 1st solo; then Take 1, Green's 2nd solo and Braff's 1st solo; ending with, Take 2, Braff's 2nd solo, to conclusion.)

- 0 - take 1	UNISSUED - Tape (Benny forgets the lyrics)
- 0 - take 2	UNISSUED - Tape
- 0 - take 3	UNISSUED - Tape
- 0 - take 4	UNISSUED - Tape
	It's Bad For Me - voc Benny Goodman, Nancy Reed
- 0 -	UNISSUED
	'S Wonderful
- 0 - n/c	UNISSUED
	I Cried For You - voc Nancy Reed
- 0 -	UNISSUED
	I Want A Little Girl - voc Art Lund

6 December 1955, New York (ref: pages 213, 319)

As Legacy suggests, Irving Jacoby filmed this session; his son Oren inserted brief clips into his "Benny Goodman: Adventures in the Kingdom of Swing." For further comment on this hour-long telecast, see under date of July 1993, herein.

Age took its toll on Mr. Jacoby's 35mm film; about an hour and 15 minutes' worth has been salvaged. Transferred to videotape, approximately half has sound, half—for whatever reason—is silent. Nevertheless, viewing it in its entirety is fascinating. While Bobby Donaldson is still setting up his kit, Benny and Claude Thornhill begin to jam on **A Fine Romance.** One by one the others join in, and they swing. Then it's take 1 of **Can't We Talk It Over,** with Benny blowing a marvelous chorus on Claude's new arrangement. (He's seen handing both arrangements to the group, so credit both charts to Thornhill.) Benny and Claude smoke incessantly the whole session, Buck, Aaron Bell and Bobby occasionally, Urbie never. Urbie keeps his coat on throughout, Buck and Bobby wear hats, the others are in shirt sleeves. Whenever Claude solos, Benny smiles, says something in an aside to Urbie. Great stuff.

7 December 1955, New York (ref: page 214)

Capitol's "Recording Records" list an initial take of matrix 20937, **Bugle Call Rag,** as the final effort this date. And they note that Harry James is to split royalties with Benny for **And The Angels Sing** and **Sing, Sing, Sing.**

ADD as the last entry to Legacy's array,

MR. BENNY GOODMAN   **7 December 1955, New York**

Personnel as per Legacy.

20937   UNISSUED
                              Bugle Call Rag

(Note that now commas are omitted from CAP's matrix numbers.)

8 December 1955, New York (ref: page 214)

Again, Harry James is specified to split royalties with Benny for this session's **Shine** and **One O'Clock Jump.**

Matrix 20946, **King Porter Stomp,** is issued on the LP, BluDisc T-1015.

"12," 14 December 1955, New York (ref: page 214)

The "Recording Records" cite but one date—14 December—for matrices 20932; 20946, 20947 and 20948; and 20951 through 20959, inclusive. Contrary to the two separate arrays in Legacy, the sheets omit the 12 December date. They do, however, list two CAP sessions: No. 5317 for the big band sides, No. 5318 for the Quintet recordings.

The single date listing contradicts the pay records the author examined in Benny's office many years ago. It contravenes the information Capitol's Bill Miller sent the author in the mid-1950s. In the late 1970s, Benny was casting about for unissued material that might be worthy of release; the author listed the Capitols for him. Benny forwarded that list to Capitol's Dave Cavanaugh, requesting transfers from the masters. Dave then sent Benny three seven-inch reels containing most of the unissued sides the author had specified, plus some transfers of recordings that had been released. Among the latter was matrix 20932, **Don't Be That Way,** dated 12 December 1955, as issued on the LP, CAP S706, et al.

In light of these persuasive attestations for a 12 December session, one is loath to accept a 14 December date only. A suggestion: let the two dates stand, unless and until there is irrefutable evidence to the contrary.

*

Matrix 20932, **Don't Be That Way,** is also on the LP, Blu-Disc T-1015, the same take issued on the LP, CAP S706, et al.

Matrices 20955, **Alicia's Blues;** 20958, **Seven Come Eleven;** and 20959, **I Got Rhythm,** were first released on the LP, Blu-Disc T-1016. Later, two sides were released on the CD, CapJap 32-5182, **Alicia's Blues** and **Seven Come Eleven.**

All seven Quintet tracks from 14 December are also on LP and CD, Mosaic MQ6-148 and MD4-148, respectively. Only take numbers available are: matrix 20955, -1; 20958, -1; and 20959, -2. Mosaic's discography omits notice of Blu-Disc T-1016's **I Got Rhythm.** Mosaic's policy, like that of many other legitimate record producers, is to ignore bootleg labels, understandably so. Reluctantly, this author, as discographer, must take notice of at least some of them.

In sum, Mosaic is to be commended for its release of Benny's small group Capitol recordings. Audio fidelity is excellent, the strict chronological/matrix programming is welcome, liner notes and discography (despite minor glitches) are intelligent, the previously unknown/unissued tracks are major contributions. Would that other producers empty their vaults in similar fashion.

17 May 1956, New York (ref: pages 215, 320)

Two tracks on a Yale/MusicMasters release revise their listing in Legacy's Addenda. Liner notes erroneously cite "16 May 1957" for them, a seeming transposition of numbers for the correct date:

The Yale University Music Library
BENNY GOODMAN, Volume 4: BIG BAND RECORDINGS   **17 May 1956, New York**

Personnel as per Legacy.

- 0 - take 1	UNISSUED - Tape
- 0 - take 2	UNISSUED - Tape
- 0 - take 3	UNISSUED - Tape
- 0 - Splice	**StLp:** MM 20201, JHS & MHS 922431. **Cas:** MM 40201, MM 5017-4, JHS & MHS 322431. **CD:** MM 60201, MM 5017-2, JHS & MHS 522431
	The Earl

(A piano chorus from take 2 is spliced into complete take 3. Thus the unalloyed takes 2 and 3 remain unissued.)

- 0 -	All issues as for "The Earl"
	More Than You Know - voc Mitzi Cottle

14, 15 December 1956, Bangkok (ref: pages 216, 217)

Goodman enthusiast Kurt Mueller released a four-CD album in December 1993, TCB(Swiss) 4301-2. Each of the four discs offers tracks from different engagements: Bangkok; Basel (page 230); Santiago, Chile (page 238); and Berlin (pages 299, 300). The latter three are noted herein chronologically; but first Bangkok, and some introductory comment:

Liner notes state that all tunes were recorded either 14 or 15 December, but fail to specify dates for individual tracks. If correct, that changes Legacy's listing of an undated concert (page 217) to a continuation of the second show of 15 December (page 216), before Benny became ill. The master tapes confirm that change: following **Sugar Foot Stomp,** Benny introduces Dottie Reid, who then sings **Anything Goes.**

The master tapes also permit keying the CD's tracks to Legacy's array: Following the relevant tune title below, the parenthetical note "(14-1)" indicates performance on the 1st show, 14 December; "(14-2)", the 2nd show, 14 December; and so on. The note "(15-2A)" signifies Legacy's undated performance.

The liner notes also fail to mention that Benny is not present for **Big John Special.** As cited in Legacy, illness forced Benny to leave the stage before it was played. And although body copy mentions guitarist Steve Jordan by name, personnel listings for the CD omit him.

Despite these glitches, collectors will welcome this first release of tracks from the Thailand engagement, meticulously re-mastered by Jack Towers.

CONSTITUTION FAIR CONCERTS   *14, 15 December 1956, Lumpini Park, Bangkok*

Personnels as per Legacy.

CD: TCB(Sw) 4301-2 - No. 1

Let's Dance (theme)	*(15-2)*
Don't Be That Way	*(15-1)*
King Porter Stomp	*(15-1)*
Trigger Fantasy - feat. Israel Crosby	*(15-1)*
Roll 'Em	*(15-1)*
One O'Clock Jump	*(14-1)*
Down South Camp Meetin'	*(15-2)*
Yarm Yen	*(14-2)*
Sugar Foot Stomp	*(15-2)*
(Big John Special - NO BG	*(15-2)*
Flying Home - OCTET	*(14-2)*
The World Is Waiting For The Sunrise - TRIO	*(14-2)*
Oh, Lady Be Good! - TRIO	*(14-2)*
Sai Fon	*(14-2)*
Stompin' At The Savoy	*(15-2A)*
(Thai National Anthem - NO BG	*(see note)*

NOTE: The Thai anthem is from the 1st show, 16 December. Benny, ill, also missed this concert. Peanuts Hucko fronted the band, played clarinet and alto sax.

December 1956, Bangkok (ref: pages 216, 217)
A 12-inch acetate, which Benny sent to disc jockey Art Ford, adds another, but undated, performance of **Rainfall (Sai Fon).** It begins with Benny's greetings to Ford. Following the rendition, Benny signs off, "See you when we get home, Art. This is Benny Goodman saying 'Good Night' (in Thai, then in English) from Bangkok, Thailand."

The 78's Gotham label bears the typewritten inscription, "Benny Goodman from Bangkok, January 21, 1957"—and nothing else. Presumably, Ford appended this inscription when he received the disc.

CONSTITUTION FAIR CONCERT   *December 1956, Lumpini Park, Bangkok*

Orchestra personnel as per Legacy.

Rainfall (Sai Fon)

USIS-VOA film, December 1956, Bangkok (ref: page 217)
Liner notes for the LP, HARLEQUIN 2028, list **Bye Bye Blues,** preceding **Sing, Sing, Sing.** No; that track is the tenor saxophone solo that introduces Part 2 of **Sing, Sing, Sing.**

10 February 1957, "The Ed Sullivan Show," New York (ref: page 218)
Early in 1991, the Ed Sullivan Estate sold separate rights to the video and audio tracks of kinescopes and videotapes of Ed's immensely popular, 23-year CBS-TV series. The successful bidders then announced their intentions to televise, or to broadcast via radio, excerpts from the "Toast Of The Town" and "The Ed Sullivan Show" hour-long telecasts.

Within months of the contract awards, a telecast was presented on independent stations in the U.S. Others followed, but to date none has included any of Benny's appearances. To the best of the author's knowledge, there have been no radio broadcasts.

At the end of 1991, the Goodman Estate authorized CD and audio cassette releases of selections from Benny's dates with Sullivan, to be included in releases titled, "Big Band All Stars." Other categories in a projected 25-volume series are devoted to rock, comedy, British performers, "vocal superstars," and Louis Armstrong.

The initial big band release was marketed in Spring 1992. It offers but two tracks by Benny, others by Basie, Hampton, Herman, James, and the Ray McKinley-led Miller band. Running time is just under 35 minutes—"compact disc," indeed—but the sound is good.

"THE SULLIVAN YEARS - Big Band All-Stars"
Benny Goodman and His Orchestra   **10 February 1957, New York**

Personnel as per Legacy.

- 0 -   **Cas, CD:** TVT 9431
                         Let's Dance

See also this release under date of 19 June 1960, herein.

16 May 1957, Stamford, CT (ref: page 219)
Both Trio medleys recorded this date are included as the final two tracks in Yale/MusicMasters Volume 8. Releases are: StLp: JHS 913685; Cas: JHS 313685; CD: MM 65093-2, JHS 513685. At a later date Volume 8 may also appear on the MHS label.

May 1957, Stamford, CT (ref: page 219)
For additional releases of the MusicMasters classical album, BENNY GOODMAN—PRIVATE COLLECTION, see under date of March/post-March 1955, herein.

29 September 1957, New York (ref: page 219)
Line missing from Legacy: "Crescendo, via CBS-TV."

9 April 1958 telecast, New York (ref: page 220)
The "augmented Goodman orchestra" included: Gene Orloff, Julius Schachter, Harry Melnikoff, Ralph Silverman, Max Hollander, Earle Hummel, George Ockner, v; Howard A. Kay, Isador Zir, viola; Maurice Bialkin, Maurice Brown, cel; Janet Putnam, harp; Harry Brewer, percussion. Rod Alexander and Bambi Linn were the dancers.

Some collectors have videotapes of this telecast. The LP, GOJ 1010, includes the opening theme.

May 1958, Brussels (ref: pages 221-225, inclusive)
Two multi-format releases, 1989's Yale/MusicMasters Volume 3, and 1990's MAGIC(E) 36, each offer some performances from Brussels that are listed in Legacy, and some that are not. All formats of the MM, JHS and MHS releases have identical contents. The MAGIC LP, however, omits some tracks that are in the MAGIC cassette and CD.

The excellent audio quality of both Volume 3 and MAGIC 36 permits positive cross-referencing between them. It also facilitates exacting comparison of their tracks to performances in the several radio broadcasts and telecasts, and all prior issues, displayed in Legacy for the Brussels engagement. Reevaluation uncovers new linkages and some errors in Legacy, detailed below.

Reviewed first are those tracks in Volume 3 and MAGIC 36 that ARE listed in Legacy. They are listed chronologically, in the order in which the source broadcasts and telecasts, and prior issues, appear in the book. This initial section—in the same order—also includes cross-references and corrections to entries in Legacy. These MM/JHS/MHS and MAGIC 36 ascriptions, and other cross-reference credits and corrections, should be ADDED to the relevant displays in the book.

BRUSSELS EUROVISION TELECAST (ref: page 221)
MAGIC 36 includes **Let's Dance; This Is My Lucky Day** (not "Oh Boy, I'm Lucky"); **The Song Is Ended; I'm Coming, Virginia; A Fine Romance; Harvard Blues,** all from this telecast.

BRUSSELS NBC TELECAST (ref: page 222)
TIME/LIFE LP STA354's **Brussels Blues** is the same performance as that on the LP, WBIB-Side IX (page 223), and on the StLp, CO CS8075 (page 223). Performance is from this telecast.

BRUSSELS FRENCH BROADCAST (ref: page 222)
Who Cares?; When You're Smiling; Sent For You Yesterday...; and **Soon,** all from this broadcast, are the same performances as those on the LP, WBIB 2-Side IV (page 222). See also Volume 3, MAGIC 36:
Volume 3 includes **Who Cares?** and **Soon** from this broadcast, and as on the LP, WBIB 2-Side IV (page 222). Note also MAGIC 36, next.
MAGIC 36 includes **Who Cares?; When You're Smiling; Sent For You Yesterday...; Soon,** all from this broadcast, and as on the LP, WBIB 2-Side IV (page 222). Note also Volume 3, above.
MAGIC 36 Cas, CD include **'Deed I Do; There's No Fool...; Goin' To Chicago,** all from this broadcast. MAGIC 36 LP includes only **Goin' To Chicago.**

BRUSSELS AFN BROADCAST (ref: page 222)
Volume 3 includes **When You're Smiling; 'Deed I Do; I'm Coming, Virginia; Harvard Blues,** all from this broadcast. **I'm Coming, Virginia** is also on sampler CDs, MM 60216, MM 5022-2.

WBIB (ref: page 222)
Volume 3 includes **Stompin' At The Savoy,** same performance as on the LP, WBIB 1-Side I.
MAGIC 36 includes **Pennies From Heaven,** same performance as on the LP, WBIB 2-Side IV.
(Other cross-references to WBIB 2-Side IV are under the Brussels French broadcast, preceding.)

WBIB (ref: page 223)
Volume 3 includes **On The Sunny Side...** and **Sometimes I'm Happy,** same performances as on the LP, WBIB 5-Side IX. Note also MAGIC 36, next.
MAGIC 36 includes **Sometimes I'm Happy,** same performance as on the LP, WBIB 5-Side IX. Note also Volume 3, above.
(Correction: The unedited version of **Brussels Blues,** WBIB 5-Side IX, should be cross-referenced to the Columbia stereo StLp CS8075 et al, NOT to the monaural releases. As noted previously, the same performance is also on the LP, TL STA354.)

COLUMBIA - BENNY IN BRUSSELS (ref: pages 223, 224)

Omission in Legacy: Inadvertently, CO StLp CS8076 was omitted from the heading, "STEREO LP's" (page 223). It embraces tracks 14-22, inclusive (page 224).

As noted previously, add the LP, TL STA354, **Brussels Blues,** to credits for the stereo releases, track 8.

BRUSSELS CONCERT, 28 May 1958 (ref: page 225)

Volume 3 includes **Pennies From Heaven** from this set at the American Pavilion. Performance is by the Octet with Frosk (not Jordan), a detail neglectfully omitted in Legacy.

Yale/MusicMasters Volume 1 (not 3) includes the complete performance of **Don't Blame Me.** (For MM/JHS/MHS catalog numbers for Volume 1, see under date of 25/26 March 1955, herein.) The author's old ears fail to hear Billy Bauer's guitar; he prefers Quartet to the liner notes' Quintet.

The foregoing concludes a review of Yale/MusicMasters Volume 3 (and Volume 1) and MAGIC 36, in respect of listings in Legacy, except for cross-references to the Westinghouse broadcasts. The author's poor tapes of them make comparisons infeasible.

Yale/MusicMasters Volume 3 also includes 10 tracks (a medley of three tunes is counted as one track) that the author has been unable to assign to listings in Legacy (again, excepting the Westinghouse broadcasts). Listed next, per their sequence in Volume 3 (its track positions precede tune titles), they should be ADDED in toto to Legacy's arrays for the Brussels engagement. Dates of performances follow tune titles. Unless otherwise qualified (the medley is an exception), all performances are by the full orchestra.

(As noted herein under date of 25/26 March 1955, JHS & MHS releases are double albums, use identical catalog numbers, combine Volumes 3 and 4; and, Volume 3 is also included in the box set, MM 65095-2).

The Yale University Music Library
BENNY GOODMAN, Volume 3: BIG BAND IN EUROPE   26-29 May 1958, Brussels

Personnel as per Legacy, Brussels Eurovision telecast, page 221; and add SEXTET—Quintet plus tpt, possibly Taft Jordan.

- 0 -   **StLp:** MM 20157, JHS & MHS 922431. **Cas:** MM 40157, MM 5007-4, JHS & MHS 322431. **CD:** MM 60157, MM 5007-2, JHS & MHS 522431

1	**Let's Dance** (theme)	(26 May)
2	**Bugle Call Rag**	(26 May)
6	**Blue Skies** - voc Jimmy Rushing - QUARTET, band in coda	(29 May)
7	**I Want A Little Girl** - voc Jimmy Rushing - QUINTET	(29 May)
9	**A Fine Romance** - voc Ethel Ennis, Jimmy Rushing	(29 May)
13	*Medley:* **I Gotta Right To Sing The Blues** - SEXTET)	
	I Hadn't Anyone Till You (orch))-all, voc Ennis	
	I've Got You Under My Skin (orch)) (all 29 May)	
16	**Flying Home** - OCTET (incl. Jordan, tpt)	(26 May)
17	**This Is My Lucky Day** - voc Ethel Ennis	(29 May)
18	**Roll 'Em**	(26 May)
19	**Baby (Bye, Bye Baby)** - voc Jimmy Rushing	(29 May)

(Liner notes incorrectly title track 19 as, "Brussels Blues." Lyrics here are those for Jimmy's "Baby (Bye, Bye Baby)," per the same tune on WBIB 1-Side II and SWH 7.)

Finally: Linkage of three MAGIC 36 tracks to Legacy listings has escaped such identification. This suggests that they may be from a broadcast or telecast unknown to the author.

Note that the Medley is on MAGIC 36 cassette and CD only, not on the LP.

? BROADCAST/TELECAST ? Unknown source(s), location(s)   10-31 May 1958, Europe

Medley: I Hadn't Anyone Till You - voc Ethel Ennis   )
*   I've Got You Under My Skin - voc Ethel Ennis) - MAGIC Cas, CD*
If I Had You - QUARTET) - MAGIC LP, Cas, CD
Good-Bye (theme)   )

4 July 1958, Newport, RI (ref: page 225)

In 1994, Sony/Columbia producer Teo Macero consulted with the author and the Goodman Estate about releasing additional tracks from Benny's Newport Jazz concert this date. Both objected on grounds that the performances are without merit. For the present at least, Teo decided to shelve the project.

7 July 1958, New York (ref: pages 225, 320)

Martha Tilton once declined Benny's long-distance telephone invitation to join him for a concert tour because, "You know, I would have loved doing it, and would have, except that he couldn't remember my name! He kept calling me 'Pops'!" But she did come to New York for this studio date, and two tunes have now been released:

The Yale University Music Library
BENNY GOODMAN, Volume 4: BIG BAND RECORDINGS   **7 July 1958, New York**

BENNY GOODMAN AND HIS ORCHESTRA

Personnels as per Legacy.

	StLp: MM 20201, JHS & MHS 922431. **Cas:** MM 40201, MM 5017-4, JHS & MHS 322431. **CD:** MM 60201, MM 5017-2, JHS & MHS 522431
- 0 -	**You Couldn't Be Cuter** - voc Martha Tilton
- 0 -	**Oh! Gee, Oh! Joy** - voc Martha Tilton

See page 320 for takes and tunes from this date that remain unissued.

14 July 1958, New York (ref: page 225)

Fleshing out this short session, the two hitherto unissued titles are now available:

The Yale University Music Library
BENNY GOODMAN, Volume 1   **14 July 1958, New York**

BENNY GOODMAN AND HIS ORCHESTRA

Personnel as per Legacy.

	StLp: MM 20142, JHS & MHS 922277. **Cas:** MM 40142, MM 5000-4, JHS & MHS 322277. **CD:** MM 60142, MM 5000-2, JHS & MHS 522277
- 0 -	**Cherokee**
- 0 -	**Macedonia Lullaby**

2 September 1958, Hollywood (ref: page 226)
    Martha Tilton sparkles in the only track issued to date from this session:

The Yale University Music Library
BENNY GOODMAN, Volume 8:   **2 September 1958, Hollywood**

BENNY GOODMAN AND HIS ORCHESTRA

Personnel as per Legacy.

- 0 -	**StLp:** JHS 913685. **Cas:** JHS 313685. **CD:** MM 65093-2, JHS 513685
	Bei Mir Bist Du Schon - voc Martha Tilton

    Later, Volume 8 may be released on the MHS label.

3 September 1958, Hollywood (ref: page 226)
    In contrast to the sole release from 2 September, all three Quintet sides are included in Volume 8. Big band—and Martha's—fans might have preferred it the other way 'round.
    A few collectors have true alternate takes of two performances, and a questionable alternate of **Easy To Love.** The Volume 8 track includes an additional chorus by Benny that is not in the author's tape copy. Both "versions" are seamless, give no hint of either an elision or an insertion. Loren Schoenberg has no recollection of adding a chorus to the release, is at a loss—as is the author—to account for this extra chorus in these otherwise identical takes.

The Yale University Music Library
BENNY GOODMAN, Volume 8: BENNY GOODMAN QUINTET   **3 September 1958,**
                                                       Hollywood

Personnel as per Legacy.

- 0 - alt take	UNISSUED - Tape
- 0 -	**StLp:** JHS 913685. **Cas:** JHS 313685. **CD:** MM 65093-2, JHS 513685
	It's All Right With Me
- 0 - "alt" ?	UNISSUED - Tape
- 0 -	Same issues as "It's All Right With Me"
	Easy To Love
- 0 - alt take	UNISSUED - Tape
- 0 -	Same issues as "It's All Right With Me"
	Who?

Volume 8 may be eventually issued on the MHS label.

7 October 1958, Stamford (ref: page 226)
Not logged for this session, but on Benny's tapes at Yale, are two takes of another instrumental. ADD them to the display in Legacy:

THE BENNY GOODMAN QUARTET   **7 October 1958, Stamford**

Personnel as per Legacy.

- 0 - take 1	UNISSUED
- 0 - take 2	UNISSUED
	Get Happy

Look for **Get Happy,** and likely one or more takes of **How Can You Forget?,** in a future Yale/MusicMasters release.

15, 17, 18 November 1958, New York (ref: pages 226, 227)
Three of the four November 1958 studio sessions are addressed by Volumes 1 and 4 in the Yale/MusicMasters series. Together they add five alternate takes to previously-issued recordings. Arbitrarily, each should be ADDED to Legacy's listings as having preceded the initial release. Note that Volume 4 slightly alters the title to, **What A Difference A Day Makes,** from that given in CO CL1324, et al.

The Yale University Music Library
BENNY GOODMAN, Volume 4: BIG BAND RECORDINGS   15 November 1958, New York

Personnel as per Legacy.

	StLp: MM 20201, JHS & MHS 922431. **Cas:** MM 40201, MM 5017-4, JHS & MHS 322431. **CD:** MM 60201, MM 5017-2, JHS & MHS 522431
- 0 - alt take	**Oh, Baby!**
- 0 -	**Autumn Nocturne** (same as 7" LP, GALA FPK703)
- 0 - alt ake	**Happy Session Blues**

THE BENNY GOODMAN ORCHESTRA   **17 November 1958, New York**

Personnel as per Legacy.

	same issues as "Oh, Baby!"
- 0 - alt take	**Benny Rides Again**

BENNY GOODMAN AND HIS ORCHESTRA   **18 November 1958, New York**

Personnel as per Legacy.

	same issues as "Oh, Baby!"
- 0 - alt take	**What A Difference A Day Makes**

The Yale University Music Library
BENNY GOODMAN, Volume 1   **same session - 18 November 1958, New York**

BENNY GOODMAN AND HIS ORCHESTRA

Personnel as per Legacy.

	StLp: MM 20142, JHS & MHS 922277. **Cas:** MM 40142, MM 5000-4, JHS & MHS 322277. **CD:** MM 60142, MM 5000-2, JHS & MHS 522277
- 0 - alt take	**Batunga Train**

19 November 1958, New York (ref: page 227)
    Targeted for eventual release in the Yale/MusicMasters series are two alternate takes by the Quintet from this session, **Diga Diga Doo** and **Whispering.** Note that most latter-day releases forsake the original title, **Digga Digga Doo.**

3 January 1959, New York (ref: page 227)

Seven of the nine tunes recorded on 2 and 3 January 1959 feature vocalist Donna Musgrove. As of this writing, even with this release, none has been issued.

The Yale University Music Library
BENNY GOODMAN, Volume 1   **3 January 1959, New York**

THE BENNY GOODMAN SEPTET

Personnel as per Legacy.

	StLp: MM 20142, JHS & MHS 922277. **Cas:** MM 40142, MM 5000-4, JHS & MHS 322277. **CD:** MM 60142, MM 5000-2, JHS & MHS 522277
- 0 -	**Diga Diga Doo**

10 April 1959, New York (ref: page 228)

A commercial videotape of the "Swing Into Spring" telecast, of indifferent sight and sound quality, is available: CLASSIC TELEVISION #171. Excerpts from the telecast are also on LP, GOJ 1011.

15, 16, 17 August 1959, Miami (ref: page 229)

Volumes 1 and 7 in the Yale/MusicMasters series together provide one take each of every tune recorded on these three sessions in Florida. Volume 7 corrects the erroneous Legacy title, "The Best Things In Life Are Free," to Irving Berlin's **The Best Thing For You;** and it specifies the instruments played by Robinson and Binnix.

Note that the three takes shown in Legacy as available via tape—**Ten-Bone, Broadway** and **Dark Shadows**—are the same takes used for Volume 7. As if to compensate, alternate takes of two tunes were considered for release, were rejected for preferred takes in Volume 7, and were made available to the author. They are listed below as, "UNISSUED - Tape."

The Yale University Music Library
BENNY GOODMAN, VOLUME 7: FLORIDA SESSIONS   **15 August 1959, Miami**

Benny Goodman, clt; Bill Harris, tbn; Flip Phillips, ts; Marty Harris, p; Leo Robinson, g; Al Simi, b; Bob Binnix, d. Arrangers: Al Cohn (AC), Freddy Crane (FC).

- 0 -	**StLp:** JHS & MHS 913104. **Cas:** MM 65058-4, JHS & MHS 313104. **CD:** MM 65058-2, JHS & MHS 513104
	I Want To Be Happy (arr AC)
	Sometimes I'm Happy (arr AC)
	Time On My Hands (arr AC)
	Ten-Bone (also on promo **CD**, MM 65099-2)
- 0 -alt take	UNISSUED - Tape
	I Want To Be Happy

The Yale University Music Library
BENNY GOODMAN, VOLUME 7: FLORIDA SESSIONS   16 August 1959, Miami

Personnel as 15 August.

- 0 -   same issues as "I Want To Be Happy"
                         Sleep (also on promo **CD,** MM 65099-2)
                         Tea For Two (arr AC)
                         Rosetta (alternatively, "Yardbird Suite")
                         Splanky
                         Sweet Miss
                         The Best Thing For You

- 0 - alt take   UNISSUED - Tape
                         Tea For Two

The Yale University Music Library
BENNY GOODMAN, VOLUME 7: FLORIDA SESSIONS   17 August 1959, Miami

Personnel as 15 August.

- 0 -   same issues as "I Want To Be Happy"
                         Someone To Watch Over Me

The Yale University Music Library
BENNY GOODMAN, VOLUME 1   same session - 17 August 1959, Miami

Personnel as 15 August.

- 0 -   **StLp:** MM 20142, JHS & MHS 922277. **Cas:** MM 40142, MM
                         5000-4, JHS & MHS 322277. **CD:** MM 60142, MM 5000-2, JHS
                         & MHS 522277
                         Broadway (arr FC)

The Yale University Music Library
BENNY GOODMAN, VOLUME 7: FLORIDA SESSIONS   same session - 17 August
                                                       1959, Miami

Personnel as 15 August.

- 0 -   same issues as "I Want To Be Happy"
                         Dark Shadows (arr FC)
                         (The) Deacon And The Elder

(As of this writing no counterpart JHS Volume 7 has been scheduled.)

18 October 1959, Stockholm (ref: pages 229, 320, 321)
    Error: Despite access to the master tapes, the author failed to note that Anita acknowl-

edges the presence of STAN GETZ, not Zoot Sims, in the Konserthuset audience. Her reference to him precedes **Four Brothers,** now on an excellent-quality CD, PHON 8801. Released in 1988, the CD offers most of the performances listed on pages 320 and 321.

Stan didn't play, either. Had that right, anyway.

28 October 1959, Basel (ref: page 230)

Disc No. 2 in the TCB(Sw) 4301-2 four-CD album offers an even dozen performances from the Basel concert, omitting two by Red Norvo's small group, and all three of Anita O'Day's vocals.

Among other shortcomings in the liner notes, collectors will find errata, e.g., the mistaken claim for its track of **Marching And Swinging:** "...apparently the only time Benny played this title was during his European tour." No; see Yale/MusicMasters Volume 1. However, it's delightful to listen to this marvelous concert anytime, and Jack Towers's transfers are up to his usual high standard.

They're much better, in fact, than the eight titles on the bootleg LP, ARTISTRY 108, released in 1989, preceding the TCB(Sw) album by four years. Also absent on the LP are the Norvo and O'Day performances, and four more Goodman cuts.

13 November 1959, New York (ref: page 231)

Volumes 1 and 5 in the Yale/MusicMasters series offer excerpts from Benny's tapes of this Basin Street East engagement. Their release affects the display in Legacy in this manner:

Only one performance in Legacy's UNISSUED - Tape display is now issued, **Marchin' and Swingin',** in Volume 1. All other performances in that display remain unissued, despite duplicate tune titles—**Let's Dance, Sleep,** and the **Medley**—included in Volume 5. These performances are from different master tapes than those detailed in the UNISSUED - Tape display.

Seven performances included in Volume 5 have counterparts in Legacy's UNISSUED (no tape) display. They are identified below by an asterisk that precedes each tune title. These titles should now be deleted from Legacy's UNISSUED (no tape) display.

Volume 5's **After You've Gone, Between The Devil And The Deep Blue Sea, Breakfast Feud,** and **I Want To Be Happy,** have no counterpart listings in Legacy, and thus are net additions to the display in Legacy.

The Yale University Music Library
BENNY GOODMAN, Volumes 1 and 5   **13 November 1959, New York**

BENNY GOODMAN AND HIS ORCHESTRA

Personnels as per Legacy.

> Volume 1: **StLp:** MM 20142, JHS & MHS 922277. **Cas:** MM 40142, MM 5000-4, JHS & MHS 322277. **CD:** MM 60142, MM 5000-2, JHS & MHS 522277

- 0 -   **Marchin' and Swingin'** (also on promo CD, MM 65099-2)

13 November 1959, continued

13 November 1959, continued

               Volume 5: **StLp:** JHS & MHS 922588. **Cas:** MM 5040-4, JHS & MHS
               322588. **CD:** MM 5040-2, JHS & MHS 522588

- 0 -   **Let's Dance** (theme)
               * **No Way To Stop It**
               * **Memories of You** - SEXTET (also on promo CD, MM 65099-2)
               (**Sleep** - feat. Phillips, Harris w/rhythm - NO BG
               Medley: **Don't Be That Way**
                             Stompin' At The Savoy
                             On The Sunny Side Of The Street
                             Rose Room (contra-melody, **In A Mellotone**)
                             Moon Glow
                             One O'Clock Jump
                             Sing, Sing, Sing
               I Want To Be Happy
               * **Gotta Be This Or That** - voc Benny Goodman
               Between The Devil And The Deep Blue Sea
               * **Body And Soul** - SEXTET
               * **(Don't Get Around Much Anymore** - Dodgion, Norvo
               w/rhythm - NO BG
               * **(Sweet And Lovely** - Phillips w/rhythm - NO BG
               After You've Gone - SEXTET
               * **(Tenbone** - feat. Phillips, Harris w/rhythm - NO BG
               Breakfast Feud

(Spellings of certain tune titles above are different than those in the liner notes.)

18 April 1960, Munich

    On this date the German radio network Bayrischer Rundfunk, Munich, broadcast what apparently is a pre-recorded tape of an interview between Benny and the German film actress Margot Hielscher, plus a snippet of Benny performing with local musicians. When and where the tape was recorded is unknown.

RADIO BROADCAST   Bayrischer Rundfunk   *Broadcast date: 18 April 1960*

Benny Goodman, clt; Klaus Wagner, tpt; Michael Meister, bjo.

...interview, Margot Hielscher, Benny Goodman
China Boy - TRIO (n/c)

19 June 1960, "The Ed Sullivan Show," New York (ref: page 233)

    You won't find this version of **Sing, Sing, Sing** in Legacy, for the very good reason that it was not televised. The telecast had ended, but the group continued to play. At the end of the performance, Benny's remarks are buried under the applause; he apparently was grumbling about playing one more tune than he had contracted for. But Sullivan tells him not to worry, "You'll get a bonus."

"THE SULLIVAN YEARS - Big Band All-Stars"
BENNY GOODMAN AND HIS ORCHESTRA   **19 June 1960, New York**

Personnel as per Legacy.

- 0 -	**Cas, CD:** TVT 9431
	Sing, Sing, Sing

See also this release under date of 10 February 1957, herein.

6 July 1960, New York (ref: pages 234, 321)

Released in 1990, Volume 5 in the Yale/MusicMasters series includes three recordings from this session. (Liner notes misdate a medley, the 6th track on the second CD. It is from the Rotary Concert of 7 February 1963, not from this studio session.)

To position the three issued takes in their correct order-of-performance, they are detailed below. Note that in this array, breakdowns are numbered, contrary to Legacy's usual practice. The reason for the change is that producer Teo Macero is heard to announce each take on the master tapes. Since he could not know in advance that the upcoming recording would be aborted, he numbers each breakdown consecutively.

The Yale University Music Library
BENNY GOODMAN, VOLUME 5   **6 July 1960, New York**

BENNY GOODMAN AND HIS ORCHESTRA

Personnel as per Legacy.

CO 54739-1 - bkdn	UNISSUED - Tape
CO 54739-2	UNISSUED - Tape
CO 54739-3	**StLp:** JHS & MHS 922588; JHS 912999. **Cas:** MM 5040-4, JHS & MHS 322588; JHS 312999. **CD:** MM 5040-2, JHS & MHS 522588; JHS 512999
	St. James Infirmary (also on promo **CD**, MM 65099-2)

(JHS 912999, 312999 and 512999 are "sampler" releases.)

CO 54741-1 - bkdn	UNISSUED - Tape
CO 54741-2	UNISSUED - Tape
CO 54741-3 - bkdn	UNISSUED - Tape
CO 54741-4	UNISSUED - Tape
CO 54741-5	UNISSUED - Tape
CO 54741-6	**StLp, Cas, CD:** same issues as for matrix CO 54739-3, except omit JHS 912999, 312999 and 512999
	Air Mail Special

6 July 1960, continued

6 July 1960, continued

CO 54742-1	UNISSUED - Tape
CO 54742-2 - bkdn	UNISSUED - Tape
CO 54742-3	**StLp, Cas, CD:** same issues as for matrix CO 54741-6
- 0 - false start	UNISSUED - Tape
CO 54742-4 ("1")	UNISSUED - Tape ("short version")
CO 54742-5 ("2")	UNISSUED - Tape ("short version")
	My Baby Don' Tol' Me - voc Jack Sheldon

Takes 4 and 5 of matrix CO 54742 are announced by Macero as, "Short version, take 1" and "Short version, take 2"; he does not change the matrix assignment. For some unknown reason, he does not number the false start.

Running times of the "short versions" of **My Baby Don' Tol' Me** are each two minutes less than complete takes 1 and 3. To reduce their running times, parts of the arrangement are eliminated.

As of this writing, other titles from this 6 July 1960 session remain unissued.

2 September 1960, Hollywood (ref: page 235)
Legacy typo: Make that CO, not "CL," CL1579, for the first-listed LP, pressing matrix XLP 51692.

30 September 1960, New York (ref: page 236)
Oops: The Bell Tel Hour was televised by NBC, not CBS.

24 January 1961, New York (ref: pages 236, 321)
Macabre musing: It didn't happen, but what a punch line if only Benny just once had said, "Over my dead body!", any of the many times he rejected the author's pleas to issue tracks from the Hawaiian sessions. Posthumously, then, an August 1993 Yale/MusicMasters release of one take each of every tune recorded the final date:

The Yale University Music Library
BENNY GOODMAN, Volume 8:

BENNY GOODMAN AND HIS ORCHESTRA   **24 January 1961, New York**

Personnel as per Legacy.

CO 65929-3	**StLp:** JHS 913685. **Cas:** JHS 313685. **CD:** MM 65093-2, JHS 513685
	Too Many Tears

24 January 1961, continued

24 January 1961, continued

CO 65930-S	Same issues as "Too Many Tears" **Willow Weep For Me**

(Splice: Take 6, with a tbn solo from take 2 substituted)

CO 65931-2	Same issues as "Too Many Tears" **Blue Hawaii**

CO 65892-8	**LP:** GRIV-Side 2 (not take "1"); plus same issues as "Too Many Tears" **Song Of The Islands**

CO 65891-4	Same issues as "Too Many Tears" **My Little Grass Shack**

CO 65877-2	Same issues as "Too Many Tears"
CO 65877-3	**LP:** GRIV-Side 2 **The Moon Of Manakoora**

CO 65893-9	Same issues as "Too Many Tears" **Sweet Leilani**

CO 65878-alt	**LP:** GRIV-Side 2 (not take "3")
CO 65878-3	Same issues as "Too Many Tears" **On The Beach At Waikiki**

Note that take numbers above, supplied by Yale, revise two originally assigned to the GRIV LP. These take numbers are cumulative, embracing complete renditions and breakdowns from prior sessions.

Eventually, Volume 8 may also be released on the MHS label.

7 September 1961, New York (ref: page 238)

Most of AFR&TS ONS 5480 is on the LP, MAGIC(E) 23.

3 November 1961, New Haven (ref: page 238)

Fittingly, excerpts from this Yale concert are planned for a future Yale/MusicMasters release.

17 November 1961, Santiago, Chile (ref: page 238)

A year after its publication, Jerry Valburn informed the author that Legacy's last paragraph on page 238 needed updating: A tape from the 1961 South American tour had turned up. He predicted a future release, a prophecy come true via the third CD in a TCB(Sw) 4301-2 album, December 1993.

The band & Sextet swing, albeit for a too-brief 41 minutes, and even if Benny sits out **Shine** and Maria Marshall's enthusiastic vocals. Note that this version of **Bill Bailey...** is Joe Lippman's score for full orchestra. Credit Jack Towers for vastly improving a muddy tape.

But again, those liner notes...! From the inside cover alone we're told **Bugle Call Rag's** three composers are actually four, as "Elmer" and "Schoebe(1)" get separate credit. (That elusive final "1" afflicts Arvell, too.) **Avalon's** composers also become a foursome, as B. G. DeSylva splits amoeba-like into "Goodman" and "DeSilva," with an "i" yet. Fanny May loses a "d" in "Balridge." She fares better than Miss Marshall, wholly absent the personnel roster. The Gershwins—plural—titled their masterpiece **I Got Rhythm,** not "I've..." Then on the first page...

Enough. Don't read. Just listen.

BENNY GOODMAN IN SANTIAGO   *17 November 1961, Gran Palace Theater, Santiago*

Personnels as per Legacy, 4 November 1961.

CD: TCB(Sw) 4301-2 - No. 3
Let's Dance (theme)
Bugle Call Rag
Don't Be That Way
(This Can't Be Love - voc Maria Marshall - no BG
(I Can't Believe That You're In Love With Me - voc Maria Marshall - NO BG
(Bill Bailey, Won't You Please Come Home? - voc Maria Marshall - NO BG
(Shine - feat. Clayton - NO BG
Avalon - SEXTET
Memories Of You - SEXTET
Body And Soul - SEXTET
Sweet Georgia Brown - SEXTET
The Man I Love - DUET
Poor Butterfly - SEXTET
I Got Rhythm - SEXTET
King Porter Stomp

Harry Sheppard earns the audience's plaudits for **I Got Rhythm;** he was equally impressive the first the author heard him, at the 4 November rehearsal. His enthusiasm for Sheppard brought an off-hand nod from Benny, nothing more. Later, when he heard tapes of the Yale concert, the author was convinced Benny had a winner in this rather obscure vibraphonist. Follow-on suggestions that Sheppard would be an asset to future groups were rejected by Benny, with no reason given. If there was a reason why Benny never hired him again, the author never discovered it.

21-26 May 1962, Seattle (ref: page 240)
Prior to its departure for Moscow, Benny's "Russian Tour" band spent six days at the Seattle World's Fair. Professionally-recorded tapes from that engagement are extant, but by and for whom they were made is unknown. Nor can they be pinpointed to a specific date, nor sequenced with certainty into discrete sets. Continuous tapings and announced intermissions, however, provide likely order-of-performances. Running times for each segment are appended.

The tapes offer previously unavailable tunes played by this orchestra, and one by a small group. There's an interesting "Anthology of Jazz," beginning with the traditional New Orleans funeral march, "Oh, Didn't He Ramble," followed by tunes identified to the ODJB, Armstrong, Whiteman, Ellington, Basie, TD, Miller, Charlie Parker/Miles Davis and Brubeck. It then segues into a 20-minute "Sing, Sing, Sing," with Benny quoting from Gershwin's "Rhapsody In Blue" and the "Star Spangled Banner" during his soli. Sparkling soli by him and by almost all of the sidemen are heard throughout, proving just how good this group was. Especially noteworthy are Benny's soli in the second, nine-minute, "The Bulgar..."

SEATTLE WORLD'S FAIR   *21-26 May 1962, Seattle*

Benny Goodman, clt; Joe Newman, Jimmy Maxwell, John Frosk, Joe Wilder, tpt; Willie
Dennis, Wayne Andre, Jim Winters, tbn; Jerry Dodgion (fl), Phil Woods, as; Zoot Sims,
Tommy Newsom(e), ts; Gene Allen, bar; Teddy Wilson, p; Turk Van Lake, g, bjo; Bill Crow,
b; Mel Lewis, d; Vic Feldman, vib. Additional arranger credits: Bob Brookmeyer (BB); Ralph
Burns (RB); Johnny Carisi (JC); Gene Casey (GC); Al Cohn (AC); Joe Lip(p)man (JL); Bill
Stegmeyer (BS). Vocalist: Joya Sherrill.

QUINTET: Feldman, Wilson, Van Lake, Crow, Lewis (NO BG)

Let's Dance (theme)
The Bulgar And Other Balkan Type Inventions (arr JC)
Meet The Band
Bye, Bye Blackbird
Show Me - voc Joya Sherrill (arr GC)
The Thrill Is Gone (arr RB)
Gershwin Medley (arr JL):
   Who Cares?   )
   Summertime   ) *- voc Joya Sherrill*
   Nice Work If You Can Get It)
   Fascinating Rhythm   )
I'm Beginning To See The Light - voc Joya Sherrill
King Porter Stomp
(possible, but unannounced, intermission)   *running time, 42:13*
Jersey Bounce
Clarinet A La King
One O'Clock Jump
Ev'rything I Love - voc Joya Sherrill (orig. EdSau arr.)
Ridin' High - voc Joya Sherrill (arr AC)
And The Angels Sing - voc Joya Sherrill
I Gotta Right To Sing The Blues - voc Joya Sherrill (arr BB)
Jumpin' At The Woodside
...announced intermission   *running time, 34:55*
Love For Sale
(Too Blue - QUINTET - NO BG
"Anthology of Jazz" (poss. arr. Bob Prince) - segue to,
Sing, Sing, Sing   *running time, 36:28*
Let's Dance (theme)
The Bulgar And Other Balkan Type Inventions
Meadowlands
A String Of Pearls
Mission To Moscow
Bach Goes To Town
And The Angels Sing - voc Joya Sherrill
"Salute To Glenn Miller" (arr JL):
   Moonlight Serenade
   I've Got A Gal In Kalamazoo
   I Know Why - voc Joya Sherrill
   Chattanooga Choo-Choo
...announced intermission   *running time, 32:43*

12, 13 June 1962, Tblisi (ref: page 240)

From the same source that produced the Seattle tapes (preceding), comes an undated one from a concert in Tblisi. Despite some flutter and inconstant gain, this tape finds Benny in a jovial mood and the band swinging as hard as it had in Seattle; apparently the controversies that marred the tour had not yet surfaced. Note that by now Benny has deleted one tune from the Gershwin medley, and that "Meet The Band" and "Titter Pipes" are different from those tracks on the RcaVictor release.

TBLISI CONCERT   *12 or 13 June 1962, Tblisi*

Orchestra personnel as for Seattle, preceding, except: Jimmy Knepper, tbn, replaces Winters, and John Bunch, p, is added.

Let's Dance (theme)
Bugle Call Rag
Meet The Band
(Titter Pipes - feat. Woods, Sims - NO BG
The Thrill Is Gone - voc Joya Sherrill
Gershwin Medley:
   Who Cares?   *)*
   Summertime   *) - voc Joya Sherrill*
   Fascinating Rhythm   *)*
I'm Beginning To See The Light - voc Joya Sherrill
Wrappin' It Up
When Buddha Smiles (n/c)

If, as some published reports have it, the sidemen were already mutinous when at the World's Fair, evidence of their disaffection is not on those tapes. They play well, and back-and-forth they offer audible encouragement and congratulation for each other's soli. The same can be said for the Tblisi tape, and their rendition of the ancient chart of "Bugle Call Rag" is a rouser. Confirmed, however, are in-print enthusiasms for Joya Sherrill; both sets of audiences obviously like her music hall-type vocals.

3, 5-8 July 1962, Moscow (ref: page 240)

Two tracks on a Yale/MusicMasters release are from the July 1962 Moscow concerts:

The Yale University Music Library
BENNY GOODMAN, Volume 4: BIG BAND RECORDINGS   **3, 5-8 July 1962, Moscow**

Orchestra personnel as per Legacy. SEXTET: Goodman, Feldman, Bunch, Van Lake, Crow, Lewis.

	StLp: MM 20201, JHS & MHS 922431. **Cas:** MM 40201, MM 5017-4, JHS & MHS 322431. **CD:** MM 60201, MM 5017-2, JHS & MHS 522431
- 0 -	**I've Grown Accustomed To Her Face** - SEXTET
- 0 -	**Swift As The Wind**

These two tracks, and those listed under the heading, "BENNY GOODMAN—RUSSIAN TOUR" on page 241, are integral, unspliced performances. But some, perhaps many, of the transfers in the RcaVictor album are deft splices of two or more recordings of a given tune from various locations in the then Soviet Union. One causative factor among several for the splices was erratic power supplies at the different concert sites. But the most compelling determinant for them is advanced by George Avakian:

"I said to Benny when we were about ready to leave that this was an important event, and we had to do it right; we'll take along a couple of RCA engineers to make the tapes. 'No, George, I've already hired a guy I know.' Thinking it was Bill Savory who I knew was friendly with Benny, I said fine, because Bill was an excellent engineer, probably better than the RCA men I had in mind. So I was dumbfounded when I learned that Benny's man wasn't Bill, instead was an audio repairman who had a shop near Benny's apartment, who used to fix Benny's Ampex recorder! His name was Carl Schindler, a nice guy, but totally out of his element; he knew nothing about balance, mike placement, whatever. His tapes were a disaster, probably cost RCA $5,000 or more for us to splice bits and pieces of them together to get the tracks for the album."

A few tracks from Benny's USSR tour tapes now at Yale are slated for future release, among them the Octet's **Honeysuckle Rose,** via MusicMasters. But unless tapes other than those at Yale are located, only a handful of tunes are available; the majority of the Archives' tapes are blank. This devastating loss is possibly attributable to their having been mistakenly bulk-erased before they were returned to Benny from RCA. (A similar situation involves the Quartet's "Together Again!" sessions' tapes, discussed under date of 13 February 1963 herein.) The author has reason to believe unimpaired tapes do exist, and he hopes that someday some of their recordings of this very good band will be released to the public.

3 February 1963, Cleveland (ref: page 242)

Save for the interview, the jazz portion of this broadcast is on cassette, ALPHORN 118.

7 February 1963, Stamford (ref: page 242)

Excerpts from the Goodman-Hackett program have been released by Yale/MusicMasters. From another source, the author has been advised that a 30-plus minute tape of Benny and the Berkshire Quartet from this engagement is in the hands of a private collector.

As cited earlier herein, the release's liner notes misassign the medley from this concert to 6 July 1960.

Legacy also carelessly errs: Bresano plays tenor saxophone, not flute, on **Easy Living.**

The Yale University Music Library
BENNY GOODMAN, Volume 5:

BENNY GOODMAN QUARTET/SEXTET   **7 February 1963, Stamford**

Personnels as per Legacy.

	StLp: JHS & MHS 922588. **Cas:** MM 5040-4, JHS & MHS 322588. **CD:** MM 5040-2, JHS & MHS 522588	

- 0 -	Medley: **Poor Butterfly**)
	                Avalon)
	                Sweet Lorraine)
	                The World Is Waiting For The Sunrise)
		- QUARTET

Medley: **Poor Butterfly**   )
              Avalon   )   - QUARTET
              Sweet Lorraine   )
              The World Is Waiting For The Sunrise   )
(**Lazy Afternoon** - Hackett w/rhythm - NO BG, Bresano
St. Louis Blues
Rachel's Dream (also on promo **CD**, MM 65099-2)
(**Easy Living** - Bresano (ts) w/rhythm - NO BG, Hackett

13 February 1963, New York (ref: page 243)

George Avakian, who produced the four "Together Again!" sessions, can think of several reasons why their master tapes, now in the Benny Goodman Archives at Yale, are blank. The most plausible—as in the case of the USSR tour tapes—is that RCA technicians erased them by mistake. All that may now exist are seven-inch backup reels made for Benny of the 13 & 14 February sessions, and a "demo" seven-inch reel George made for Benny, suggestions for future releases.

Those backup reels include most, but not all, of the complete takes listed in Legacy for 13 & 14 February, plus aborted takes only inferred in Legacy, and between-take rehearsals and comment. In 1994 Loren Schoenberg, who plans Yale/MusicMasters releases, suggested that the Archives' tapes be issued in toto, less elisions for "clinkers and blips." Mindful of Benny's abhorrence of release of takes he'd not approved, and especially of clinkers, the Goodman Estate denied permission to do so. It then assented to a more modest release, Volume 10 in the Yale/MusicMasters series, detailed herein.

The summary displays of the 13 & 14 February sessions are comprised of Yale's tapes, Avakian's tape, and the author's tapes. (He has some tracks that Yale does not.) These summaries represent everything now known to be extant. Substitute them in their entireties for those in Legacy.

The Yale University Music Library
BENNY GOODMAN, Volume 10:

THE BENNY GOODMAN QUARTET	**13 February 1963, New York**

Personnel as per Legacy.

Take 1	UNISSUED - Tape
Take 2 - bkdn	UNISSUED - Tape
Take 3	UNISSUED - Tape
Takes 4,5 - bkdns	UNISSUED - Tape (two consecutive aborted takes)
Take 6	**CD:** MM 65129-2. **Cas:** MM 65129-4
	Together

Take 1	UNISSUED - Tape
Take 2	UNISSUED - Tape
Take 3 - bkdn	UNISSUED - Tape
Take 4	**LP:** VI LPM2698, et al
Take "S"	**CD:** MM 65129-2. **Cas:** MM 65129-4
	Who Cares?

(The MM release is a splice, take 1 through the vibes soli, take 2 to completion.)

Take 1	UNISSUED - Tape
Take 2	UNISSUED - Tape
Take 3	UNISSUED - Tape
Take 4 - edited	**CD:** MM 65129-2. **Cas:** MM 65129-4 (minor editing)
	September Song

(The first three takes are not on the Archives' tapes.)

13 February 1963, continued

13 February 1963, continued

Take 1	UNISSUED - Tape
Take 2 - bkdn	UNISSUED - Tape (aborted take plus rehearsal)
Take 3	UNISSUED - Tape
Take 4 - complete	UNISSUED - Tape
Take 4 - edited	**CD:** MM 65129-2. **Cas:** MM 65129-4
	Just One Of Those Things

(The MM release is the truncated version described in Legacy, via Avakian's demo. It also blends the first half of Benny's first chorus to the last half of his second. The complete version is not on the Archives' tapes.)

Take 1	UNISSUED - Tape
	Love Sends A Little Gift Of Roses

(Not on the Archives' tapes.)

14 February 1963, New York (ref: page 243)

The Yale University Music Library
BENNY GOODMAN, Volume 10:

THE BENNY GOODMAN QUARTET   **14 February 1963, New York**

Personnel as per Legacy.

Take 2	UNISSUED - Tape
Take 3 - bkdn	UNISSUED - Tape
Take 4	UNISSUED - Tape
Take 5	**CD:** MM 65129-2. **Cas:** MM 65129-4
	Love Sends A Little Gift Of Roses

Takes 1,2,3,4 - bkdns	UNISSUED - Tape (four consecutive aborted takes)
Take 5	UNISSUED - Tape
Take 6	UNISSUED - Tape
Take 7 - bkdn	UNISSUED - Tape
Take 8	UNISSUED - Tape
Take 9	UNISSUED - Tape
Take 10	**LP:** VI LPM2698, et al
Take "S"	**CD:** MM 65129-2. **Cas:** MM 65129-4
	Dearest

(The MM release is spliced: First chorus, take 9; piano solo, take 8; drum solo, take 5; take 9 to completion.)

14 February 1963, continued

14 February 1963, continued

Take 1	UNISSUED - Tape
Take 2 - bkdn	UNISSUED - Tape
Take 3	UNISSUED - Tape
Take 4	UNISSUED - Tape
Take "S"	**CD:** MM 65129-2. **Cas:** MM 65129-4
	Oh, Gee! Oh, Joy!

(The MM release is spliced: First chorus, take 4; to the coda, take 3; to completion, take 4. Note correct punctuation of tune title.)

Take 1	UNISSUED - Tape
Take 2	UNISSUED - Tape
Take 3 - edited	**CD:** MM 65129-2. **Cas:** MM 65129-4
	Bernie's Tune

(Teddy loses his theme during his piano soli; the MM release blends and bridges an awkward gap. Thus take 3, as performed, is unissued.)

Take 1	UNISSUED - Tape
Take 2	**CD:** MM 65129-2. **Cas:** MM 65129-4
	East Of The Sun (And West Of The Moon)

Mid-May 1963, Basin Street East, New York (ref: page 244)

In 1987 a retrospective album of Barbra Streisand's then 25 years in show business was being assembled. Her personal manager/attorney sought tape copies of her three outstanding renditions from this engagement. After consultation with the Goodman Estate, the author declined to provide them.

14 June 1963, Mexico City (ref: page 244)

The last track on Yale/MusicMasters Volume 5 is from the Terrazza Casino rehearsal tape, cited in Legacy's text following the mid-May 1963 Basin Street East display:

The Yale University Music Library   **14 June 1963, Mexico City**
BENNY GOODMAN, Volume 5

Benny Goodman, clt; Bobby Hackett, tpt; Modesto Bresano, ts; John Bunch, p; Jimmy Rowser, b; Ray Mosca, d.

	StLp: JHS & MHS 922588. **Cas:** MM 5040-4, JHS & MHS
	322588. **CD:** MM 5040-2, JHS & MHS 522588
- 0 -	**I Found A New Baby** (sic)

26 August 1963, New York (ref: page 244)

As noted, the backup seven-inch reels are absent any recordings from the sessions of 26 & 27 August. Thus the seven tracks from this date released in RcaVictor's 1964 album, "Together Again! The Benny Goodman Quartet," are the only recordings of those takes now known to exist; and note that apparently **It Had To Be You** is lost to us forever.

However, George Avakian's demo tape does include the three recordings listed as "UNISSUED—Tape" in Legacy's display, plus a rehearsal that preceded **Four Once More.** All four tracks are in Volume 10.

To eliminate redundancy, the RcaVictor releases are not repeated. Thus, ADD the following to the display in Legacy:

The Yale University Music Library
BENNY GOODMAN, Volume 10

THE BENNY GOODMAN QUARTET   **26 August 1963, New York**

Personnel as per Legacy.

Take 3   **CD:** MM 65129-2. **Cas:** MM 65129-4
                           Somebody Loves Me

- rehearsal -   **CD:** MM 65129-2. **Cas:** MM 65129-4
                           "Four Once More"

Take "S"   **CD:** MM 65129-2. **Cas:** MM 65129-4
                           But Not For Me

(The MM release is spliced: Take 3, plus the last four and 3/4 bars from take 2. Note that this corrects an omission in this splice as listed in Legacy.)

Take 5   **CD:** MM 65129-2. **Cas:** MM 65129-4
                           It's All Right With Me

27 August 1963, New York (ref: page 245)

Avakian's tape also provides one unissued track from this date, leaving **Soft Lights And Sweet Music, Nice Work If You Can Get It, From This Moment On** and **If Dreams Come True** wasted efforts. Again, the single RcaVictor track from this session is not repeated; simply ADD the following to Legacy's array:

The Yale University Music Library
BENNY GOODMAN, Volume 10

THE BENNY GOODMAN QUARTET   **27 August 1963, New York**

Personnel as per Legacy.

Take 3-1/2   **CD:** MM 65129-2. **Cas:** MM 65129-4
                           Liza

6 May 1964, New York (ref: page 246)

Royal goof in Legacy: The 6 May concert did indeed feature the Original Quartet, Benny, Lionel, Teddy and Gene, and it was so reviewed by John Wilson the next day in the New York Times. This unpardonable mistake was first brought to the author's attention by Hal Davis, later by John Wilson, collector Mike Romano, and others.

Hal Davis, Benny's friend, publicist and traveling companion over decades, produced the concert at the instance of his aunt, who then was head of Wiltwyck's fund raising committee from her position on its board of trustees. Lionel and a big band, Arthur Godfrey's group, Bil Baird's puppets, Martha Wright, and the De Paur Chorus also participated.

16, 17 June 1964, Hollywood (ref: pages 246, 247)

Three tracks on Yale/MusicMasters Volume 4 are from the studio sessions on these dates. Liner notes credit all three cuts to 17 June, but the author believes **People** is the previously-unissued cut from the 16th:

The Yale University Music Library
BENNY GOODMAN, Volume 4: BIG BAND RECORDINGS   ? 16 June 1964, Hollywood

BENNY GOODMAN AND HIS ORCHESTRA

Personnel as per Legacy.

	StLp: MM 20201, JHS & MHS 922431. **Cas:** MM 40201, MM 5017-4, JHS & MHS 322431. **CD:** MM 60201, MM 5017-2, JHS & MHS 522431
- 0 -	**People**

17 June 1964, Hollywood

	same issues as "People"
- 0 - alt take	**Them There Eyes**
- 0 -	**A Room Without Windows**

(If "People" is from 17 June, it's an alternate take to the issues on LP, CAP T2157, et al.)

17 September 1965, Hollywood (ref: page 248)

Suggested alternative spelling of the name of Danny Kaye's vocal duet partner: Caterina Valente.

Let's Dance is not on the LP, MU 30JA5195. See 24 October 1965, next.

24 October 1965, New York (ref: page 249)

Let's Dance LP attributions are correct here. Omitted in error: **Yesterday** is also on the LP, FEST 246; **King Porter Stomp** is also on the LP, RAR 21.

19 May 1966, New York (ref: page 249)

The WNEW broadcast is on cassette, STAR LINE SLC-61095.

3, 4 June 1966, New York (ref: page 249)

Six tracks on Yale/MusicMasters Volume 6 are from Benny's tapes of this Rainbow Grill engagement. One of them—**Look For The Silver Lining**—is the same performance as that in the 3 June Legacy display. The remaining five are additions to the text.

The author was startled to see Herbie Hancock, certainly an atypical Goodman sideman, as Hank Jones's replacement on the 3rd. His style, reminiscent of Milt Buckner's "locked-hands" manner of playing, with a smattering of George Shearing thrown in, seemed to lure Benny into bypaths he rarely explored, not even in the Capitol bop band era. For example: the full rendition of **Oh, Lady Be Good!**, in the 3 June Legacy display, has a running time of 8:18. It opens with Benny's chorus, clearly identifying the Gershwins' familiar classic. Considered for inclusion in Volume 6, this performance was edited down to 6:07 by eliminating that chorus, plus one by Attile Zoller. What's left is barely recognizable, so unthematic are Benny's and Cheatham's follow-on soli.

The Yale University Music Library
BENNY GOODMAN, Volume 6: RAINBOW GRILL, '66 and '67   3, 4 June 1966, New York

BENNY GOODMAN SEXTET / QUINTET

Sextet personnel as per Legacy. QUINTET: Sextet, less Cheatham. Annette Saunders, voc.

	StLp: JHS 912836. **Cas:** MM 5047-4, JHS 312836. **CD:** MM 5047-2, JHS 512836
- 0 -	**Avalon**
	Embraceable You - QUINTET
	Sweet Georgia Brown
	Look For The Silver Lining - voc Annette Saunders (3 June)
	By Myself - voc Annette Saunders
	Honeysuckle Rose

Three more performances were considered for inclusion in Volume 6, but were also omitted therefrom. These should be added to the unissued cuts in Legacy:

BENNY GOODMAN SEXTET/QUINTET   *same dates*

Personnels as preceding.

These Foolish Things - QUINTET
It's A Most Unusual Day - voc Annette Saunders
Cheerful Little Earful - voc Annette Saunders

28, 29 June 1967, New York (ref: pages 252, 253)

Together, Yale/MusicMasters Volumes 1 and 6 include 11 performances from Benny's 1967 Rainbow Grill tapes. Volume 1's two tracks, **Sweet Georgia Brown** and **Lullaby In Rhythm** were recorded 28 June, per liner notes. Volume 6 cites 28 and 29 June collectively, with no further specification.

However, the author can assign a 28 June date to two tracks on Volume 6. Both are the performances listed in Legacy's "June 28—First Show, First Reel" array. . . after a fashion: Thirty-nine seconds of Joe Newman's solo on **Oh, Lady Be Good,** and a few bars of the drum intro to **I've Found A New Baby,** are edited out of those tracks on Volume 6.

Note that Volume 1's **Sweet Georgia Brown** and Volume 6's **Between The Devil And The Deep Blue Sea** are NOT the performances in Legacy's "June 28—First Show, First Reel" listing. These are different; those in Legacy remain unissued.

The Yale University Music Library
BENNY GOODMAN, Volume 1   **28 June 1967, New York**

Benny Goodman Septet. Personnel as per Legacy.

- 0 -   **StLp:** MM 20142, JHS & MHS 922277; JHS 912870. **Cas:** MM 40142, MM 5000-4, JHS & MHS 322277; JHS 312870. **CD:** MM 60142, MM 5000-2, MM 60216, JHS & MHS 522277; JHS 512870
Sweet Georgia Brown

- 0 -   same issues as "Sweet Georgia Brown," except omit MM 60216, JHS 912870, JHS 312870, JHS 512870
Lullaby In Rhythm

(MM 60216, JHS 912870, JHS 312870 and JHS 512870 are "sampler" releases.)

The Yale University Music Library
BENNY GOODMAN, Volume 6: LIVE AT THE RAINBOW GRILL   **28 June 1967, New York**

Benny Goodman Septet. Personnel as per Legacy.

- 0 -   **StLp:** JHS 912836. **Cas:** MM 5047-4, JHS 312836. **CD:** MM 5047-2, JHS 512836
Oh, Lady Be Good! (28 June, 1st show/reel - edited)
I've Found A New Baby (28 June, 1st show/reel - edited)

                                28, 29 June 1967, New York

- 0 -   same issues as "Oh, Lady Be Good!"
Between The Devil And The Deep Blue Sea
I Guess I'll Have To Change My Plan
There Is No Greater Love (BG obligato, no audible Sims)
Don't Be That Way
(Come Rain Or Come Shine (no audible BG)
St. Louis Blues
All The Things You Are (no audible Newman)

(As of this writing, an MHS counterpart Volume 6 release was not scheduled. When and if it is, it likely will have the same catalog numbers as those used for the JHS issues.)

The author is unable to specify dates, shows, or Benny's tape reels, for the following June 1967 Rainbow Grill performances, which have become available to him:

BENNY GOODMAN SEPTET   *28, 29 June 1967, New York*

Personnel as preceding.

Come Rain Or Come Shine - Sims w/rhythm - BG, Newman in coda
I Will Wait For You
Sweet Lorraine
Honeysuckle Rose
Moon River - Newman w/rhythm - BG, Sims in coda
The Birth Of The Blues
(I Would Do) Anything For You
The Man I Love - BG w/rhythm - Newman, Sims in coda
After You've Gone

26 June 1969, New York (ref: page 255)

The author does not have a copy, but is advised that an "excellent" audio-quality tape of this Schaefer Music Festival is extant.

7–10 October 1969, New York (ref: page 256)

All of the issued takes in the several multi-LP Reader's Digest's albums are on the CD, BRIDGE(SW) 100.021-2.

20 February 1970, Stockholm (ref: page 258)

Correct the subsidiary credit for **Stealin' Apples** to LON SPB 21, et al, instead of the mis-print, LON "STA354."

LON SPB 21, et al, is now available on CD, LON 820-471-2, whose liner notes err in some particulars.

4 March 1971, Munich (ref: page 260)

Don't Be That Way is on a hard-to-find LP, VANTAGE 512.

28 September 1971, Toronto (ref: page 262)

Evidently considered for inclusion in the CBC-TV "In The Mood" telecast, but omitted from it (or else it is simply missing from the author's audio tape of the concert), is a performance by the Quartet:

"IN THE MOOD"   CBC Television Network   *28 September 1971, Toronto*

Benny Goodman, clt; Derek Smith, p; unknown b, d.

Poor Butterfly - QUARTET

14 October 1971, Hackensack, NJ (ref: page 263)

A tape of this concert, described as being of the "finest" quality, is reported to the author, who has been unable to obtain a copy.

1, 2 December 1971, New York (ref: page 264)

Yale/MusicMasters contemplates devoting a future release solely to some of the better takes from this Sextet session. (The author vividly recalls that his control room criticism of Benny's indifferent playing caused Urbie to turn green.)

25, 26 May 1972, Paris (ref: page 266)

A Swedish group assembling a video retrospective of vibraphonist Lars Erstrand's work, wishing to include in it excerpts from this telecast, sought clearances from the Goodman Estate and others in 1992. As of this writing, nothing has eventuated.

8 July 1972, Waterloo Village, NJ (ref: page 266)

This concert is not detailed in Legacy because of the poor audio quality of the author's audience-recorded cassette. He is informed that a tape whose sound is "superior" is extant.

18, 19, 20 August 1972, Toronto (ref: pages 266, 267)

These three concerts were not arrayed in Legacy because the author's tapes of them failed his standard for inclusion. New tapes, supplied by a correspondent who prefers anonymity, are excellent, merit full exposition. Note, too, the corrected spelling of the bandsmen's names, provided by Canadian John Nelson.

Two tunes—identified by asterisks preceding their titles—and dialogue between Benny and MC Elwood Glover, were spliced from this first concert into the CBC-FM broadcast of 12 January 1973.

TORONTO CONCERT   *18 August 1972, Canadian National Exhibition, Toronto*

Benny Goodman, clt, and the Guido Basso Orchestra: Guido Basso, Arnie Chycoski, Erich Traugott, Al Stanwyck, tpt; Rob McConnell, Butch Watanabe, Teddy Roderman, Ron Hughes, tbn; Eugene Amaro, Moe Koffman, Cary Morgan, Jerry Toth, Rick Wilkins, reeds (Koffman doubles on flt); Derek Smith, p; Ed Bickert, g; Don Thompson, b; Ron Rooley, d.

QUINTET: Goodman, rhythm section
SEXTET: Quintet plus Peter Appleyard, vib.

(...introduction and Basso theme - NO BG
Let's Dance (theme)
Don't Be That Way
On A Clear Day
Avalon - SEXTET
Poor Butterfly - SEXTET
(...dialogue, Benny and Glover
(Swingin' Shepherd Blues - Koffman, flt, w/rhythm - NO BG
Roll 'Em
Love For Sale - Smith w/rhythm - BG in coda
MEDLEY: The Man I Love   )
*   Somebody Loves Me)*
*   * Fascinating Rhythm) - SEXTET*
*   * Oh, Lady Be Good!)*
(...dialogue, Benny and Glover
A String Of Pearls
Tin Roof Blues - Appleyard w/rhythm - BG in coda
Yesterday
Stealin' Apples
Memories Of You - QUINTET
King Porter Stomp
Good-Bye (theme)

The introduction and Basso's theme, and one Sextet rendition (identified by an asterisk preceding the tune title), were spliced from the 19 August concert into the CBC-FM broadcast of 12 January 1973.

TORONTO CONCERT   *19 August 1972, Canadian National Exhibition, Toronto*

Personnels as for 18 August.

(...introduction and Guido Basso theme - NO BG
Let's Dance (theme)
Don't Be That Way
Avalon - SEXTET
Poor Butterfly - SEXTET
On A Clear Day
Roll 'Em
...encore, Roll 'Em
Stealin' Apples
(...dialogue, Benny and MC Glover
Sweet Georgia Brown - SEXTET
*Stompin' At The Savoy - SEXTET
After You've Gone - SEXTET
Honeysuckle Rose - SEXTET, plus tpt, tbn, reeds from Basso's orchestra
King Porter Stomp
Memories Of You - QUINTET
The World Is Waiting For The Sunrise - SEXTET
Good-Bye (theme)
...encore, A String Of Pearls
...encore, Oh, Lady Be Good! - SEXTET

The 20 August concert provided the bulk of CBC-FM's 12 January 1973 broadcast, "Showcase '73—Benny Goodman at the 'EX'." Omitted from the broadcast are four small-group performances from the 20th; they are so noted below. As related previously, two Sextet renditions from the 18th, and the intro and one Sextet rendition from the 19th, were spliced into the broadcast.

Benny's younger daughter, Benjie, is introduced from the audience at the end of the concert.

Gene Krupa was the featured soloist with Basso's orchestra the following week at the "Ex," 27 August. His appearance was taped and broadcast via CBC-FM on 15 December 1972, as one program in a series titled, "Showcase '72." A stereo tape of his concert is prized by Krupa collectors, for it proved to be one of his last performances on radio. Ill with leukemia, Gene accedes to Basso's aside, "Do you want to take a breather?" Then Basso announces to the audience, "Gene is resting," and the band plays two numbers without him.

TORONTO CONCERT   *20 August 1972, Canadian National Exhibition, Toronto*

Personnels as for 18 August, EXCEPT: DAVE McMURDO, tbn, replaces Watanabe, and MOE WEINSLAG replaces Wilkins.

(...introduction and Guido Basso theme - NO BG
Let's Dance (theme)
Don't Be That Way
I Want To Be Happy - SEXTET

20 August 1972, continued

20 August 1972, continued

Rose Room - SEXTET
Love For Sale - Smith w/rhythm - BG in coda
(Swingin' Shepherd Blues - Koffman, flt, w/rhythm - NO BG
Roll 'Em
(...dialogue, Benny and MC Glover
Tin Roof Blues - Appleyard w/rhythm - BG obligati   *) omitted*
Shine - SEXTET   *) from*
Honeysuckle Rose - SEXTET, plus tpt, tbn, reeds   *) CBC-FM*
Avalon - SEXTET   *) broadcast*
Stealin' Apples
A String Of Pearls
King Porter Stomp
Good-Bye (theme)
(...closing announcements

13 April 1973, Patchogue, NY (ref: page 269)

    Noting Legacy's plaint that a tape of the Skills Unlimited benefit had not been discovered, Jack Ellsworth, who contracted Benny's Septet for this dance date, thoughtfully has provided one. Owner of jazz & swing oriented radio station WLIM, Patchogue, Jack used his long friendship with Benny to get a 25% reduction in the contract, down from $6,000 to $4,500.

    Save for an electrical fault during Urbie Green's stellar reading of **Star Dust,** the reel tapes provide good audio quality. Urbie was in good form throughout, and for this one night at least, he was the star of the group.

SKILLS UNLIMITED BENEFIT   *13 April 1973, Patchogue, NY*

Personnels as per 11 April 1973, Legacy, plus TRIO: Benny, Bunch, Hinton.

Indiana - QUINTET
Here's That Rainy Day - TRIO (g, d inaudible)
Thou Swell - QUINTET
(Jitterbug Waltz - Sims w/rhythm - NO BG
(Come Rain Or Come Shine—Sims w/rhythm - NO BG
(The Girl From Ipanema - Bunch w/rhythm - NO BG
(Star Dust - Green w/rhythm - NO BG
A Smo-o-o-oth One
Sweet Georgia Brown
(Satin Doll - Pizzarelli w/b, d - NO BG
Medley: Don't Be That Way
       Stompin' At The Savoy
encore: Stompin' At The Savoy
(Body And Soul - Sims w/rhythm - NO BG
Too Close For Comfort - Sims w/rhythm - BG in coda
My Melancholy Baby - QUINTET
Seven Come Eleven
Good-Bye (theme)
I Guess I'll Have To Change My Plan - QUINTET
Avalon
Good-Bye (theme)

31 August, 1 September 1973, Toronto (ref: pages 271, 272)

Professionally-recorded tapes of this 1973 CNE engagement are excellent, an adjective inappropriate for the big band's performances. Those by the small groups are quite good, but those by the full orchestra are ragged, seemingly ill-rehearsed, executed at agonizingly slow tempi. There are long pauses between renditions, apparently caused by Benny's wondering what to play next. The single noteworthy exception is a complete **Good-Bye,** signature of the 31 August concert.

Tune titles and order-of-performances listed in Legacy for this concert set, including the CBC-FM broadcast, are correct. See herein under date of 18 August 1972 for revised spellings of some Basso sidemen.

20 September 1973, Syracuse, NY (ref: page 272)

Benny played a benefit for the Syracuse Symphony at Loew's State Theater this date. He performed with the symphony, and with his own group—Polcer, Masso, Klink, Bunch, Stewart and Corsello. No tapes have been discovered.

16 July 1974, Long Island, NY

The author is advised that a "superb" 90-minute tape of a concert at the Westbury Music Fair, this date, is being mastered for an eventual CD release. No details are available at this writing.

27 July 1974, Rochester, NY (ref: page 274)

Collector Elliot Forman's audience recording of Benny's concert this date falls below the author's standard for detailing. Too bad, because Benny had a stellar group: Chris Griffin, Urbie Green, Zoot Sims, Hank Jones, Bucky Pizzarelli, Slam Stewart and Ronnie Bedford.

9 August 1974, Jefferson, NH (ref: page 274)

Full title of this engagement is, "White Mountain Art & Music Festival." In its first half, Benny performed the Mozart Concerto with a symphony orchestra. The second half was reserved to his Quintet.

Reading in Legacy that no tapes of this concert were known to exist, Goodman enthusiast George Palma asked his son Donald, principal bassist in the symphony, to investigate. Don did recall he had been given a reel tape, searched, finally found it: a 35-minute excerpt of the Quintet's segment.

Thanks to the Palmas, father and son, for this welcome accession to the Goodman legacy from the Granite State:

"White Mountain Art & Music Festival"   *9 August 1974, Jefferson, NH*

Benny Goodman, clt; Hank Jones, p; Bucky Pizzarelli, g; Slam Stewart, b; Grady Tate, d. DUET: Goodman, Jones

I Know That You Know
You Must Meet My Wife
Satin Doll - feat. Pizzarelli
After You've Gone

9 August 1974, continued

9 August 1974, continued

Play, Fiddle, Play - feat. Stewart
Send In The Clowns - DUET
(The Very Thought Of You - Jones solo
On the Sunny Side Of The Street

7 October 1974, Helsinki (ref: page 275)

This concert was videotaped by Finnish TV, Channel 1, not Swedish TV. Channel 1 televised its tape "soon after" the concert, thus preceding those in Sweden by several months.

26 October 1974, Gaithersburg, MD (ref: page 275)

Another audience recording of the Shady Grove concert adds non-Goodman performances to the listing in the book. These are shown as they occurred, and are prefaced by a parenthesis.

SHADY GROVE CONCERT   *26 October 1974, Gaithersburg, MD*

Personnels as per Legacy.

I Want To Be Happy - QUINTET (n/c - intro clipped)
You Must Meet My Wife - QUINTET
I Know That You Know - QUINTET
That's A Plenty
(The Girl From Ipanema - Klink w/rhythm - NO BG
(Oh, Lady Be Good! - Stewart w/rhythm - NO BG
Poor Butterfly - QUINTET
(That's All - Gravine w/rhythm - NO BG
Seven Come Eleven
(I Love You - Stamm w/rhythm - NO BG
Entertainer Rag
Medley: Don't Be That Way
*   Stompin' At The Savoy*
The World Is Waiting For The Sunrise - QUINTET
(The Very Thought Of You—Jones p solo - NO BG
Avalon - QUINTET - full group in coda
Slipped Disc
Sing, Sing, Sing
And The Angels Sing - QUINTET
Sweet Georgia Brown

27, 28 January "1975," Los Angeles (ref: page 281)

Typographical error: Make that 1976, for the Copland Concert.

30 June 1976, Stamford (ref: page 283)

Transposition: Correct catalog number for **Somebody Loves Me** is CD, LON 820 179-2.

4 July 1976, Highland Park, IL (ref: page 283)

Four rehearsal cuts are available from this Ravinia engagement: **Dearly Beloved, Chicago, Remember,** and **Makin' Whoopee.**

7 August 1976, Stanhope, NJ (ref: page 284)

Omitted in error from Legacy: (**I Can't Get Started**—Tate w/rhythm—NO BG), immediately preceding **I've Found A New Baby.**

17 November 1976, Grand Rapids, IA (ref: page 285)

Likely the personnel that accompanied Benny in the midwest—Vaché, Hamilton, Bunch, Collins, Moore and Kay—were with him for this concert. And correct spelling to DaveNport, Iowa, this paragraph.

2 May 1977, New York (ref: page 287)

Reputedly, a "quite good" tape of this Lincoln Center appearance is extant. The author's tape is quite bad.

2 July 1977, Vienna, VA (ref: page 287)

Typographical error: Philip D. LANG, not "Lane," arranged **Rhapsody In Blue.**

18 July 1977, Los Angeles (ref: page 287)

Because the date supplied with an interview tape sent to the author could not have been correct, notice of an NBC telecast was deliberately omitted from Legacy. (Date was one year off.) On his late night "Tomorrow" program, host Tom Snyder interviews Benny and Les Brown, and they all chat with Doris Day via telephone.

27 November 1977, Miami (ref: page 289)

Omitted in error from Legacy: **Love Me Or Leave Me,** vocal by Susan Mellikian, immediately precedes the medley, **Don't Be That Way/Stompin' At The Savoy.**

17 January 1978, New York (ref: page 290)

In addition to a legitimate half-dozen tracks from the 40th Anniversary Concert, a deceptive CD, SOUNDSATIONAL 4009, also includes six non-Goodman tracks, interspersed with other Goodman dubs. This fraud is cloned on another CD, Big Band Spectacular S-4562.

25 November 1978, Elmira, NY (ref: page 292)

Although brief excerpts of this concert at the Clemens Center were televised, no videotapes or audio tapes are known to exist. Benny was accompanied by Bob Zottola, Wayne Andre, Buddy Tate, John Bunch, Wayne Wright, Major Holley and Connie Kay.

2 December 1979, Syracuse, NY (ref: page 296)

Faulty operation of a cassette recorder lost two-thirds of this 90-minute concert. Equalized and pitch-corrected, what's left is rather good audio, captures Benny playing quite well:

SYRACUSE CONCERT 2 December 1979, Onandaga County Civic Center, Syracuse, New York

Benny Goodman, clt; Bob Zottola, tpt; Britt Woodman, tbn; Al Klink, ts; John Bunch, p; Bucky Pizzarelli, g; Slam Stewart, b; Bobby Rosengarden, d.

DUET: Goodman, Pizzarelli
QUINTET: Goodman, Bunch, Pizzarelli, Stewart, Rosengarden

Oh, Lady Be Good! - voc Slam Stewart - QUINTET
Here's That Rainy Day - QUINTET
Avalon - QUINTET
Bewitched - DUET
The World Is Waiting For The Sunrise - voc Slam Stewart - QUINTET
That's A-Plenty
Indiana

7, 8 November 1980, Berlin (ref: pages 299, 300)

Excerpts from the Berlin concerts of 7 and 8 November 1980 constitute the fourth CD in the TCB(Sw) 4301-2 album. It's a plus for collectors, for the bulk of it is from the second concert, hitherto unavailable to but a few. (The first concert was televised, and tapes of it abound.) Appended after the tune titles, "(7)" and "(8)" specify the source dates. Note that track 11, **Stompin' At The Savoy,** mysteriously excises the **Don't Be That Way** intro to the medley that was performed.

BERLIN CONCERTS   *7, 8 November 1980, Berlin*

Personnel as per Legacy.

CD: TCB(Sw) 4301-2 - No. 4

Oh, Lady Be Good!	*(8)*
Here's That Rainy Day - TRIO	*(8)*
"Harry Pepl's Blues"	*(8)*
Avalon	*(8)*
Poor Butterfly	*(8)*
Air Mail Special	*(8)*
You Must Meet My Wife - TRIO	*(8)*
Medley: Don't Be That Way	
* Stompin' At The Savoy*	*(8)*
If I Had You	*(7)*
The World Is Waiting For The Sunrise	*(7)*
Stompin' At The Savoy	*(7)*
Bei Mir Bist Du Schon	*(7)*
Sing, Sing, Sing	*(8)*
Good-Bye (theme)	*(8)*

Collectors might have had these Berlin tracks a decade sooner. In the early 1980s, with few of his legitimate, royalty-producing records on store shelves, Benny reviewed his unissued tapes, seeking material he hoped would interest producers. He had Loren Schoenberg—who the author had induced Benny to hire as an office assistant after he'd fired Muriel Zuckerman for the nth time—prepare a cassette of selected Berlin cuts. It was offered to London, Columbia and Evergreen in turn, as evidence of how well Benny was still performing. All turned it down.

True, Benny did play well. But he had a more compelling reason for trying to sell this particular cassette. The trip to Berlin had been pain free, carefree, and importantly, expense free. He'd had lush accommodations, a chauffeured limousine courtesy of Chancellor Schmidt, gourmet meals, all at practically no cost. Production expenses for the master tapes—studio, engineers—were nil. Release payments to his four accompanists would be modest. Thus, sale of this material would have been a bonanza for Benny, but it was not to be.

4 September 1981, Copenhagen (ref: page 301)

With permission granted by the Goodman Estate, this telecast was released on a commercial videotape, KULTUR 1351, "Benny Goodman at the Tivoli," in 1993. Save for a few "tears" the video is quite good, audio excellent. Contents listing, however, contains some errors: guitarist's name is misspelled, some tune titles are wrong. See Legacy, instead.

And Legacy also errs: it's SLUKEFTER, not "Skulfeter."

16 July 1982, Pori, Finland (ref: page 305)

Portions of this concert—omitting **Air Mail Special, Poor Butterfly,** and **Don't Be That Way/Stompin' At The Savoy**—were televised, and fortunate Finns have videotapes. Kirjurinluoto Park was the locale.

24 July 1982, West Germany (ref: page 305)

Embarrassing error: Tune is **Seven Come Eleven,** not "Slipped Disc." Omission: Ella is accompanied by the Quintet.

16 August 1982, Ontario (ref: page 305)

An audience recording of a portion of the Stratford Shakespearian Festival is below the author's standard for detailing. Accompanying Benny for certain are John Bunch and Chris Flory, and likely Phil Flanigan and Chuck Riggs.

7 October 1985, New York (ref: page 310)

For its 1990 fund appeal, PBS-TV was granted permission by executors of the Goodman Estate to include a Quintet performance from this dinner dance that was omitted from the 1986 telecast. The Quintet appears in the final segment of the program:

"MERV GRIFFIN'S 'ECHOES OF THE BIG BANDS'"   PBS-TV Network   7 October 1985,
Marriott Marquis Hotel, New York

Televised regionally via PBS-TV stations, beginning in August 1990.

7 October 1985, continued

7 October 1985, continued

Benny Goodman, clt; Red Norvo, vib; Dick Hyman, p; Slam Stewart, b; Louis Bellson, d.
Indiana

As of December 1995, WNET-TV has not exercised its option to release a commercial videotape of the original telecast. However, independent producers have approached the Goodman Estate with a proposal to do so, and negotiations are ongoing.

17–19 January 1986, Purchase, NY (ref: page 312)

As of this writing, only two recordings from Benny's last studio sessions have been released. One is an authorized issue, the final track on Yale/MusicMasters Volume 1. The other is a "vanity" issue, a seven-inch LP produced privately to celebrate the 65th birthday of the owner of the Phontastic label. Pressed in very limited quantities, the latter is quite rare.

For obvious reasons, the author looked forward eagerly to listening to the tapes of these sessions. Privileged to do so in 1986, he was disappointed in what he heard. Perhaps realization seldom measures up to anticipation. But even upon current review, the performances are not what the author believes they should have been. For a full six months, the core personnel of this orchestra had been rehearsed exhaustively. In the opinion of the author, these recordings do not reflect that effort.

These sessions were not a Park Recording venture; all aspects of them were paid for by the Musical Heritage Society/MusicMasters. They represent a considerable expense. In future, MusicMasters may release more of these recordings, in an effort to recoup its investment. But it is mindful of Benny's reputation for excellence, and it has no intention of diminishing that reputation. At a guess, future releases from these tapes will be few indeed.

BENNY GOODMAN AND HIS ORCHESTRA   **18 January 1986, Purchase, NY**

Personnel as per Legacy.

- 0 -   **StLp:** MM 20142, JHS & MHS 922277. **Cas:** MM 40142,
                               MM 5000-4, JHS & MHS 322277. **CD:** MM 60142, MM
                               5000-2, JHS & MHS 522277
                               Blue Room

("Blue Room" appears to be the last of the six takes—including a false start—of this tune.)

BENNY GOODMAN AND HIS ORCHESTRA   **19 January 1986, Purchase, NY**

Personnel as per Legacy.

- 0 - take 1   UNISSUED
- 0 - take 2   **7" LP:** ARO 65
                               Wrappin' It Up

(Its label characterizes ARO 65 as an "EP," but in fact it is recorded at 33-1/3 rpm.)

6 November 1986, New York

A "Tribute to Benny Goodman" was given at the Century Club, New York on this date. A videocassette especially made for the event includes excerpts from several of Benny's films, and from the 3 May 1983 Pittsburgh Concert (Legacy, page 307). Benny's daughter Rachel, who hosted the tribute, gave copies of the videocassette to those who attended.

June 1987

A year after Benny's death, subscribing radio stations of the United Stations Programming Network began to broadcast a retrospective titled, "The Benny Goodman Story—Long Live Swing." The three-hour program included dubs of his commercial recordings, and an interview with Benny.

16 January 1988, New York

Bob Wilber and his Big Band performed a "Gala 50th Anniversary Recreation" of the 1938 concert in newly-refurbished Carnegie Hall. Personnel included some sidemen who had worked for Benny, among them Doc Cheatham, Al Grey, Buddy Tate, John Bunch and Panama Francis.

Others who have presented "musical tributes" to Benny are Walt Levinsky's orchestra, and small groups led by Peanuts Hucko and Buddy DeFranco. The Goodman Estate vigilantly monitors these events, makes certain they are never billed as, "...and the Benny Goodman Orchestra."

17 May 1988, New York

With other honorees, Benny was inducted this date in the Emerson Radio Hall Of Fame. His former secretary and factotum, Muriel Zuckerman, accepted the posthumous award.

10 February 1989, Hollywood

Producer Elliott Kastner announced plans for a second biographical feature film about Benny, scheduled to begin in the spring of this year. As of this writing, nothing has happened.

October 1989, Berkeley, CA

As evidence of his induction into the Jewish-American Hall Of Fame, a plaque dedicated to Benny was installed in the Magnes Museum, Berkeley. Bronze, silver and gold medals, replicas of the plaque, are available from the museum for $20, $85, and $1,000, respectively.

October 1989, New York

James Lincoln Collier's **Benny Goodman and the Swing Era** (Oxford University Press), drew generally favorable reviews, in contrast to some adverse criticism accorded his controversial bios of Louis and the Duke. A flowing chronology, the book is necessarily eclectic, drawn from many sources. These are fully credited in a 24-page addendum, cross-referenced by number to passages in the text. Thus the reader can distinguish between Collier's original work, such as his personal interviews, and that of others. Glenn Miller's theme is mistakenly identified as "Sunrise Serenade," but such errata are overbalanced by a fair assessment of both Benny and his music.

Conversely, many lifetime jazz cognoscenti and record collectors find unfair appraisal in another 1989 Oxford University Press book, Gunther Schuller's **The Swing Era.** They read in it a pervasive bias toward black musicians that perforce depreciates the talents and accomplishments of Caucasians, Benny among them. They sense in it the popular "politically correct" vogue of the times that degrades Western culture in general. The message in this medium is, if it's black it's hot, if it's white, it's not. To coin a word, call it Afrodisia.

December 1990, Springfield, VA

A serviceman involved in the World War II V-Disc program announced approval by the U.S. Department of Defense of his commercial release of those recordings. Two years later, a very few small independent radio stations advertised three cassettes for sale by the "V-Disc Corporation," $29.95 for the set. Their 36 tracks were absent any by Benny. Ditto a second release.

Undated, 1990

St. Vincent Island, West Indies, issued postage stamps honoring such jazz luminaries as Basie, Bechet, Ellington, Goodman, Holiday, James, Krupa, Parker, Bud Powell, Reinhardt and Lester Young. Denominations range from 10¢ (James) to $5 (Holiday/Basie, Parker/Powell). Benny's is 25¢, topping Sidney's by a dime.

27 April 1991, New York

Harry Goodman was interviewed this date on the program, "Traditions In Swing," WKCR-FM, New York. Prompted by host Phil Schaap, Harry recounts incidents from the early days in Chicago and New York, speaks briefly about the Swing Era. Interspersed with illustrative recordings, the interview lasts about 90 minutes. Harry and his wife Carol were in Manhattan so that he might donate a harpsichord to the Juilliard Institute.

Harry reveals that Benny plays the trumpet transition in Pollack's **My Kinda Love** (VI 21944 A) "...because Jimmy (McPartland) couldn't make it. So Benny says, 'I'll take it,' picked up (Jimmy's) trumpet and made the transition." Other interesting tidbits crop up throughout; a tape's worth a listen. Harry's memory slips, however, when he states emphatically that he played tuba only, never string bass, while with Pollack. See entry herein, ? 10 August 1929. The camera gotcha, Harry.

Winter 1991, New York

How Am I To Know, from the 30 July 1952 Columbia Sextet session (Legacy, page 205), is background music for a major U.S. bank's radio and TV commercials. Well into 1995, it's still being aired nationwide. Offhand, can think of no other record so employed for that length of time.

Spring 1992, Stockholm

Phontastic began release of six consecutively numbered CDs, 7667 through 7672, in a series titled, "Portrait Of A Year In Music." Each CD offers hit songs from the years 1939 through 1944, inclusive; and each contains one or more Goodman tracks. Liner notes give specific details, with one exception: in PHON 7669, **On The Sunny Side Of The Street** is the third take listed in Legacy, page 131, as first released on the LP, Blu-Disc 1004.

22 May 1992, Berkeley, CA

Johnny Carson appeared for the last time as host of NBC-TV's "The Tonight Show," as did his foil Ed McMahon and Doc Severinson and his excellent orchestra. Through his long tenure, Carson had as guests most of the major jazz instrumentalists and vocalists of the era.

20 September 1992, Westport, CT

A "Command Performance in honor of the King of Swing," to benefit the Fairfield County Stage Company, presented Tony Randall, Margaret Whiting, Lynn Roberts and Ken Peplowski's All-Stars, among others; Gene Rayburn was MC. Gil Glynn was on hand to obtain additional endorsements for his campaign to have Benny awarded the Presidential Medal of Freedom. A letter from then candidate, now President Bill Clinton, endorsed Gil's efforts.

5 December 1992, Washington, D.C.

Lionel Hampton was one of six personalities honored by the Kennedy Center for the Performing Arts; the videotaped ceremony was televised via CBS-TV on 30 December. This was the 15th annual presentation; Benny received his award on the fifth, 5 December 1982.

11 December 1992, New York

WNEW-AM, the station that first broadcast Martin Block's treasured "Make Believe Ballroom," and later featured droll William B. Williams (his Friars Club roast of Don Rickles is both hilarious and unquotable), converted from music to an all-news format under new ownership. WQEW-AM, a **New York Times** outlet, took up the torch, hired some of 'NEW's on-air personnel.

January 1993, Ocean, NJ

MusicMasters reissued the first five Volumes in its Yale University Music Library series—six CDs in all—in a handsome box set, 65095-2. New catalog numbers for the individual releases, Volumes 1 through 5 respectively are: 65000-2; 65006-2; 65007-2; 65017-2; and 65042-2.

A 36-page catalog, featuring a useful index of the personnel, and some unfamiliar photographs, is included. Unfortunately, it repeats a glaring error in Volume 5, misassignment of a medley from the Rotary Concert of 7 February 1963, in error to the studio session of 6 July 1960.

January 1993, New York

Provided by Yale University from its Benny Goodman Archives, an exhibit of Benny's memorabilia opened in the Rainbow Room, Rockefeller Center, on 22 January. It remained on display into October.

March 1993, New York

In work for a half-dozen years, Ross Firestone's **Swing, Swing, Swing, The Life & Times of Benny Goodman** (W. W. Norton & Company) clones the format used in Collier's **Benny Goodman and the Swing Era:** It pieces together a chronology from a massive array of print and audio sources, interspersing them with the author's real-time interviews. The sources are "noted" in a 42-page addendum. But here Firestone's approach differs from Collier's. His source credits are by chapter, but they are in alphabetic, not chronologic, order. Nor are they cross-referenced by page number to their employment in the text. Thus it is impossible in many instances to link source to text. Further, some print/audio source statements are in quotation marks in the text, which may lead the naive to assume that such remarks were made by Benny and others directly to Firestone. This is of course untrue, and is misleading.

April 1993, New York

Goodman fans eagerly awaited a two-CD Columbia set whose advance publicity promised "14 previously unissued" air checks from Benny's heyday, in addition to those in the CO SL-180 "Jazz Concert No. 2" album. Available this month on multi-format CO 48836 et al, "Benny Goodman On The Air (1937–1938)" proved something less than the "Best Value" its cover boasts: Liner notes notwithstanding, all 14 had been issued before, most of them on LPs some 40 years earlier.

Eleven are on the Rose/Sunbeam LPs, October–November 1937. Two, **Moten Swing** and **Bumble Bee Stomp,** are not only in the Dr. Jazz "Air Play" and related releases, but also are in a multi-format Columbia issue, CO 40350. And, incredibly, **Nagasaki** is in the "Jazz Concert No. 2" album itself.

Further defects: The Rose/Sunbeam tracks are so far off pitch (slow) that listening to them is painful. **In The Shade Of The Old Apple Tree** is from the broadcast of 13 October 1937, not 23 October. And Gene Goodman did not substitute on trumpet for Ziggy Elman on that 13 October date; as stressed in Legacy, Gene never played any instrument in the band, then or ever.

One might expect such deception and poor repro from bootlegs. But from a major label? Never. Shame, Sony, shame.

July 1993, Great Britain

An hour-long TV presentation, "Benny Goodman: Adventures in the Kingdom of Swing," was first telecast via ITV on its late night "The South Bank Show." In December 1993, PBS stations throughout the U.S. featured it during their funds drives. A commercial copy is available, Columbia No. 49186, VHS format.

The video was produced by Oren Jacoby, whose father Irving co-produced 1953's "The Silent Night," which included Benny in its soundtrack. Jacoby senior also filmed the 6 December 1955 Columbia recording session, excerpts of which are in Benny's "Adventures." Silent footage of Art Rollini's 16mm films of late 1930s band personnel, and of Vido

Musso's 16mm films of Benny's 1941 Pound Ridge housewarming, are excerpted for inclusion. Very rare 35 mm sound film of the Benny Goodman Quintet with Red Norvo, from the Army/Navy Screen Magazine production "Rehearsal Time," is a highlight welcomed by film collectors.

Because proximate film is non-existent, film/music/commentary are not always in sync, e.g. the Billie Holiday sequence. But those lapses are more than compensated for by live interviews with Benny's family members and associates. Helen Ward Savory's remarks are startlingly personal, Jimmy Maxwell's tribute sadly poignant.

In sum, a must for every Goodman fan, a treat for anyone interested in excellent television viewing.

31 August 1993, Orange, MA

Goodman collector Ron Senet and his wife attended, and audio-taped, a psychic reading with the medium Elwood Babbitt. (Babbitt is the author of several books about psychic phenomena, has been "tested" by the University of New Hampshire.) Including responses from the Senets, a two-minute, 50-second dialogue occurred during the reading. Verbatim, it is:

"I don't know if you can hear me?"
(Yes, we can hear you.)
"I feel like I've drowned in a sour note discord, but this Cole person said I could enter this body that I must have had some time on earth, and that if I made the mouth go, I would be talking with people on the earth. Is that true, or are you in another dimension or. . . (last word unclear)?"
(No, we are here on earth.)
"Why, then, I address you. I don't know as I believe it as I want to believe it, but I am interested only because I've been directed to you, and you can convey my best to those individuals I guess that still survive on your world. And whether they believe it or not, I am and was Benny Goodman."
(Oh, Benny!)
"I wanted—or the force wanted—me to speak to you."
(Oh, thank you, Benny!)
"I shall be, now that this, this, this what do you call it, a measure of force that has been opened, I'll try to talk to you until I can believe the difference between us."
(You cut him off. Was he finished? Yes.)

Spiritual contacts evidently are random, usually unanticipated, and in this case were not prompted or otherwise sought by the Senets. The "voice" is low, thick, hesitant, not unlike Benny's speech when the author spoke with him a few days before his death. What startled the author and his wife—both openminded, but skeptical—was the rising inflection of the voice's "I guess," very much Goodman-like.

"Cole" is "Jim Cole," Babbitt's spirit world intermediary, self-described as a "psychic engineer," able to convert psychic energy to a level humans can tolerate. In an entirely different voice, Cole wraps up this segment by promising to assist Benny in future, ". . . because he is truly interested in being able to speak to you."

In the event of another contact, the author has suggested a question that only Benny could answer.

More later. Maybe.

21 October 1993, New York

"Benny Goodman Revisited: 1993" was presented this date in Carnegie Hall by the Carnegie Hall Jazz Band, Jon Faddis directing. In the 17-piece orchestra were former Goodmanites Urbie Green and Jerry Dodgion; among the guest soloists were Milt Jackson and Walt Levinsky.

24 June 1994, Miami

Effervescent Maria Marshall's radio interview granted WLRN-TV's Ed Bell this date rebuts Benny bashers: "He was very kind and generous with me. The thing is, whatever anyone has to say about Benny being tough and all, he really wasn't. The only things he wanted were for everyone to be on time, do a good swinging job, concentrate, have fun, and you'd never hear a peep out of him. That's fair, isn't it?" Sure is, Maria.

June 1994, Pleasantville, NY

The Reader's Digest's four-cassette/four-CD album, "The Big Bands Live!," bally-hoo'd as "A Collector's Edition of Original Broadcast Performances," contains three tracks by Benny, **I Got Rhythm, Flying Home** and **Memories Of You.** All are from the 24 December 1939 "Spirituals to Swing" Carnegie concert. So much for truth in advertising, at least insofar as Benny's concerned.

August 1994, Washington

Despite unceasing effort by Gil Glynn of Baton Rouge over the past decade, Presidents Reagan, Bush and Clinton have not been persuaded to award the prestigious Presidential Medal of Freedom, the Nation's highest award to civilians, to Benny Goodman. Gil has amassed hundreds of warm endorsements for his cause from the elite of the worlds of academia, government, industry, the media, music and show business. Forwarded to the White House, these recommendations have gotten a cursory "under consideration," nothing more.

Benny did a lot for the United States. He sold both WW II War Bonds and U.S. Savings Bonds, subscriptions in the millions of dollars. His tours for the Department of State to the Far East, Europe and the U.S.S.R. promoted not only the culture of his country, but also its political ideology. His life-long allegiance to the Democrat Party—as far back as 1940, he campaigned for Franklin Roosevelt—may have dissuaded Republicans Reagan and Bush. But Reagan, a Swing devotee, had Benny perform at the White House, praised him lavishly; Bush is a graduate of the Law School at Yale, where Benny's Archives are housed. Democrat Clinton, also a Yale Law School graduate, and an amateur musician himself, would seem to have every good reason to grant Benny that honor. His awards this month once again ignored Benny, who richly deserves the medal.

September 1994, Mars

To fill otherwise unprogrammed air time, TV stations occasionally schedule "infomercials," commercials thinly disguised as entertainment. To promote its "The War Years" set of releases, Time-Life produced a half-hour videotape that offers film clips over sound bites of hit records, both from the WW II era. Enthusing about the included track of Benny's **Somebody Else Is Taking My Place,** actor/host George Kennedy makes this out-of-this-world pronouncement: "Peggy Lee. . .backed by Glenn Miller and his orchestra!" Can't wait to see those liner notes.

September 1994, Paris

In its "Masters Of Jazz" series, the French label MEDIA 7 began this month to issue, over time, eight CDs that highlight Charlie Christian soli. Sources are eclectic, embracing both studio and location dates with Benny Goodman and others. Volumes 1 through 8, bearing catalog numbers MJCD 24, 29, 40, 44, 67, 68, 74 and 75, have been auditioned by English correspondent Jeremy Mitchell. He rates their transfers—evidently, all from previously-released recordings—as satisfactory.

The author finds accompanying discographical detail, as to personnel, locations, dates, tune titles and matrices, in main to be accurate. (Note that the liner notes cite the revised dates for Benny's first-half 1940 Columbia sessions, per Legacy, page 317, evidence of some care in research.) But MEDIA 7's assignment of take numbers is baffling: Following each matrix, it appends take numbers in order-of-performance, ignoring preferential take numbers visible on shellac records and those identified in liner notes of legitimate releases. For example, it appends take "3" to matrix CO 29028, **Royal Garden Blues,** 7 November 1940, for the shellac 78, CO 35810. Its take is, of course, -1, embossed on the record and denoted in both specialized and general discographies. Use Legacy to correct MEDIA 7's idiosyncratic take numbering system.

MEDIA 7 also fails in its announced goal of including in its eight CDs every performance in which Christian solos. One instance: Benny's big band Columbia recording of **Li'l Boy Love** has a Christian solo (see entry in this text under "3 July 1940," true date 25 June 1940); it's absent in MJCD 44. Also missing are the newly-revealed relevant Goodman small-group recordings in this text, and applicable combo performances in the section on Savory's air checks herein. Beyond those omissions are possible Christian soli that may be in several hours' worth of Benny's big band air checks, August 1939–June 1941, in private collections only, never released on record. Charlie did play in the orchestra, as well as in the Sextets and Septets, and some of these performances may include his soli.

In sum, no discographer or issuing agency should claim totality. In the author's experience, it's unattainable.

December 1994, Washington, D.C.

Overdue, Benny's good friend Morton Gould was honored by the Kennedy Center for the Performing Arts on 3 December, together with Kirk Douglas, Aretha Franklin, director Harold Prince and Pete Seeger. Readers will recall that Benny received his award from the Center a dozen years earlier.

Summer/Fall 1995

Inquiries received about three consecutive 1947 tracks of **A Song Was Born** in the RcaFr (Jazz Tribune) two-CD album 66605-2 prompted review of the soundtrack of the film in which it was featured and prior releases (Legacy, pages 187, 188), vis a vis the CD. Comparisons of all available versions revealed:

Essentially, the ET WOR 3177-Part B track is the master take for all versions, including that in the movie's soundtrack. Absent vocals by the Golden Gate Quartet and Jeri Sullivan, it is the take used for the initial track of the tune on RcaFr 66605-2.

A "mini-take" (coda only), however, was recorded and substituted for the WOR ET's ending, when the performance was inserted into the soundtrack. This alternate ending is easily identifiable; Bellson solos on his drums, not on the cymbals he played for the "master" take. Also, instrumental soli by TD, Louis, Charlie, Benny and Lionel were all abridged when the insertion into the soundtrack was made; portions of each retained solo, however, are all from the WOR ET take. This truncated version, with the drum-solo windup, is also on ViJap NB-6013, et al; and it is the second of RcaFr 66605-2's three tracks. (Note that vocal interjections during the rendition, heard in the soundtrack and in kindred releases, are not in the WOR ET. They were overdubbed later.)

The third track of the tune on RcaFr 66605-2 has nothing to do with the film, nor with Benny Goodman. It's by Louis's own septet, with Barney Bigard playing clarinet.

*

The Vintage Jazz folks who brought you the welcome V-Disc alternates (q.v. this text, under beginning date 9 December 1943) now offer a new label and some old material: Six consecutively-numbered VIPER'S NEST CDs, VN 171–176 inclusive, re-re-reissuing Boris Rose's "Madhattan Room" broadcasts. But: these are clean transfers, and those more concerned about listening to the music rather than acquiring first issues, may welcome these, too. (See Legacy, beginning on page 74.)

*

The U.S. Postal Service, which seems to issue commemorative stamps weekly in an attempt to reduce its recurring deficits, tapped the jazz fan market earlier this year by immortalizing Louis and the Duke (as if either needed it). Then on 18 September it began to sell a pane of 10 stamps honoring other Afro-Americans who've contributed to America's sole original art form. USPS hadn't yet caught up with racial integration; to jazz fans, Elvis doesn't count.

But wait! A year later, September 1996, USPS is slated to recognize the talent and stature of bandleaders Benny Goodman, Count Basie, Jimmy Dorsey, Tommy Dorsey and Glenn Miller. (Sorry, Artie, you'll have to wait your posthumous turn.) That same month songwriters Harold Arlen, Hoagy Carmichael, Dorothy Fields and Johnny Mercer—all of whom had some association with Benny—are also to receive their due from USPS. And if present plans materialize, Benny's stamp will be reproduced as the cover of a MusicMasters box set.

So: A belated nod to USPS; better late—as it often is—than never.

October 1995, Stockholm

Six PHONTASTIC CDs, each embracing two "Camel Caravan" broadcasts, are now available. They are:

PHON CD 8841: 10 and 17 August 1937
PHON CD 8842: 24 and 31 August 1937
PHON CD 8843: 16 November 1937 and 30 August 1938
PHON CD 8844: 6 and 13 September 1938
PHON CD 8845: 20 and 27 September 1938
PHON CD 8846: 2 and 9 September 1939

All 12 programs have been previously released, in whole or in part, on various labels. The PHON CDs are complete, however, and have been remastered using the costly CEDAR process. Within the limitations imposed by source acetates recorded more than half a century earlier, the CDs offer excellent audio fidelity.

Note that one track in producer Anders Ohman's souvenir Christmas 1994 CD, PHON XMCD 94, is also in PHON CD 8845. It's the Trio's "Don't Let That Moon Get Away," from the "Camel Caravan" of 20 September 138 (Legacy, page 91).

Wrappin' It Up for 1995

One more time, a president of the United States failed to award the Medal of Freedom to Benny Goodman. In the author's opinion, some of 1995's honorees were deserving, a few but marginally so. Surely Benny's contributions to the nation should have placed him at the top of this year's modest roster. Watergate, Irangate, WhiteWatergate, and now Goodman gets the gate.

Untruth In Advertising #1: CANBY CD 1009, "Radio Days," dubs the 20 August 1952 Blue Note broadcast, as on the LP, MARK 736 (Legacy, page 206). But its advertising falsely claims two tunes not broadcast, thus enticing misled collectors to buy the CD. Too, its liner notes boast novel personnel: Terry Gribbs (sic), vibes; Ted Wise (sic), bass; and Morrie Fell (sic), drums. Sick.

U I A #2: GRAMMOPHONO 2000 CD 78519, "Benny Goodman—The Classical Repertoire From Mozart to Gershwin," continues the canard in re' Benny and "An American In Paris," first perpetrated by the CD, HUNT 534. See comment in the text under date 14 November 1943

U I A #3: Yet another bootleg CD—I won't dignify it by naming it—clones 1938 "Camel Caravan" programs previously pirated via LPs. Its mail-order ads snidely trumpet, ". . .Goodman's leading discographer knew nothing about . . ." these broadcasts, or words to that effect. Must be the leading discographer responsible for U I A #s 1 and 2, above.

Let's end the year on some positive notes:
The New York Times, 19 December 1995, applauds the growing success of Wynton Marsalis's "Jazz At Lincoln Center" concerts and notes that they are concurrent " . . . when general interest in jazz is booming." Further along, the article adds, "There has also been criticism of what is seen as a paucity of white players in the (Lincoln Center) programs." Wynton, jazz can and should be color-blind; Benny proved that long ago.

The 2-CD set, RHINO R272169, "Lullaby Of Broadway," includes the extended Speak-O-Phone version of "Hooray For Hollywood" (Legacy, page 70). Quite a few bucks for but one four-minute-plus track by Benny, but this CD can be classified as a first issue.

Finally, the compleat collector need not despair of acquiring 1995's private PHON release, XM CD-95. Its only included Goodman contribution is "You're Driving Me Crazy" from the "Camel Caravan" broadcast of 13 September 1938 (Legacy, page 90). That track is on PHON CD 8844 and other prior releases.

Early Days, 1996

Good note: The Trio's "China Boy," excerpted from NBC-TV's "Allen In Movieland," 2 July 1955 (Legacy, page 211), is on two commercial videotapes: "Legends of Jazz Drumming, 1920–1950," DCI Music Video VHO-248; and on "Steve Allen In Hollywood," Video Resources, no catalog number specified. First listed is the better value.

Bad note: Sony SP CD A 26058, "Dick Haymes with Harry James & Benny Goodman," Art-lessly errs on one of its three Goodman inclusions: The vocalist on track 8, "I've Got A Gal In Kalamazoo," is London, not Haymes! Liner notes give the proper date for Haymes's recording, but offers London's mx CO 32795-1, 14 May 1942 (Legacy, page 136) instead.

Sad note: Report from France states that Benny's brother Harry suffered a debilitating stroke, but is recuperating, thank you. Sadder still, a report from Chicago informs that Benny's sister Ida (Mrs. Winsberg) has passed on, but does not provide details.

THE SAVORY GOODMAN AIR CHECKS

Two men have given posterity more of Benny Goodman's most memorable music than have any others. By chance they share three Goodman-engendered attributes: Neither has been recognized adequately for his contributions. One caused the most famous concert in all of Jazz history to be recorded; the other made it possible for the world to hear it. And both can claim the beauteous Helen Ward as wife.

They are Albert Marx and William A. Savory. Marx has been accorded belated credit for having preserved the 1938 Carnegie Hall concert on wax; but to his death in 1991 he was bitter that the Columbia album failed even to mention his name. Too, those same liner notes ignore Savory, who spent weeks restoring the acetates to the state that he could transfer them to tape successfully. George Avakian does acknowledge the use of Savory's recordings and his engineering skill for the ill-named Columbia "Jazz Concert No. 2" release; but the successor M-G-M/Book-Of-The-Month "Treasure Chest" albums do neither. The author apologizes for his oversight in the latter, and now would make amends.

Bill Savory, Charter Member and Fellow of the Audio Engineering Society, studied physics, electrical engineering, mathematics and collateral disciplines over time at Harvard University, the University of Chicago, Catholic University and Columbia University. In 1938 the National Vocarium engaged him to construct and operate a system to reproduce Edison cylinders electronically. He joined Columbia in 1940, helped operate and maintain its new Chicago studios. He was commissioned an officer in the U.S. Naval Reserve in 1943, served on active duty in World War II, Korea and Vietnam, attaining the rank of Commander. After WW II, he returned to Columbia as a member of the team that developed the long-playing record. Next he became chief engineer for Angel Records/EMI, remained there until 1960. Kindred employment, over the next three decades, continued his life's work. His last position was senior scientist for Tracor Applied Sciences; retired, he now is a consultant to that firm. Amidst all this activity, and with frequent recalls to Navy service, Bill founded his own recording company, Lyricon Records, Inc., in 1980. Ten years earlier, in September 1970, he had wed Helen Ward, with whom he shares music and memories at their home in Falls Church, Virginia. Helen is also busy preparing her autobiography.

Those are the bare bones of Bill's career. Let's flesh it out with events that relate to Benny Goodman:

The Depression forced Bill to leave Harvard in 1935 and seek employment. His musical background (he's a pianist) and acquired knowledge of sound reproduction were attractive to custom recording companies in New York. He worked for several, whose primary business was transcribing radio broadcasts for bandleaders and others, and for sponsors and advertising agencies. Early on he decided Benny's band was best, so he made duplicate discs for his own pleasure.

Many of the broadcasts were in late evening via WABC (CBS), WOR (Mutual) and independent WNEW; when Benny's "Camel Caravan" switched networks in 1939, NBC became dominant. Bill delivered some recordings himself, and in so doing struck up a friendship with Gene Goodman. But his association with Benny began because of their mother, Dora. She enjoyed a Jewish-language broadcast, but couldn't get it at times on her radio:

"The left side works fine, but the right side don't," and would Benny please get it fixed. Benny asked Gene to see if "the guy who's making those records for me" would come to their home in Jackson Heights and repair the radio and get Mom off his ear. Bill did, earned Benny's gratitude, and that incident began a lifelong relationship between them. In future it was, "Muriel, find Bill Savory!" whenever Benny was faced with anything he didn't like about the way his band was being recorded or broadcast.

Bill had made no attempt to exploit his Goodman air checks until the third week in November 1950, and then only by request. He was assigned to replay the spliced tapes of Copland's "Concerto For Clarinet And String Orchestra," which Benny had recorded the week before. That session had not gone well, and now Benny and Dave Oppenheim, the Masterworks Department producer, were evaluating the edited version in Studio C in Columbia's facilities at 799 Seventh Avenue. Benny didn't like what he heard, decided some passages would have to be done over. (He never liked the release; in 1963, he re-recorded the Concerto for Columbia for a second release.) Dispirited, he sat alone in the studio, prudently avoided by all present.

Thinking to cheer him, Bill approached, said, "Benny, how'd you like to hear some good music?" Scoffingly: "Oh yeah, what've **you** got?" "Stay here, I'll put it on the monitor." He did, a big band number on one of his acetates, title forgotten. The effect was immediate: "Hey, that's great, great! When did we do that? Say, do you have any more things like that?" "Lots." "Well, how about making me some tapes, I think I can do something with them." Bill complied, and the result is history, the magnificent Columbia air checks album, released in 1952. And a sidelight: Columbia judged the material worthy of its Masterworks label, chose George Avakian to produce it. Unaware of the background, George called Bill: "I'm doing a new album for Benny and I want you to engineer it. It's some of the best things he's ever done; wait'll you hear it, you'll love it!" "I know," and Bill told him the story.

Bill's fragile discs were preserved with meticulous care, in jackets, in tin containers, all encased in wooden crates. Over the years they were stored in various places, the bulk of them finally in a loft over Benny's garage (later converted into a studio) in Stamford. They remained there until shortly after Benny died, and that precipitated a crisis of sorts: Under the terms of Benny's will, Yale University was bequeathed almost all of his memorabilia—less whatever Rachel and Benjie chose to take—to establish and fund the Goodman Archives. "Memorabilia" included Benny's recordings, and the author watched as Yale's representatives gathered them up—along with everything else in sight—from Benny's apartment and office in the Manhattan House. Realizing that Yale would soon repeat the removal at Benny's home in Connecticut, aware that Bill's discs were there, and fearing that Yale—unknowingly—would seize them, the author intervened. He phoned Bill, told him to get to Stamford ASAP, retrieve his acetates. And he phoned Benny's attorney and co-executor of his estate, Bill Hyland, to inform him that certain recordings at Stamford were not Benny's, and were not to go to Yale. Bill (Savory) rented a small station wagon, drove to Stamford. Finding the wagon too small, he exchanged it for a larger one, filled it with his discs, got them safely home. The author was relieved because, despite his urgings over decades, the acetates had never been transferred to tape. At last that process could begin.

The transfers took time. First, there were experiments with various solvents to clean the acetates, restore them to pristine condition, essential to preparing discs more than half a century old for successful taping. Next, more experimentation with styli, then a lengthy period of modifying off-the-shelf pickup heads and turntables, in order to extract everything possible from the acetates. Not until the end of 1991 was Bill content to begin the transfers, to a digital cassette deck and reel-to-reel recorders. First were his 10- and 12-inch discs, followed by his 16-and 17-inch transcriptions. All were on tape by mid-1994, with this caveat: Helen and Bill own a second home in California, and some acetates and tapes—contents unlisted on their crates—are stored there. It may become necessary to have them shipped to Virginia, because some transcriptions have on them air checks by more than one performer. Although he concentrated on Goodman, Bill also recorded other popular artists of the Big Band Era off the air. There are tracks by Basie, Berigan (with the CBS house band), Bob Crosby, Ellington and Miller, the small groups of Louis Jordan and John Kirby, and others. Bill believes there likely are Goodman cuts on such undedicated transcriptions.

Now that the Goodman acetates are on master tapes suitable for reproduction, will at least some of those transfers become available to the public? Bill estimates that he has enough attractive, good audio-quality material to constitute five CDs, even when duplicate tunes performed by identical personnels are eliminated. (But who among us wouldn't relish more than one new air check of the Sextet's **Honeysuckle Rose,** featuring Charlie Christian?) The Goodman Estate would welcome such releases, for they represent Benny and his small groups and orchestras during their peak years; the Estate wants to enhance Benny's reputation, and Bill's acetates will do just that. An eager market for them seems assured, confirmed by the judgments of potential issuers and global distributors. Further, Bill has his own label, also a possible means of public access. But the obstacle to issuance is—to date—the American Federation of Musicians' posture in regard royalties for its members. It insists on imposing today's scale, not the rates that obtained when the broadcasts occurred, a half-century or more in the past. That level of expense—currently, about $270 per musician/vocalist, for each 15 minutes on record—makes release infeasible, too risky for anyone to chance. At present, then, likelihood of public availability to Bill's Goodman material is in limbo.

Ultimate disposition of this valuable, unrivaled aggregation of air checks by Goodman and others is also uncertain. Both public and private institutions would embrace their acquisition, but no discussions with such repositories have gone forward. Bill now has but two desiderata in mind to govern their eventual placement: One, an Archive will be established in the family name, Desavouret, Anglicized when Bill's father emigrated from France. And two, this massive collection will remain intact. Other factors that may modify these intentions and decide the acetates' fate are the opportunities that present themselves in future.

*

Personal assessment:

I wrote in Legacy that I considered (unnamed) Bill's ". . . treasure trove to be the major source of future releases of Goodman air checks from his most desirable years." Although I've heard but a few of the transfers, that opinion is confirmed: If issued, these off-the-air performances will match those in the Columbia and M-G-M albums, track for track. New tunes extend the Goodman recorded repertoire: Benny is so excited by Harry James's soli in "Mr. Ghost Goes To Town" that he blows a police whistle instead of his clarinet. "I'm Hatin' This Waitin' Around" would be Peg LaCentra's debut with Benny on record; ditto "One Alone" sung by actor John Boles. Successive excellent soli by Russin, Elman, Brown and Goodman highlight an early 1938 "Bugle Call Rag," as Krupa drives the band to its limits. Dave Tough tears up "I'm A Ding Dong Daddy (From Dumas)" when the Quartet guests on an Eddie Cantor broadcast. And Benny blows a chorus on a Christmas 1942 "Rose Room" by the Quintet that is unlike anything I have of his on record or tape.

There are disappointments, certainly not among the cuts I've heard, but because I likely will never hear some performances I've long anticipated. Bill recorded six tunes onto four acetates, broadcast during the band's disastrous spring 1935 engagement at the Roosevelt Hotel, New York. Those discs, and a duplicate set, were delivered to Benny. Bill eventually retrieved one set; the other has disappeared. Despite many attempts to restore those acetates to reproducible condition, Bill has not succeeded, and those recordings are lost to us.

I do not recall either having seen or heard the band play "Sing, Sing, Sing" during Tough's tenure. Of the many broadcast playlists I have covering relevant periods in 1938 and 1941, only one lists that tune. It's a CBS broadcast, 30 April 1938, Benny's closing night in the Madhattan Room, and the log specifies that Tough is featured. I think Davey would have done something special with that Goodman classic, but an acetate of it is not among those available to date.

There is only one listing in Legacy for "The Siren's Song," the RcaVictor recording of 7 April 1939; Jerry Jerome remembers its studio playback vividly. Jimmy Mundy's arrangement begins in the key of C, and Benny blows a modest introduction. Then it modulates to D-flat, and Jerry comes on with a warm tenor sax solo. Listening to the monitor, Benny "ray-ed" Jerry, huffed, "Hell, that thing sounds like you're the leader, not me!" That did not augur well for the chart's future. Again, there's only one air check of the tune in my program logs, a sustaining broadcast from the Roof Garden of the Ritz-Carleton, Boston, 17 June 1939, not on Bill's acetates at hand. Benny had a long memory.

Minor regrets, surely, in view of what is extant:

ACETATES

Certain conditions apply to this array:

1. All of the 300-odd air checks following are "new"; that is, none appears in Legacy or in any other publication. (Exception: Complete performances that now displace prior listings of partial availabilities.) Thus they do not encompass the full contents of Savory's Goodman transcriptions, which also include hundreds more entries in Legacy, or in the text of this work.

2. The tabulation is in chronological order, and where known, in order-of-performance. For example, the 3 March 1937 CBS sustaining broadcast from the Hotel Pennsylvania: **Let's Go Slumming On Park Avenue** and **Liza** were played, in that order, immediately preceding the **Sometimes I'm Happy** listing in Legacy.

If the order-of-performance is unknown or uncertain, tunes are listed in the order in which they were transcribed.

3. In main, dates and locales cited, as inscribed on the discs or written on their labels or jackets, are confirmed by program logs. ("Logs" are playlists of broadcasts, supplied to the author over time by Bill Harper, Bob Inman, Jim Maher, Sheila Stead, the R. J. Reynolds Company, and others.) Agreement between Savory's data and the program logs assures the accuracy of those details.

There are a few conflicts between information on the discs and on the playlists. Causative may be multiple tracks, from undifferentiated broadcasts, on Savory's 16- and 17-inch transcriptions; or, the logs may be in error. These discrepancies are noted in the array.

A few air checks on undated acetates cannot be assigned specifically at this time; research is continuing. These are listed in what is considered to be appropriate time frames.

Where known, station or network sources are given.

Personnel for the entries may be inferred from those cited in Legacy for relevant time periods.

"LET'S DANCE"   NBC   2 February 1935, New York

King Porter Stomp
Blue Moon - voc Helen Ward
China Boy

"LET'S DANCE"   NBC   23 March 1935, New York

It's Easy To Remember - voc Helen Ward (arr SM)

"RADIO CITY DANCE PARTY"   NBC   13 July 1935, New York

Every Little Moment

"ELGIN REVIEW"   NBC   12 May 1936, Chicago

China Boy - TRIO

"ELGIN REVIEW"   NBC   2 June 1936, New York

Let's Dance (theme)
I've Found A New Baby
I Can't Get Started - voc Helen Ward - TRIO, segue to band (arr JM)
Someday, Sweetheart - TRIO
Would You? (n/c - interrupted by commercial)
Robins And Roses - voc Helen Ward
('Way Down Upon The) Swanee River (arr FH) (n/c - BG/Dowling comedy routine)
(I Would Do) Anything For You - TRIO 32 bars, segue to band
Good-Bye (theme)

"CAMEL CARAVAN"   CBS   1 September 1936, Steel Pier, Atlantic City

Minnie The Moocher's Wedding Day

Hotel Pennsylvania 20 February 1937, New York

This Is My Last Affair - voc Frances Hunt
I Got Rhythm - QUARTET
Star Dust

Hotel Pennsylvania 21 February 1937, New York

Anything Goes (arr SM) (n/c - mid-b'cast break)
Swing Low, Sweet Chariot
Limehouse Blues - QUARTET

Hotel Pennsylvania   CBS   27 February 1937, New York

Changes

Hotel Pennsylvania   CBS   3 March 1937, New York

Let's Go Slumming On Park Avenue - voc Frances Hunt
Liza - QUARTET

Hotel Pennsylvania   CBS   4 March 1937, New York

Ridin' High
You're Here, You're There, You're Everywhere (arr JM)

"CAMEL CARAVAN" CBS 9 March 1937, New York

Old Man River

Hotel Pennsylvania CBS 10 March 1937, New York

Bugle Call Rag
Stompin' At The Savoy - QUARTET
Roll 'Em
Good-Bye (theme)

Hotel Pennsylvania Mutual 11 March 1937, New York

Clap Hands, Here Comes Charlie
Remember
You're Laughing At Me - voc Frances Hunt
He Ain't Got Rhythm - voc Frances Hunt
Oh, Lady Be Good!
Limehouse Blues - QUARTET (unspliced)
I Can't Lose That Longing For You - voc Frances Hunt
Honeysuckle Rose

Hotel Pennsylvania CBS 13 March 1937, New York

More Than You Know - TRIO
Camel Hop
Liza - QUARTET

"CAMEL CARAVAN" CBS 23 March 1937, New York

Sugar Foot Stomp (complete)

Hotel Pennsylvania CBS 23 March 1937, New York

Let's Dance (theme) (**LP:** CO ML/OL 4613, et al - see text)
Chlo-e (Song Of The Swamp)
I've Got My Love To Keep Me Warm

Hotel Pennsylvania Mutual 25 March 1937, New York

Alexander's Ragtime Band (n/c)
You're Laughing At Me - voc Frances Hunt
Somebody Loves Me
Sweet Is The Word For You - voc Frances Hunt (arr SM)

"CAMEL CARAVAN" CBS 13 April 1937, New York

Oh, Lady Be Good!
September In The Rain - voc Frances Hunt
Nagasaki - QUARTET
Minnie The Moocher's Wedding Day (see text this date)

Hotel Pennsylvania 13 April 1937, New York

Nagasaki - QUARTET

Hotel Pennsylvania   Mutual   15 April 1937, New York

Hallelujah!
Good-Bye (theme)

"CAMEL CARAVAN"   CBS   27 April 1937, New York

Nagasaki - QUARTET
Roll 'Em

"MAKE BELIEVE BALLROOM"   WNEW   29 April 1937, New York

Oh, Lady Be Good! - TRIO (first two bars clipped)
I've Found A New Baby
Good-Bye (theme)
(See text this date for "Minnie The Moocher's Wedding Day.")

Hotel Pennsylvania   Mutual   29 April 1937, New York

'Cause My Baby Says It's So (arr JM)
Mr. Ghost Goes To Town
There's A Lull In My Life - voc Peg LaCentra
Sometimes I'm Happy

"CAMEL CARAVAN"   CBS   4 May 1937, New York

I Want To Be Happy
Never In A Million Years - voc Peg LaCentra

"CAMEL CARAVAN"   CBS   11 May 1937, New York

Alexander's Ragtime Band
Sweet Sue-Just You - QUARTET
Peckin' (Benny cites Harry James)

"CAMEL CARAVAN"   CBS   18 May 1937, New York

Jam Session
Big John Special

"CAMEL CARAVAN"   CBS   25 May 1937, New York

I'm Hatin' This Waitin' Around - voc Peg LaCentra
Avalon - QUARTET

"CAMEL CARAVAN"   CBS   1 June 1937, New York

Madhouse (n/c)
They All Laughed - voc Peg LaCentra
L'Heure Bleu (The Hour Of Parting) (This arrangement not Sauter's, not now extant.)

"CAMEL CARAVAN"   CBS   8 June 1937, New York

Marie - QUARTET

"CAMEL CARAVAN"   CBS   7 September 1937, Palomar Ballroom, Los Angeles

I Surrender, Dear - Red Norvo, vib, w/orch. (intro only)
So Rare - voc Martha Tilton

"CAMEL CARAVAN"   CBS   14 September 1937, Pan American Casino, Dallas

Don't You Know Or Don't You Care? - QUARTET
Bugle Call Rag

"CAMEL CARAVAN"   CBS   28 September 1937, Cleveland

St. Louis Blues
Me, Myself And I - voc Martha Tilton
I'm Getting Sentimental Over You - TRIO (complete)
Wrappin' It Up
That Old Feeling - voc Martha Tilton
Caravan
Good-Bye (theme)

"CAMEL CARAVAN"   CBS   5 October 1937, Baltimore

In The Shade Of The Old Apple Tree
Honeysuckle Rose
Limehouse Blues - QUARTET
Loch Lomond - voc Martha Tilton, Benny Goodman
One O'Clock Jump

"CAMEL CARAVAN"   CBS   12 October 1937, New York

Satan Takes A Holiday
Let's Have Another Cigarette - voc Martha Tilton (n/c)
Ciribiribin
Roses In December - TRIO
I Got Rhythm - QUARTET

"CAMEL CARAVAN"   CBS   19 October 1937, New York

Roll 'Em
Pop-Corn Man - voc Martha Tilton
At The Darktown Strutters' Ball

"CAMEL CARAVAN"   CBS   26 October 1937, New York

Once In A While - voc Martha Tilton
Life Goes To A Party
In A Mist - p solo, Jess Stacy

"CAMEL CARAVAN"   CBS   2 November 1937, New York

After You've Gone - QUARTET, plus Dave Newman, Emilio Caceres, v's
Farewell, My Love - voc Martha Tilton
Vieni, Vieni - QUARTET (ending only, following news break)
(See also 30 November 1937 "Camel Caravan.")

Hotel Pennsylvania   CBS   3 November 1937, New York

If It's The Last Thing I Do - voc Martha Tilton (n/c)
Liza - QUARTET
Camel Hop
Bob White - voc Martha Tilton
Good-Bye (theme)

Hotel Pennsylvania   CBS   5 November 1937, New York

Vieni, Vieni

"CAMEL CARAVAN"   CBS   9 November 1937, New York

Blue Skies
Once In A While - TRIO
China Boy - Emilio Caceres Trio, orch. in coda
I'm A Ding Dong Daddy (From Dumas) - QUARTET
Blossoms On Broadway - voc Martha Tilton
Life Goes To A Party
Good-Bye (theme)

Hotel Pennsylvania   CBS   17 November 1937, New York

Once In A While - TRIO
Good-Bye (mid-b'cast theme)
Sweet Stranger (n/c)
Vieni, Vieni
I've Hitched My Wagon To A Star - voc Martha Tilton
If It's The Last Thing I Do - voc Martha Tilton

Hotel Pennsylvania   CBS   24 November 1937, New York

You Showed Me The Way - voc Martha Tilton
Big John Special

"CAMEL CARAVAN"   CBS   30 November 1937, New York

When It's Sleepy Time Down South
China Boy - TRIO
*   The Lady Is A Tramp - voc Martha Tilton
*   (Not in log; likely from 2 November 1937 "Camel Caravan.")*

"CAMEL CARAVAN"   CBS   21 December 1937, New York

Someday, Sweetheart - TRIO
One O'Clock Jump
Vibraphone Blues - voc Lionel Hampton - QUARTET
Bei Mir Bist Du Schon - voc Martha Tilton

Hotel Pennsylvania   CBS   25 December 1937, New York

Liza - QUARTET
I Wanna Be In Winchell's Column - voc Martha Tilton

(NOTE: An uninscribed disc defies identification of its date/locale source. This Goodman-Wilson-Krupa performance is likely—but not certainly—from the year 1937. If so, suggested possibilities are the "Camel Caravan" broadcast of 16 February, or a CBS sustaining broadcast from the Hotel Pennsylvania of 24 November.)

? 1937 ?

Nobody's Sweetheart - TRIO

"CAMEL CARAVAN"   CBS   4 January 1938, New York

Swing Low, Sweet Chariot

"CAMEL CARAVAN"   CBS   11 January 1938, New York

Solid Mama
Body And Soul - TRIO
Let That Be A Lesson To You - voc Martha Tilton
Dizzy Spells - QUARTET
Don't Be That Way

"CAMEL CARAVAN"   CBS   18 January 1938, New York

Good-Bye (theme)

"CAMEL CARAVAN"   CBS   25 January 1938, New York

Liza - QUARTET
Bugle Call Rag
Good-Bye (theme)

"SATURDAY NIGHT SWING CLUB"   CBS   29 January 1938, New York

Avalon - QUARTET
Where Or When - TRIO

"CAMEL CARAVAN"   CBS   8 March 1938, New York

Ti-Pi-Tin
'S Wonderful - voc Martha Tilton
Always And Always - TRIO (Goodman, Wilson, Hampton - d)
I've Found A New Baby
oooOO-OH Boom! - voc Martha Tilton
Sweet Georgia Brown - QUARTET (Goodman, Hampton, Wilson, poss. Jo Jones, d)
King Porter Stomp

"CAMEL CARAVAN"   CBS   15 March 1938, New York

Don't Be That Way (feat. Hampton, d)
Sweet Sue-Just You
Lullaby In Rhythm (announced as, "Honey Chile")
The World Is Waiting For The Sunrise - QUARTET (unknown d)
Serenade To The Stars - voc Martha Tilton (arr ES)
Ti-Pi-Tin

Hotel Pennsylvania   CBS   15 March 1938, New York

I Got Rhythm - QUARTET (unknown d) (n/c - 24 bars missing)

Hotel Pennsylvania   CBS   19 March 1938, New York

I Love To Whistle - voc Martha Tilton (arr ES) (n/c - intro excised)
Sweet As A Song - voc Martha Tilton
Oh, Lady Be Good! (extended 2-part performance)
(NOTE: This was Dave Tough's first night with the band.)

"CAMEL CARAVAN"   CBS   22 March 1938, New York

Love Me Or Leave Me
I've Got To Sing - Bea Lillie, comedy voc
If I Could Be With You (One Hour Tonight)
One O'Clock Jump ("Two O'Clock" version)

Hotel Pennsylvania   CBS   26 March 1938, New York

Sugar - QUARTET
Roll 'Em (extended performance)
Ti-Pi-Tin

Hotel Pennsylvania   CBS   2 April 1938, New York

Ciribiribin
Blue Skies
Lullaby In Rhythm (announced as, "Honey Chile")

"THE EDDIE CANTOR PROGRAM"   CBS   4 April 1938, New York

I'm A Ding Dong Daddy (From Dumas) - QUARTET
(NOTE: Program occasionally announced as, "Eddie Cantor's Camel Caravan.")

Hotel Pennsylvania   Mutual   7 April 1938, New York

Lullaby In Rhythm
After You've Gone - TRIO
Please Be Kind - voc Martha Tilton
Don't Be That Way - QUARTET
How'd Ya Like To Love Me? - voc Martha Tilton (arr FH)
Clarinet Marmalade - to station break

Hotel Pennsylvania   10 April 1938, New York

King Porter Stomp
Sweet Sue-Just You
I Let A Song Go Out Of My Heart - voc Martha Tilton (n/c)

Hotel Pennsylvania   CBS   16 April 1938, New York

How'd Ya Like To Love Me? - voc Martha Tilton
Melancholy Baby
Lullaby In Rhythm (n/c - intro excised)
That Feeling Is Gone (n/c - ends before vocal)
Big John Special
Dizzy Spells - QUARTET
Serenade To The Stars - voc Martha Tilton
I Can't Give You Anything But Love, Baby

Hotel Pennsylvania   CBS   23 April 1938, New York

Always

"CAMEL CARAVAN"   CBS   3 May 1938, Boston

I Let A Song Go Out Of My Heart - voc Martha Tilton

"CAMEL CARAVAN"   CBS   10 May 1938, New York

At A Perfume Counter
I Must Have That Man - p duet, Stacy, Wilson
Joseph, Joseph - voc Martha Tilton
I Married An Angel - voc Martha Tilton (first time on air)

Roseland Ballroom   Mutual   13 May 1938, New York

Shine On, Harvest Moon
(I've Been) Saving Myself For You - voc Martha Tilton (arr ES)

"CAMEL CARAVAN"   CBS   24 May 1938, Boston

Cowboy From Brooklyn - voc Martha Tilton
Oh, Lady Be Good! - duet: Stacy, p; Wilson, harpsichord

Footguard Hall   CBS   26 May 1938, Hartford, CT

Sweet Sue-Just You
Melancholy Baby
I'm A Ding Dong Daddy (From Dumas) - QUARTET

"CAMEL CARAVAN"   CBS   19 July 1938, New York

You Leave Me Breathless - voc Martha Tilton
Good-Bye (theme)
(NOTE: Goodman on vacation, this broadcast)

Steel Pier   Mutual   20 August 1938, Atlantic City

House Hop
Dizzy Spells - QUARTET
I Never Knew
Where Or When - TRIO
Love Me Or Leave Me
Music, Maestro, Please - voc Martha Tilton

Coliseum   CBS   31 August 1938, Detroit

Russian Lullaby
Blue Interlude - voc Martha Tilton (n/c)
At Sundown
Dear Old Southland
Honeysuckle Rose (n/c - intro clipped)

Coliseum   CBS   1 September 1938, Detroit

I Know That You Know
Melancholy Baby
- one chorus, unidentified pop tune
I Can't Give You Anything But Love, Baby
Sweet Sue-Just You
(NOTE change in locale from entry in Legacy, same b'cast)

"CAMEL CARAVAN"   CBS   20 September 1938, Kansas City

Good-Bye - theme, in its entirety

Aragon Ballroom   Mutual   10 October 1938, Chicago

Sing You Sinners
Wrappin' It Up

Aragon Ballroom   station WGN   12 October 1938, Chicago

'S Wonderful - QUARTET
I Never Knew
Nobody's Sweetheart - TRIO (Goodman, Wilson, Hampton—d)
The Yam (arr ES) - to signoff

"CAMEL CARAVAN"   CBS   18 October 1938, Palace Theater, Milwaukee

Who's Sorry Now? (arr JM)
Have You Forgotten So Soon? - voc Martha Tilton - QUARTET
I Never Knew
You're Lovely, Madame - voc Martha Tilton
I'm A Ding Dong Daddy (From Dumas) - QUARTET
What Goes On Here In My Heart? - voc Martha Tilton (arr JM)
Alexander's Ragtime Band - clarinet quintet w/orch.

"CAMEL CARAVAN"   CBS   25 October 1938, New York

My Reverie - voc Martha Tilton

"CAMEL CARAVAN"   CBS   1 November 1938, New York

Alexander's Ragtime Band
Dance Of The Russian Peasant - Dave Rubinoff, v, w/orch.
Reverie - Dave Rubinoff, v, w/orch.

Waldorf-Astoria   CBS   2 November 1938, New York

Always
At Sundown
Madhouse
What Goes On Here In My Heart? - voc Martha Tilton
Body And Soul - TRIO
Sweet Sue - Just You
My Reverie - voc Martha Tilton
Good-Bye (theme)

Waldorf-Astoria   3 November 1938, New York

I'll Always Be In Love With You - voc Martha Tilton
What Have You Got That Gets Me? - voc Martha Tilton
Oh, Lady Be Good! - TRIO
Blue Interlude - voc Martha Tilton

"CAMEL CARAVAN"   CBS   8 November 1938, New York

A-Tisket, A-Tasket (n/c)
What Have You Got That Gets Me? - voc Martha Tilton
Heart And Soul - voc Martha Tilton

(NOTE: Lack of program logs for the "Camel Caravan" broadcasts of 15 and 22 November 1938 makes it impossible to prove Martha Tilton missed both of them. However, there seem enough extant performances from each to suggest she had a two-week hiatus, and that Mildred Bailey and actor John Boles filled in for her.)

"CAMEL CARAVAN"   CBS   15 November 1938, New York

All Of Me
From The Land Of Sky Blue Water - voc Mildred Bailey
Don't Be That Way - voc Mildred Bailey - QUARTET
Good-Bye (theme)

"CAMEL CARAVAN"   CBS   22 November 1938, New York

Ciribiribin
Waitin' At The Gate For Katie - voc John Boles
One Alone - voc John Boles
Dizzy Spells - QUARTET
Farewell Blues

"CAMEL CARAVAN"   CBS   6 December 1938, New York

Smiles
At The Darktown Strutters' Ball
Pick-A-Rib - QUARTET

"CAMEL CARAVAN"   CBS   13 December 1938, New York

Three O'Clock In The Morning - clarinet duet, Goodman, Ken Murray
The Blues In My Flat - QUARTET
My Heart Belongs To Daddy - feat. Ziggy Elman, tpt
Blues In My Heart - QUARTET

"FITCH BANDWAGON"   CBS   18 December 1938, New York

Smoke House (Rhythm)
Bach Goes To Town
Good-Bye (theme)
(NOTE: Broadcast may have emanated from the Waldorf-Astoria)

"CAMEL CARAVAN"   CBS   20 December 1938, New York

I Have Eyes - voc Martha Tilton
Some Of These Days - TRIO: Goodman, clt; Phil Baker, acc; Don Budge, d.

Waldorf-Astoria   prob. Mutual   21 December 1938, New York

Clarinet Marmalade
Bach Goes To Town
The World Is Waiting For The Sunrise - TRIO
Deep In A Dream - voc Martha Tilton (n/c)
Wrappin' It Up
(NOTE: Announcer identifies himself as MELVIN Allen.)

Waldorf-Astoria   Mutual   22 December 1938, New York

Always
Hot Foot Shuffle
Stompin' At The Savoy - QUARTET
Life Goes To A Party
They Say - voc Martha Tilton (n/c)
*   *This Can't Be Love - voc Martha Tilton (arr JM) (not in log)*
*   *Farewell Blues (not in log)*
(Note corrected arranger credit for "This Can't Be Love.")

"CAMEL CARAVAN"   CBS   27 December 1938, New York

My Blue Heaven
Deep In A Dream - voc Martha Tilton
Opus 1/2 - QUARTET
I Cried For You - feat. Dave Matthews, as (arr JM)
Ode To A Cement Mixer - feat. Joe Venuti, v
I Know That You Know - TRIO
Smoke House (Rhythm)
Good-Bye (theme)

(NOTE: Comment preceding the Columbia air checks album's track of "Roll 'Em" (Legacy, "February 1938, Pittsburgh," page 82) is still applicable; date and locale of this performance have not been determined. Similarly, discussion preceding the WNEW broadcast of "I Know That You Know" (Legacy, "poss. July 6, 1938," page 88) still obtains. Savory believes a somewhat later date in 1938 may be more nearly correct.)

(NOTE: Next two "Camel Caravan" broadcasts are from the Open Air Bandstand, Treasure Island, Golden Gate Exposition.)

"CAMEL CARAVAN"   NBC   8 July 1939, San Francisco

If I Didn't Care - voc Louise Tobin
Wait 'Til The Sun Shines, Nellie - voc, announcer Bert Parks

"CAMEL CARAVAN"   NBC   15 July 1939, San Francisco

Boy Meets Horn - feat. Chris Griffin, tpt (complete)
Well, All Right! (Tonight's The Night) - voc Benny Goodman, Louise Tobin (arr FH)
I Surrender, Dear - QUARTET
Roll 'Em

"CAMEL CARAVAN"   NBC   5 August 1939, Hollywood Bowl, Hollywood

Bolero

(NOTE: All remaining "Camel Caravan" broadcasts are probably from the Waldorf-Astoria.)

Waldorf-Astoria   CBS   22 November 1939, New York

Spring Song
Swingtime In The Rockies
Flying Home - SEXTET
All The Things You Are - voc Kay Foster (arr EdSau)
Smiles
Absence Makes The Heart Grow Fonder (arr FH)
Good-Bye (theme)

"CAMEL CARAVAN"   NBC   2 December 1939, New York

Scatter-Brain - voc Mildred Bailey
Peace, Brother! - voc Mildred Bailey

Waldorf-Astoria   4 December 1939, New York

Honeysuckle Rose - SEXTET

Waldorf-Astoria   6 December 1939, New York

In The Mood
Oh, Johnny! Oh, Johnny! Oh! - voc Kay Foster
Roast Turkey Stomp (later, "Seven Come Eleven") - SEXTET
Cherokee (arr EdSau)

"CAMEL CARAVAN"   NBC   9 December 1939, New York

Bolero
I Didn't Know What Time It Was - voc Mildred Bailey
Pick-A-Rib - SEXTET

Waldorf-Astoria   21 December 1939, New York

Remember
Honeysuckle Rose - SEXTET
Swingtime In The Rockies
Good-Bye (theme)

"CAMEL CARAVAN"   NBC   30 December 1939, New York

One O'Clock Jump (complete)
(Benny introduces "Camel Caravan" replacement Bob Crosby)
Good-Bye (theme)

(NOTE: Neither the title nor the sponsor of Alec Templeton's weekly radio program, next, was inscribed on the disc by Bill Savory. He does recall that Benny was so enamored of his duet with the impish Englishman that he contemplated releasing it, coupled with **Improvisation** (Legacy, page 154). Sadly, he never did.)

SPONSORED RADIO BROADCAST   NBC   15 January 1940, New York

Sweet Reed - DUET: Benny Goodman, clt; Alec Templeton, p.
Quintet for Clarinet and Strings - Menuetto (Mozart): Benny Goodman, clt; J. Stopak, M. Silverman, v; H. Brodkin, viola; D. Sadenberg, cel.

(NOTE: Source of the next broadcast is also unknown. Absent from the contemporary Sextet complement is Charlie Christian.)

?   16 January 1940, New York

I Got Rhythm - QUINTET

Wardman Park Hotel   2 February 1940, Washington, D.C.

Indian Summer - voc Helen Forrest
Busy As A Bee (I'm Buzz, Buzz, Buzzin') - voc Helen Forrest
Hallelujah!
Good-Bye (theme)
(NOTE: Occasion was a Georgetown University prom.)

Cocoanut Grove   22 March 1940, Los Angeles

Memories Of You - QUINTET (Charlie Christian absent)

Cocoanut Grove   5 April 1940, Los Angeles

Soft Winds - SEXTET
Cocoanut Grove (Announcer: "Now, Benny dedicates one to the ladies—Cocoanut Groove. . .!")

Cocoanut Grove   19 April 1940, Los Angeles

I Surrender, Dear - SEXTET
Wrappin' It Up

Hotel Sherman   NBC   20 July 1941, Chicago

Perfidia (Tonight) - voc Helen Forrest
Tuesday At Ten
Soft As Spring - voc Helen Forrest
Good Evenin', Good Lookin'! (n/c)
Let The Doorknob Hitcha - voc Cootie Williams

(NOTE: Benny's was but one of 40 orchestras broadcast in a marathon 12-hour Coca Cola "Spotlight Bands" special presentation this Christmas Day. Ambient sound suggests his locale might have been a service camp rather than New York City.)

"SPOTLIGHT BANDS"   Blue Network   25 December 1942, unknown locale

Roll 'Em
Rose Room - QUINTET

(NOTE: On one of what may have been a series of programs, titled, "CBS After Dark Dance Session," Benny and the band were broadcast from the New Yorker. The specific date is unknown.)

"CBS AFTER DARK DANCE SESSION"   CBS   November 1943, New York

Let's Dance (theme)
Down South Camp Meetin'
A Journey To A Star - voc Ray Dorey
Mission To Moscow
I'm Bidin' My Time
Let's Dance (station break)
Bugle Call Rag

TAPES

After serving in World War II, and with the Big Band Era rapidly coming to its close, Bill recorded few broadcasts for his own pleasure. (The Goodman air checks he transcribed need no further exposition, for all are included in Legacy.) In future—after Navy duty in Korea—he would tape Goodman performances as a professional, employed for that specific purpose. His initial commission is a major contribution to the Goodman oeuvre, and warrants background:

The occasion was the first concert of the reconstituted Goodman orchestra, the beginning of the planned six-week 1953 tour. In fact the engagement was an out-of-town rehearsal, in accord with Benny's lifelong insistence on preparedness. More, he was having difficulty with his own playing, in reverting to the embouchure he'd always used, prior to studying with Reginald Kell. He not only wanted to hear how the band played, but he had to hear how he performed. Besides—thinking of the 1938 Carnegie concert—it might turn out to be something special. He therefore hired his favorite engineer to tape the concert.

Bill packed his modified ElectroVoice microphones, a pre-amp/line-amp mixer of his own design, and a massive Ampex 351P (monaural) recorder, drove them to New Hampshire on a rainy night in April. He soon had a problem with Benny: Mistakenly convinced that a single overhead mike was used to record his 1938 Carnegie concert (actually, there were three), he insisted that the solo mike be removed. Result, Helen Ward's vocals are but dimly audible on tape, courtesy of the p. a. system . . . which intermittently failed during the evening. (Bill's problem now is to restore Helen's vocals, by means of ". . . a high-speed attack and release time limiter, together with a continuously-variable parametric filter . . .", whatever they are.) Withal, the overflow audience was enthusiastic, Benny and the band both played well, and a good time was had by all. And importantly, the single overhead omnidirectional mike captured the instrumentals ". . . in exquisite detail, you can hear the guys breathing. . ." on the 15 ips tapes.

This unique recording—the sole 1953 concert taped while Benny was present—deserves release. If only the union will be reasonable about royalties, we may someday get to hear two hours' worth of history.

MANCHESTER CONCERT   10 April 1953, Carousel Ballroom, Manchester, NH

Benny Goodman, clt; Charlie Shavers, Ziggy Elman, Al Stewart, tpt; Vernon Brown, Rex Peer, tbn; Clint Neagley, Willie Smith, as; George Auld, Sol Schlinger, ts; Teddy Wilson, p; Steve Jordan, g; Israel Crosby, b; Gene Krupa, d. Helen Ward, voc.

TRIO: Goodman, Wilson, Krupa

. . .warmup, introduction
Let's Dance (theme)
Down South Camp Meeting
Blue Room
Sometimes I'm Happy
Sugar Foot Stomp
Don't Be That Way
(What Can I Say, Dear) After I Say I'm Sorry - voc Helen Ward (arr FH)
What A Little Moonlight Can Do - voc Helen Ward
Always
Bugle Call Rag
I'll Never Say "Never Again" Again - voc Helen Ward
Roll 'Em
And The Angels Sing - voc Helen Ward
Milenberg Joys (arr FH)
Cherry
Ridin' High
China Boy - TRIO
Memories Of You - TRIO
Nice Work If You Can Get It - TRIO
The World Is Waiting For The Sunrise - TRIO
The Glory Of Love - voc Helen Ward
Alexander's Ragtime Band
Wolverine Blues
'Deed I Do - voc Helen Ward
Blue Skies
It's Been So Long - voc Helen Ward
The Dixieland Band - voc Helen Ward
You Turned The Tables On Me - voc Helen Ward
(I Would Do) Anything For You
Sing, Sing, Sing

*

As stated earlier, some of Bill's acetates and tapes are housed in the Savorys' property in southern California. No, make that "were" housed: The 17 January 1994 earthquake that struck the area damaged their home and garage, causing the recordings to be removed to bonded storage while repairs are in progress. Only property owners are permitted access to the warehouse, preventing Bill's tenant from forwarding the transcriptions to Virginia. What Goodman broadcasts they include is unknown, and thus the foregoing listings are unavoidably incomplete at this time.

It is idle to speculate what Bill's acetates may add to the listing. But although they cannot be detailed, Bill is certain that two sets of tapes are in that warehouse. One set embraces two shows at Ciro's, Hollywood, September 1960, possibly two hours' worth of performances by that excellent group. At Benny's insistence, and over producer Irving Townsend's protests, Bill recorded this Columbia session as Benny's "personal engineer." Whether Bill's tapes of these shows include tracks on Columbia's release (Legacy, page 235) won't be known until comparisons can be made. However, they may not, for two reasons: One, Bill is positive that Jack Sperling played drums on the shows he recorded, and that Jerry Dodgion was not present. And two, Benny made a sidebar agreement with Townsend: He, Benny, would pay all of the engineering costs, and would own the "Savory" tapes, if for any reason those tapes were unsatisfactory. No one now knows how that turned out.

The second set of tapes consists of performances from the May/June 1961 engagement at Disneyland, approximately three hours' worth. Again, Bill was on hand as Benny's personal engineer for this Westinghouse production. And once more, comparisons will have to be made when the tapes are available to determine if any of their tracks duplicate those on the Westinghouse souvenir LP/telecast, and the delayed KTTV-TV telecast (both, Legacy, page 237). Bill recalls that a fireworks display was contemporaneous with the beginning of the band's stint, may be audible on the tapes.

A discographer's work is never done. Damn that earthquake.

GOODMAN ARRANGEMENTS

In 1988 Yale University published a massive catalogue of the more than 1,500 arrangements in its Benny Goodman Archives. Of these, 26 were donated by Benny to Yale the year before he died. Fifteen were acquired at auction (Sotheby's, London) in 1989. All the rest were bequeathed to Yale under the provisions of Benny's will in 1986.

The principal section of the work lists the swing band and small group manuscripts alphabetically by title, detailing—where available—the name of the arranger, the date of the chart, and its score, individual parts and key, plus miscellaneous notes. A goodly number are neither signed nor dated. But because of proven examples of handwriting and other clues, confident ascriptions to some of these have been made. Still, 240-odd out of a total of approximately 1,475 in the big band/small group category remain uncredited.

(Note that there are not 1,475 different **tunes.** For example, there are five arrangements of **Don't Be That Way.** Usually, such duplicates are later revisions, adding a fourth trumpet, a third trombone, a fifth saxophone, etc., to the original. And over time, Benny commissioned different arrangers to chart the same tune.)

Following the main section are two similarly-structured separate categories. One is for 32 "orchestral arrangements" (those including strings); the second is devoted to the complete sets of arrangements for both the 1958 and 1959 "Swing Into Spring" television programs.

The catalogue concludes with two useful compilations. The first names the arrangers alphabetically, credits assignable charts to them, alphabetically by tune title. The final section details the dated charts chronologically, alphabetically by tune title for each year.

Titled **The Benny Goodman Papers—MSS 53,** hard bound, 8 1/2 × 11, 318 pp, the catalogue is available by purchase from Yale University. All inquiries should be directed to: Yale Music Library, P.O. Box 5469 Yale Station, New Haven, CT 06520.

NOTE: A revision to the catalogue adds an addendum, the 15 arrangements purchased at auction in 1989. Five of them are listed—in part—in the initial press run; 10 are additions.

Not listed in the catalogue (save for some duplicates) are 57 arrangements "on deposit" at Yale in the Benny Goodman Archives. They remain the property of the depositor, who acquired them in incredible fashion:

Picnicking with relatives on a Long Island beach in the 1950s, a young girl saw a man get out of a "big white convertible," throw a batch of papers into a dumpster, drive off. Curiosity moved her to rummage in the trash, find the discards—57 original, handwritten arrangements, and a half-dozen fragments. More than a third of them were signed: Eddy Sauter, Danny Rose, Joe Lipman (note spellings), and Spud Murphy, James R. Mundy, Johnny Thompson, Red Kent, Harry James, et al. Some few have the sidemen's names pencilled in on their parts; e.g., Spud Murphy's 14 May 1935 **I'm In Love All Over Again** specifies "PeeWee," "Ralph," "Jerry," "Red," "Jack," "Hymie," "Toots," "Arthur," "Dick," "Frankie," "Al," "Harry" and "Gene." And some of them include comments— Benny's ?—per the unsigned chart of **Carry On,** which has parts for brass, reeds and drums only: "Give us some fucking rhythm."

Thirty-odd years later, now the proprietor of a book store, the lucky lady wrote Benny, asked whether he or the author would be interested in her treasure trove. Several months later (typical), Benny gave the letter to the author, asked him to "check this out, willya,

Russ?" He did; phone calls and correspondence elicited their provenance and authenticity, and an intimation that they'd be "available." Was Benny interested in buying them?

No, Benny was not. Besides, huffily, "They're mine; they belong to me. Why should I buy them, she should give them to me." The author then debated whether to make an offer for the arrangements on his own. But thinking to do so would jeopardize his relationship with Benny—if ever The Man found out—he decided not to. He's been sorry ever since.

The Archives include a list of these arrangements. Those interested in purchasing the catalogue might request a copy of the list.

Not in the Archives at Yale are approximately 250 arrangements Benny donated to the New York Public Library in the years 1979–1984. Some duplicate those in the Archives, and some are "shared" by the Archives and the Library: one has the score, the other the individual parts, of a given arrangement. "Shared" manuscripts are of course listed in the catalogue, but the majority of those in the Library's repository at Lincoln Center are not.

Circumstances attendant to Benny's donations to the NYPL are worth recounting:

In the late 1970s Benny's tax accountant recommended to him that he seek write-offs against his considerable income. Discussion eventually centered on charitable donations, then targeted Benny's forty-odd years' accumulation of arrangements. They seemed to qualify under federal tax laws, and were attractive from several standpoints: They were valuable; they would be welcomed by such institutions as public and collegiate libraries; Benny no longer had use for the great majority of them; and there were so many that the process could go on for years.

Several steps were necessary to effect the submissions. First, Benny had to find the manuscripts he wished to donate. Many had recently been brought from a rented storage facility at 50th and Broadway; they were dumped into five-drawer filing cabinets in his office at 200 East 66th Street, mixed in haphazardly with those already at hand. An inventory list of those—at one time—in the rental property, and an outdated Rolodex file of those supposedly kept in the office were utterly useless. So, when the spirit moved him, Benny simply opened a file drawer at random, flipped through the contents, pulled out whatever struck his fancy, and piled them on a desk.

Next, a list had to be prepared that detailed each arrangement, citing title, arranger, key, score, parts and provenance (label and catalog number of a Goodman recording, if one had been made, date of the chart), and the tune's composer(s). Benny would name the arranger (if the manuscript was unsigned), determine the key. Office aides would do the rest. Frank Driggs, then Loren Schoenberg, fleshed out the first three submissions; the author completed the balance.

Finally, a dollar value had to be assigned to each manuscript. Benny made those decisions. Those submissions that the author prepared ranged in price from a low of $1,500 for Joe Lip(p)man's 1961 arrangement of **Song Of India,** to $7,500 for Morton Gould's orchestral **I Got Rhythm.** Then Benny's valuations were certified by a noted rare-book dealer and antiquary, now deceased, who happened to be a good friend.

All went swimmingly until the U.S. Internal Revenue Service began to take exception to the values assigned to the arrangements. This caused a review of all the submissions, and led to downsizing the valuations and additional back taxes. During negotiations with the IRS and Benny's attorneys, Benny told the author that it could cost him as much as $50,000 in back taxes and penalties.

*

The Benny Goodman Papers supplements arranger credits cited in Legacy. The arrangers are:

Albam, Manny (MA)
Bassman, George (GB)
* Byers, Billy (BB)
Clayton, Buck (BuC)
Cohn, Al (AC)
Evans, Gil (GE)
Henderson, Fletcher (FH)
Jenkins, Gordon (GJ)
Karlin, Fred (FK)
Kincaide, Deane (DK)
Kirkpatrick, Don (DoK)
Levant, Oscar (OL)
Lip(p)man, Joe (JL)
Martin, Skippy (SkM)
Masso, George (GM)
* May, Billy (BM)
Mundy, Jimmy (JM)
Murphy, Spud (SM)
Newsom(e), Tommy (TN)

O'Farrill, Chico (C O'F)
* Pleis, Jack (JP)
Powell, Mel (MP)
Roumanis, George (GR)
Sampson, Edgar (ES)
Sauter, Eddie (EdSau)
Schutt, Arthur (AS)
Stegmeyer, Bill (BS)
Thompson, Johnny (JT)
Todd, Tommy (TT)
* Valentine, Jerry (JV)
Van Lake, Turk (TVL)
* Wayne, Chuck (CW)
Wilder, Alec (AW)
Wilkinson, Ralph (RW)
Williams, George (GW)
Williams, Mary Lou (MLW)
Woode, Henri (HW)

(An asterisk precedes the names of those arrangers due first-time credit.)

*

Listed below by tune titles are renditions in Legacy that lack arranger ascriptions. Credits are based on the Yale publication. Additional arranger designations are in the text of this work. Relevant pages in Legacy are cited.

Absence Makes The Heart Grow Fonder   FH   106
All The Things You Are   EdSau   107
Anything Goes   SM   48, 52
Begin The Beguine   FH   97
Benny's Bugle (orch)   SkM   120
Blame It On My Youth   OL   47
Blue Skies (1946 voc version)   JM   169
Blue Views   CW   193
Bye Bye Blues   MLW   192
Carioca   JP   175
Cherokee   EdSau   106
Clap Your Hands   FH   97
Come Rain Or Come Shine   RW   169
Complainin'   EdSau   147
Cookin' One Up   prob. MP   192
Could Be   JM   95
Could You Pass In Love?   ES   88
Day I Let You Get Away, The   JM   56
Delia's (ms: Delia) Gone   GE   215

Don't Take Your Love From Me   EdSau   130
Drip Drop   JT   142
East Of The Sun   JL   54
East Of The Sun   GR   238
Egg Head   CO'F   198
Embraceable You   EdSau   123
Flying Home (orch)   SkM   122
For Me And My Gal   JT   140
G'Bye Now   SkM   121
Girl From Ipanema (ms: Ipenema), The   TN   247
Goodnight My Love   JM   62
How'd Ya (ms: How'dja) Like To Love Me?   FH   84
How Sweet You Are   EdSau   148
Hundred Years From Today, A   AS   41
I Can't Believe That You're In Love With Me   SM   48
I Got Rhythm (orch)   FH   69
I Hate To Lose You (I'm So Used To You Now)   FH   190
I Just Couldn't Take It, Baby   AS   41
I Love To Whistle   ES   87
If It's True   EdSau   125
I'll Get By   prob.   AW   128
I'm Building Up To An Awful Letdown   HW   56
I'm Growing Fonder Of You   GB   47
I'm In A Crying Mood   FH   190
Indiana ("Donna Lee")   MLW   192
It All Comes Back To Me Now   EdSau   119
It's Wonderful   FH   78
Jubilee   GW   223
Just An Idea   MLW   197
Lady Who Didn't Believe In Love, The   DoK   139
Lambeth Walk, The   JM   90
Lamp Is Low, The   FH   100
Little Man Who Wasn't There, The   FH   104
Love For Sale   JL   241
Lover Man   MP   195
Lullaby Of Broadway, The   GJ   48
Ma Belle Marguerite   CO'F   195
Mandy Is Two   EdSau   135
March Of The Swing Parade   ES   90
Memphis Blues   FH   82
Merry-Go-Round Broke Down, The   JM   72
My Best Wishes   ES   88
My Heart Tells Me   EdSau   147
My Ideal   JT   154
My Last Goodbye   EdSau   106
My Prayer   EdSau   107

MEDLEY, Ennis vocals   DK   221, 223

Nearness Of You, The   TVL or AC   227
Night In Manhattan   FH   59
Oh, Lady Be Good! (orch)   FH   74
One I Love Belongs To Somebody Else, The   GW   320
Pound Ridge (ms: Same Time Tomorrow)   SkM   123
Rockin' Chair   EdSau   108
Rosalie   prob. BuC   178
Rosie The Riveter   EdSau   141
(I've Been) Saving Myself For Bill   EdSau   142
Shirley Steps Out   MP   190
Sing   GM   272
Singin' In The Rain   JM   97
Small Fry   FH   92
So Long, Farewell   FK   230
Spin A Record   CO'F   198
Spring Is Here   MA or AC   227
Stolen Love   BM   247
Strike Up The Band   BS   235
Sweet As A Song   FH   83
Sweet Georgia Brown (orch)   EdSau   148
Sweet Sue-Just You (orch)   FH   85
Swinging (ms: Swingin') A Dream   FH   107
Swingin' Down The Lane   FH   96
Tappin' The Barrel   AS   41
Thanks A Million   JM   55
That Foolish Feeling   JM   68
That Naughty Waltz   JM   73
This Time It's Real   FH   88
This Year's Kisses   JM   64
Ti-Pi-Tin   ES   83
Too Marvelous For Words   GW   320
Truckin'   FH   55
Twilight In Turkey   JM   72
We'll Meet Again   MP   135
What Goes On Here In My Heart?   JM   87
When Yuba Plays The Rhumba On The Tuba   JM   98
Where Do I Go From You?   FH   112
Who Can I Turn To?   EdSau   130
Why Don't We Do This More Often?   JV   198
Yam, The   ES   90
You Didn't Know Me From Adam   JL   47
You Turned The Tables On Me   MLW   192
You Was Right, Baby   FH   or   ES   (arr. unassigned)   164
You Went To My Head   ES   85
You'd Be So Nice To Come Home To   EdSau   or   FH   (2 arr's)   142
You're A Sweetheart   FH   79
You're Always There   BB   198
You're The Top   GB   48

1958, 1959 "Swing Into Spring": Buster Davis contributed to the vocal arrangements of both programs.

Alternatives, corrections, oddities:

Behave Yourself (small group)   FH   190
Don't Wake Up My Heart   FH, not JM   87
Let's Dance, 1934 original, signed "Sammy Bassman"
Smo-o-o-oth One, A (orch)   SkM,   not   EdSau   123
This Can't Be Love   JM, not JL (typo) 92
Undecided   only extant arr, EdSau   93
You Go To My Head   EdSau, not ES   89

GOODMAN FILMS, VIDEOTAPES

There is active and growing interest among collectors in Benny Goodman's motion pictures and his appearances on television. To gauge the extent of both held privately, the author consulted with Bob Bierman, Ken Crawford, Oren Jacoby and Don Wolff of the United States; Eric Gee, Canada; Arend Buck, Germany; Yasuo Segami, Japan; and other correspondents.

Singly or severally, those named above, plus the author, have the following,

FILMS:

All films listed in Legacy, page 324, either complete or Goodman sequences from them, some on videotape. Commercial videotapes of some films are cited in the text of this work. Others include "Upbeat In Music," Embassy/Nelson Home Video 01725; and "One A.M.," in the "Charlie Chaplin Cavalcade," details vague. Newsreel and TV news clips spanning decades, from the 1938 Carnegie concert through Benny's demise, abound. Excerpts from both the movies and news sources are in many Goodman- or jazz-related TV programs.

Some films not listed in Legacy are also extant. Those below preceded by an asterisk (*) are excerpted in 1993's, "Benny Goodman: Adventures in the Kingdom of Swing." Selected newsreel footage is noted.

* Silent 16mm film of the Pollack orchestra on Atlantic City's boardwalk, July 1928. Benny and Glenn Miller mug for the camera (Pollack's?), other band personnel remain in the background.

Vitaphone No. 1573, Dave Rubinoff's orchestra, unknown date in 1933. Included in the anthology videotape, "Heroes Of Pre-War Music Series, Rare Bands Volume 3." The 10-minute Vitaphone/Warner Bros. musical captures Benny accompanying Rubinoff in one sequence, taking a four-bar bass clarinet solo in another.

* Art Rollini's silent 16mm film of the 1937 Goodman orchestra, various locations.

Newsreel footage, silent & sound, Madison Square Garden, c. May/June 1941.

* Vido Musso's silent 16mm film of Benny's housewarming, September 1941, Pound Ridge, CT. The nine-minute, 30-second footage screens Benny, his mother, and Alice (Hammond); and Mildred Bailey, Sid Catlett, Charlie Christian, Peggy Lee, Jimmy Maxwell, Lou McGarity, Vido Musso, Clint Neagley, Red Norvo, Mel Powell, Cootie Williams, possibly Billy Butterfield and Skip Martin, and unidentified others.

Outtakes, "Upbeat In Music (March Of Time)," discovered in the Library of Congress. Filmed 16 November 1943, Hotel New Yorker, NYC.

* Army/Navy Screen Magazine "Rehearsal Time," U.S. Gov't. 35mm sound film of the Benny Goodman Quintet, c. late 1944–early 1945, uncertain location. Complete film runs less than five minutes.

* Irving Jacoby's 35mm sound/silent films of a Goodman studio recording session. See text for details, under date of 6 December 1955.

Newsreel footage, silent, the Goodman orchestra, 26 November 1956, Denham Auditorium, Vancouver, B.C. Note that Martha Tilton was the band's vocalist during its West Coast concerts, prior to its departure for the,

* Far East tour, 1956–1957, from USIS and private sources, 16mm & 35mm, sound and

silent. Full extent of this footage is unknown; Benny's Archives at Yale have a number of cans of film that are as yet undocumented.

Newsreel footage of the May 1958 European tour, including the clip with Bill Holden, 30 May 1958, reprised on the 15 June 1958 "Ed Sullivan Show."

Newsreel footage, sound & silent, the 16 January 1968 Carnegie anniversary party.

Private-source 16mm silent film, excerpts of the 18 August 1973 Saratoga Springs, NY, concert.

(There is a difference of opinion among collectors in regard to at least three Laurel & Hardy two-reelers, "Blotto," "Brats," and "Perfect Day." Commercial videotape releases of the comedies—e.g., VIDEO TREASURES SV9309, et al—have musical soundtracks that offer Goodman-like clarinet soli. A film historian says these tracks were recorded and added in 1936, when Stan and Ollie's popularity caused their early movies to be re-released; and that the original prints were sans music. Since it is highly unlikely Goodman would have anonymously recorded a soundtrack when he'd achieved national acclaim, some contend the clarinet soli cannot be his. Those who champion his participation believe the soundtracks are from the late 1920s, had been retained in Hollywood since then, and that they are not those recorded in 1936.)

Next, correspondents report videotapes of Goodman's television appearances certain to be extant; note that a few of them are also on 16mm film. "TEXT" is a reference to this work, not to Legacy.

TV / VIDEOTAPES:

Art Of Performing: 4 May 1967
Aurex Jazz Festival '80: 3 September 1980 (also on laserdisc, TOMEI(Jap) LO78-3131); 7 September 1980
Bad Segeberg Jazz Festival: 24 July 1982 (ZDF-TV telecast)
Bell Telephone Hour: 27 October 1961; 6–7 August 1966
Brussels NBC Telecast: 25–31 May 1958 (also, 16mm film)
Sid Caesar Show: 1 November 1954
Dick Cavett Show: 1 November 1979
Perry Como Show: 23 March 1957; 19 October 1957; 18 November 1959
(Merv Griffin's) Echoes Of The Big Bands: TEXT, 7 October 1985
Evening At The "Pops": 9 May 1974
Mitzi Gaynor Show: 16 March 1978
Benny Goodman: Adventures in the Kingdom of Swing: TEXT, July 1993
Benny Goodman: Let's Dance, A Musical Tribute: 7 October 1985
Benny Goodman Show: May–June 1961
Benny Goodman: Tivoli Theatre Concert: 13 March 1972 (excerpts also on videocassette, VIDJAZZ 30)
Benny Goodman Tribute: TEXT, 6 November 1986
Grammy Awards: 25 February 1986
Merv Griffin Show: 20 May 1976; 15 October 1979; 30 September 1980; 18 February 1982
John Gunther's High Road: 14–15 May 1958 (also, 16mm film)
In The Mood: 28 September 1971; see also TEXT, same date (also, 16mm film)
Jazzhus Slukefter Concert: 4 September 1981; see also TEXT, same date
Kennedy Center Honors: 5 December 1982
Rene Kollo TV Show: 5 September 1981
Monsanto Special—Benny Goodman: January 1974 (excerpts also on videocassette,

VIDJAZZ 30)
NBC Magazine: January 1981
Omnibus: 25 January 1953
Pittsburgh Concert: 3 May 1983
Pori International Jazz Festival: 16 July 1982; see also TEXT, same date
Signature: 24 November 1981
Soundstage: The World Of John Hammond: 10 September 1975 (PBS telecast)
Ed Sullivan Show: 10 February 1957; 30 May 1958; 19 June 1960 (see also TEXT, same date)
Swing Into Spring: 9 April 1958 (see also TEXT, same date); 10 April 1959 (see also TEXT, same date) (9 April 1958 also on 16mm film)
Timex All Star Swing Festival: 23 October 1972 (also on videocassette, VESTRON MA1048; and on laserdisc, LOB(Jap) LVD-521 and TOSHIBA-EMI(Jap) TOLW-3131)
Today Show: 30 October 1979
Tonight Show: 20 June 1967; 22 June 1978; 17 January 1980
"20/20" and Troy Concert: 10 November 1979
Waterloo Village Concert: 1 October 1985
Wedding Reception: 8 March 1985
Wolf Trap Telecast: 2 July 1977
World Of Benny Goodman: televised 24 January 1963 (also, 16mm film)

Noteworthy news-source Goodman telecasts include:

Carnegie Hall Rehearsal: Excerpts (sound), 27 June 1973
Carnegie Hall Concert: Excerpts (sound), 29 June 1973
Carnegie Hall Rehearsal: Excerpts (sound), 17 January 1978
Carnegie Hall Concert: Excerpts (sound), 17 January 1978
Los Angeles City Council Awards: Benny plays "Bye, Bye Blackbird," accompanied by a civic brass band. Unknown date, poss. mid-July 1979.

Three 1990s' PBS one-hour telecasts each include brief sequences involving Goodman:

Carnegie At 100: Newsreel clips, 1938 Carnegie concert; Lionel Hampton reminisces about the 1938 Carnegie concert.

John Hammond, From Bessie Smith to Bruce Springsteen: Excerpt from "Omnibus," 25 January 1953; newsreel clips, 1938 Carnegie concert.

Frank Sinatra, The Voice Of Our Time: Newsreel clip, Frank onstage at the Paramount with the Goodman orchestra, December 1942/January 1943 (silent).
(NOTE: Frequently, tracks from the Columbia album are added to silent newsreel footage of the 1938 Carnegie concert for TV programs. No sound film of that concert has ever been discovered.)

Goodman-related, if minimally: "Solo Flight," a videotape retrospective of Charlie Christian produced by Garydon Rhodes. Digitally refined, the tape is slated for commercial release by V.I.E.W. Video.

Noteworthy 1995 academic videotape: "The Life And Times of Benny Goodman." Produced by Dr. Jack Newton for his "Jazz Music In American Society" lectures at Appalachian State University. Forty minutes, photos, film, TV clips, running commentary over background music (the last not always in time sync with visual presentations). Highlight, a Soviet film (w/sound) of Benny's classical/jazz performances in Kiev, summer 1962. Via telephone, Red Norvo, Mel Powell, Art Rollini, Helen Ward and the author speak briefly about Benny.

Collectors' challenge: A 16 mm film of the "I Remember Illinois" telecast, 21 August 1967 (Legacy, page 253), is in the Chicago Public Library. To date, the library has not permitted its duplication.

Legacy errata: Latterday access to certain videotapes corrects some entries in Legacy. For example, omit Benny from the vocal credits for "Sing, Sing, Sing" in the 23 March 1957 Perry Como Show. And surely that's not Mel Powell on the 19 November 1957 Como TVer; who is that pianist? Wider dissemination of videotapes now held by relatively few collectors likely will provide further refinements.

Finally: Only one correspondent was alert enough to videotape Benny's TV promo for the three-LP Hall of Music album, televised in 1979.

The foregoing compilations of Goodman films and videotapes are in aggregate those reported extant as of December 1995. Neither list should be considered definitive, for it is probable that additions to both—especially the latter—will eventually be divulged by collectors not in our survey. The lists are offered as a guide to the growing fraternity who prize Benny's sight-and-sound performances.

MEMORABILIA PRICE GUIDE

In addition to their primary interest in his recordings, Goodman enthusiasts also collect memorabilia. Prices paid, or bids made, over the past 10 years for examples in each category are given below. Collectors are cautioned that documented provenance is the sine qua non of certain artifacts.

Arrangements: $10,000, at auction, for 15 original arrangements (scores plus parts), handwritten between 1935 and 1976. Represented are both Hendersons, Gordon Jenkins, Spud Murphy, Mel Powell, Eddie Sauter, others.

Audio tapes, air checks: Bid, $1,000 per unreleased half-hour "Camel Caravan" broadcast. Bid/paid, $200–$500 per hour, other unreleased Goodman broadcasts/telecasts, dependent upon vintage. Reel tape specified, minimum 7.5 ips, for repro.

Audio tapes, unissued studio recordings: Bid/paid per one recording, $25–$500, dependent upon vintage. Reel tape specified, minimum 7.5 ips, for repro.
   (Rare issued recordings, $10 and up per dub, usually via cassette.)

BOOKS:
The Kingdom of Swing by Benny Goodman (full title on cover), Stackpole Sons, 1939: $250, autographed, excellent condition, but sans dust jacket.
BG-Off The Record, Gaildonna Publishers, 1958 (only printing): $150, mint, with dust jacket.
BG-On The Record, Arlington House, 1969 (first press run): $75, mint, with $10 price dust jacket. (Successor printings by other publishers readily available for much less.)

Cigarette lighter: $52.50, "Metro" (Japanese), Zippo-type, unused, boxed. Has one-inch square plastic insert on face, colored red or green, "B/clt/G" logo. Given as preferred souvenir in the 1960s.

Clarinet: Benny donated an apparently unused Selmer to a New York TV station for a funds drive. It brought $2,500 at auction. It was re-sold in the '90s for $15,000. Fully documented.
   Although the rarest of Goodman memorabilia, there is an unknown number of his clarinets held by musicians unaware of their provenance. Reason: Benny donated them from time to time to conservatories such as Philadelphia's Settlement Music House, for use by indigent students.
   A present from him, the author's Selmer is one that Benny played during his "Sauter period," 1939–1941, according to an insurance record of the clarinet's serial number. It is not for sale.

Collection, recordings: $81,000, for Carl Kendziora's extensive Goodman collection, consisting of air check acetates, shellac 78s, tapes, test pressings, et alia. Absent some original issues (non-U.S. reissues substituted), rarer Goodman studio group recordings, 16-inch transcriptions. Test pressings of previously-unissued recordings, and some air checks, released on LPs.

Key chain: $25, metal, four and a half inches overall, including one-inch square logo same as on cigarette lighter, q.v. Preferred souvenir, 1960s.

Pen: $150, Tiffany & Co., sterling silver, boxed, compliments of Park Recording Company. Very few given as personal present, 1970s.

Pencil: $15, shaped as clarinet, metal and plastic, silver print on black w/Selmer identification plus "Benny, King of Swing" or "Compliments of Benny Goodman." Many given as souvenirs, 1950s on.

Personal letters: Handwritten & signed by Benny Goodman on letterhead stationery. No sales reported; those who have them are keeping them.

Photographs: Wide ask/bid/paid price range, $5–$400, dependent upon Goodman signature only or his plus band personnel, vintage. Signature(s) must be authentic.

PRINT MATERIALS: Wide bid/paid price range, dependent upon vintage, whether or not autographed. Some examples:
Life Magazine, 1 November 1937 "Life Goes To A Party" edition, good condition. $25 paid. Not autographed.
Playbill, "Swingin' The Dream" (1939), $75 paid. Not autographed.
Program, "Skills Unlimited" benefit (1973), 60 pp, bio, disco, good photos, etc., excellent condition, $30 paid. Not autographed.
Program, "The Kennedy Center Honors" (1982), massive, many photos, excellent condition, $100 asked. Not autographed.

Record jacket (with records), Columbia SL-180 "1937/38 Jazz Concert No. 2," FAKE signature, $15. Cover in fair condition, records in excellent condition.
Many collectors have one or more Goodman albums with genuine signatures. Some reported paid prices, up to $35.

Script, photocopy, assigned to Benny, 28 September 1937 "Camel Caravan," $10. Not autographed.
Many other photocopies of such memorabilia as checks, playbills/programs and the like, $5 up. Most not autographed.

Recordings: Despite an abundance of microgroove and digital reissues, original copies of rare records, especially less common alternate takes, command high prices. Some early studio group shellacs—"dime store," ME-PE-PAT, CO export, for example—as much as $500. But bargains are still out there: At Ken Crawford's 1991 collectors' "bash," Charley Braun bought five records for $7. Among them, a VG+ copy of VI 25808, "Pop-Corn Man."
Test pressings of unissued Victor's have sold for as much as $1,000. Test pressings/reference recordings of unissued Columbia's, up to $500.
Transcriptions: Acetates, unique, $500. Pressings, up to $200.

Videotapes: Ask, unique, range of $2,500–$5,000. Relatively rare, bid/paid, to $100. Commercially released, retail. Many equivalent trades among collectors, no $ involved.

NECROLOGY

Since submission of the manuscript for Legacy (1986), too many of Benny's associates have also passed on. Among them are:

ALEXANDER, Elmer "Mousey": 9 October 1988 in Seminole Community Hospital, Longwood, FL, age 66, of heart and kidney failure.

AULD, George (John Altweger): 8 January 1990 at his home in Palm Springs, CA, age 70, of lung cancer.

BAILEY, Pearl (Mrs. Louis Bellson): 17 August 1990, en route to Thomas Jefferson University Hospital, Phila., age 72, of a heart attack.

BERNSTEIN, Leonard: 15 October 1990 at his Manhattan apartment, age 72, of lung failure.

BRADLEY, Will (Wilbur Schwichtenberg): 15 July 1989 at his home in Flemington, NJ, age 78. Cause not revealed.

BUDWIG, Monty: March 1992, age 62. Details unknown.

BUTTERFIELD, Charles William "Billy": 18 March 1988 at his home in North Palm Beach, FL, age 71, of heart failure.

CALLENDER, George Sylvester "Red": 8 March 1992 at his home in Saugus, CA, age 76, of thyroid cancer.

CLAYTON, William "Buck": January 1992 at his home in New York, age 80. Details unknown.

COPLAND, Aaron: 2 December 1990 at the Phelps Memorial Hospital in North Tarrytown, NY, age 90, of respiratory failure following pneumonia.

CORB, Morty: 13 January 1996, in Las Vegas while on a short vacation there, age 79, of an aneurism.

DAVIS, Hal: 13 May 1990, in Sarasota, FL. Details unknown.

ELDRIDGE, David Roy: 26 February 1989 in Valley Stream, Long Island, NY, age 78. Cause not revealed.

EVANS, Gil: 20 March 1988 in Cuernavaca, Mexico, age 75, of peritonitis.

FAIN, Sammy: 6 December 1989 at the UCLA Medical Center, Los Angeles, following a heart attack.

FREEMAN, Lawrence "Bud": 15 March 1991 at the Warren Burr Pavilion, a nursing home in Chicago, age 84, of lung cancer.

GETZ, Stan (Stanley Gayetsky): 6 June 1991 at his home in Malibu, CA, age 64, of cancer of the liver.

GOODMAN, Irving: 7 July 1990, at his home in Tarzana, CA, age 76, of a heart attack. His widow Agnes wrote that his unexpected death was shocking because ". . . just a few days before he told me he never felt better." She adds that their son John is a pianist who has a quartet that plays classical music; and that their granddaughter Elise is a violinist who at age 11 performs with a local youth symphony orchestra. She closes with, "So with musical talent on both sides of the family, maybe the Goodman legacy will live on with one of the grandchildren."

GOULD, Morton: 21 February 1996 in Orlando, FL, age 82. One of few from whom Benny readily accepted suggestions and criticism, Morton died in his sleep the evening before he was to conduct seminars at Disney World. According to his son David, maestro Gould had not been ill, and the cause of his death was unknown.

GREEN, Johnny: 15 May 1989 at his home in Beverly Hills, CA, age 80. Cause not disclosed.

HALL, Al: 18 January 1988 in Roosevelt Hospital, New York City, age 72, of lung cancer.

HAMMOND, John: 10 July 1987 at his Manhattan apartment, age 76. Several years earlier John had suffered a disabling stroke, but the proximate cause of his death was not revealed.

HOLLEY, Major: 25 October 1990 at a friend's home in Maplewood, NJ, age 66, of a heart attack.

JACKSON, Oliver: 27 May 1994 in New York City, age 61, cause not given.

JORDAN, Steve: 13 September 1993, Alexandria, VA, age 74. No other details.

KAY, Connie (Conrad Henry Kirnon): 30 November 1994, in his sleep at his New York home, age 67. Proximate cause not disclosed.

KINCAIDE, Deane: May 1992, age 81. Details unknown.

KLEIN, Emanuel "Mannie": 31 May 1994, in the St. Joseph Medical Center, Burbank, CA, age 86. Cause not revealed. Sad commentary: The nation's press took no notice of the passing of Mannie Klein, possibly the most versatile, and most underrated, trumpet player in all of Jazz.

KLINK, Al: Mid-March 1991, in Florida, age 75. Details unknown, except that Al performed in that state just three days before his death.

LEWIS, Mel (Melvin Sokoloff): 2 February 1990, at the Cabrini Hospice in New York City, age 60, of lung cancer.

LUND, Art: 31 May 1990 in Salt Lake City, UT, age 75, of cancer of the liver.

MALTBY, Richard: 19 August 1991 at St. John's Hospice, Santa Monica, CA, age 77. Cause not cited.

MARX, Albert J.: c. May/June 1991, in California, details unknown. We're forever in his debt for his recording of Benny's 1938 Carnegie Hall concert.

MASTREN, Al: February 1992, age 74. Details unknown.

McKINLEY, Ray: 7 May 1995 in Largo, FL, age 84, cause not disclosed. Best known as featured drummer/vocalist with the Dorsey Brothers, Jimmy Dorsey, Will Bradley, Glenn Miller (AEF) and his own orchestra, Ray and Teddy Wilson both debuted with Benny Goodman on a May 1934 Columbia recording session.

McPARTLAND, James "Jimmy" D.: 13 March 1991 at his home in Port Washington, NY, age 83, of lung cancer. Just prior to his death, he and his former wife, Marian (Page) Mc-Partland, were remarried.

MONDELLO, Nuncio Francis "Toots": 15 November 1992 at Lenox Hill Hospital, New York, age 81, of prostate cancer.

NEWMAN, Joe: 5 July 1992 at Mt. Sinai Hospital, New York, age 70, following a stroke.

NORMAN, Fred: 19 February 1993 at St. Luke's Hospital, New York, age 82, of pneumonia. Among his other arrangements for Benny were his own tunes, **Smoke House (Rhythm)** and **Hot Foot Shuffle.**

NORTH, Alex: 8 September 1991 at his home in Los Angeles, age 80, of cancer. His **Review for Clarinet and Orchestra** was commissioned by Benny.

PARISH, Mitchell: 31 March 1993 at New York Hospital, New York, age 92, following a stroke. Benny's and Tommy Dorsey's back-to-back Victor release of **Star Dust,** for which Parish wrote the lyrics, was the first hit recording of Hoagy Carmichael's immortal ballad.

PASS, Joe: 24 May 1994 at the University of Southern California-Norris Cancer Center, age 65, of cancer of the liver.

REUSS, Allan: 4 June 1988 in California, age 72, of cancer of the pancreas. Benny had paid him the ultimate compliment: "We didn't realize how much he meant to the band until he left us."

RICH, Bernard "Buddy": 2 April 1987 at Bel-Air, CA, age 69, of a brain tumor. Among others, Frank Sinatra, Johnny Carson, Sammy Davis Jr. and Artie Shaw spoke at a memorial service for him.

RODNEY, "Red" (Robert Chudnick): 27 May 1994 in New York City, age 66, cancer.

ROLLINI, Arthur: 31 December 1993 at Ocala, FL, age 81, of various causes, following a four-month illness. The author, who'd kept in touch with Art regularly, was stunned when notified of his death by Art's widow, Elizabeth; Art had never complained of being ill.

ROSE, David: 23 August 1990 at St. Joseph's Hospital, Burbank, CA, age 80, of heart failure.

STACY, Jess Alexandria: 1 January 1995 in the Hospital of the Good Samaritan, Los Angeles, age 90, of congestive heart failure. The New Year was off to a sad start with Jess's death, the author's favorite of all the pianists who'd played for Benny. If there is a heavenly chorus, they'll find no one better than Jess to accompany them.

STEWART, Leroy "Slam": 10 December 1987 at his home in Binghamton, NY, age 73. Cause of death not disclosed, but Slam had suffered from congestive heart failure for some time.

TOUGH, Dave—correction: His death certificate reveals Dave died 9 December 1948, not 6 December, as erroneously stated in Legacy and elsewhere.

VAN HEUSEN, Jimmy (Edward Chester Babcock): 6 February 1990 at his home in Rancho Mirage, CA, age 77, of pneumonia, after a long illness.

VOORHEES, Donald: 10 January 1989 at Burdette Tomlin Memorial Hospital, Cape May Court House, NJ, age 85, of pneumonia.

WASSERMAN, Eddie: May 1992, age 69. Details unknown.

ZUCKERMAN, Muriel: 15 December 1990 in her apartment in New York City, of a second stroke, following the first that had occurred four weeks earlier. Age not disclosed.

INDEX OF TUNE TITLES: TEXT

A primary goal of this work is to publish information about previously undocumented Benny Goodman recordings whose status has evolved since the completion of the manuscript for *Legacy* (1986). This index is comprised of such recordings, both studio and location in origin. Illustrative of its contents are examples from the text:

Page 8, the caption, "4 April 1935, New York (ref: page 51)." Reference to page 51 of *Legacy* reveals that take 2, **Hunkadola,** was recorded during the studio session (page 9) this date, but that its existence was unknown in 1986. Issued in 1991, its tune title thus qualifies for entry in this index.

Page 10, the caption, "29 March 1936, Chicago." Absence of a page reference to *Legacy* informs the reader that this broadcast was unknown to the author in 1986, and so it is not listed in *Legacy*. Discovered in 1993, its three tunes are included in this index, in alphabetical order.

A few tune titles in the text are omitted from this index. Such tune titles are documented in *Legacy,* and their entry in the text adds but minor collateral data about them.

After You've Gone (Henry Creamer-Turner Layton), 4, 41, 43, 46(2), 47, 48(2), 57, 75, 80, 99, 114, 116, 118
Ain't Misbehavin' (Fats Waller-Andy Razaf-Harry Brooks), 50, 54, 55, 81
Ain'tcha Glad? (Fats Waller-Andy Razaf), 6
Air Mail Special (Good Enough To Keep) (Charlie Christian-Benny Goodman), 34, 76, 82, 100, 121
Alicia's Blues, 86
All I Do Is Dream Of You (Arthur Freed-Nacio Herb Brown), 7
All The Cats Join In (Alec Wilder-Eddie Sauter-Ray Gilbert), 46
All The Things You Are (Jerome Kern-Oscar Hammerstein), 26, 113
And The Angels Sing (Ziggy Elman-Johnny Mercer),104(2), 119
"Anthology Of Jazz"—Medley, 104
(I Would Do) Anything For You (Alexander Hill-Roberto Williams-Claude Hopkins), 75, 76, 79, 81, 114
As Long As I Live (Harold Arlen-Ted Koehler), 28
As Long As We Still Believe, 50
Astaire, The, 64
At The Darktown Strutters' Ball (Shelton Brooks), 9, 12, 43
Autumn Nocturne (Kim Gannon-Josef Myrow), 95
Avalon (Vincent Rose-B. G. DeSylva-Al Jolson), 80, 103, 106, 112, 115, 116, 117(2), 119, 121(2)

Baby. *See* Bye, Bye Baby
Baby, Won't You Please Come Home? (Charles Warfield-Clarence Williams), 54
Bach Goes To Town (Alec Templeton), 20, 26, 104
Bannister Slide, The (Benny Goodman-Gillian Duckworth), 65
Basin Street Blues (Spencer Williams), 22
Batunga Train (Bobby Gutesha-Benny Goodman), 95
Bedlam (Benny Goodman-Wardell Gray), 73

Before (Sergei Rachmaninoff, adapted by Toots Camarata & Reginald Connelly), 40
Behave Yourself (Alex Kramer-Joan Whitney), 69
Bei Mir Bist Du Schon (Jacob Jacobs-Sholem Secunda-Sammy Cahn-Saul Chaplin), 93, 121
Benny Rides Again (Eddie Sauter), 95
Benny's Bop (Benny Goodman), 71
Benny's Bugle (Benny Goodman-Count Basie), 29
Bernie's Tune (Bernie Miller-Mike Stoller-Jerry Lieber), 109
Best Thing For You, The (Irving Berlin), 97
Between The Devil And The Deep Blue Sea (Harold Arlen-Ted Koehler), 99, 113
Bewitched (Richard Rodgers-Lorenz Hart), 33, 121
Beyond The Sea (La Mer) (Charles Trenet-Jack Lawrence), 69
Birth Of The Blues, The (B. G. DeSylva-Lew Brown-Ray Henderson), 34, 114
Blue Hawaii (Leo Robin-Ralph Rainger), 102
Blue Interlude (Benny Carter-Manny Kurtz-Irving Mills), 7
Blue Lou (Edgar Sampson-Irving Mills), 73
Blue Room, The (Richard Rodgers-Lorenz Hart), 123
Blue Skies (Irving Berlin), 59, 91
Blue Views, 71
Bluebirds In The Moonlight (Leo Robin-Ralph Rainger), 25
Blues, The (Traditional), 22
Blues In The News (Johnny Mercer), 60
Blues In The Night (Harold Arlen-Johnny Mercer), 37
Body And Soul (Johnny Green-Robert Sour-Edward Heyman-Frank Eyton), 12, 49, 57, 59, 75, 80, 82, 99, 103
Boot Whip (Hi Ho Trailus) (Roy Eldridge), 76
Bop Hop (Chico O'Farrill), 73
Breakfast Feud (Benny Goodman), 30, 32, 99
Broadway (Sidney D. Mitchell-Archie Gottler-Con Conrad), 97
Brother Bill (Louis Armstrong), 74(2)
Brussels Blues (Jimmy Rushing-Benny Goodman), 90, 91
Buckle Down, Winsocki (Hugh Martin-Ralph Blane), 36
Bugle Call Rag (Jack Pettis-Elmer Schoebel-Billy Meyers), 8, 43, 86, 91, 103, 105
Bulgar And Other Balkan Type Inventions, The, 104(2)
Bumble Bee Stomp (Fletcher Henderson-Henri Woode), 19
But Not For Me (George Gershwin-Ira Gershwin), 79, 110
Buy, Buy For Baby (Irving Caesar-Joseph Meyer), 2
By Myself (Howard Dietz-Arthur Schwartz), 112
Bye, Bye Baby (Jimmy Rushing-Count Basie), 91
Bye, Bye Blackbird (Ray Henderson-Mort Dixon), 104
Bye, Bye Blues (Fred Hamm-Dave Bennett-Bert Lown-Chauncy Gray),71

Cabin In The Sky (Vernon Duke-John LaTouche), 29
Camel Hop (Mary Lou Williams), 16
Campus Crawl, 3
Can't We Be Friends? (Paul James-Kay Swift), 15
Can't We Talk It Over? (Ned Washington-Victor Young), 85

Caprice XXIV Paganini (Skippy Martin), 36

Changes (Walter Donaldson), 19

Chattanooga Choo Choo (Harry Warren-Mack Gordon), 104

Cheerful Little Earful (Harry Warren-Ira Gershwin-Billy Rose), 112

Cherokee (Ray Noble), 93

Chicago (Fred Fisher), 120

China Boy (Dick Winfree-Phil Bouteljie), 23, 80, 99

Clap Your Hands (George Gershwin-Ira Gershwin), 23

Clarinade (Mel Powell), 49, 52

Clarinet A La King (Eddie Sauter), 34, 104

Clouds (Gus Kahn-Walter Donaldson), 8

Come Rain Or Come Shine (Johnny Mercer-Harold Arlen), 114

Companionate Blues (Jack Pettis-Al Goering), 3

Concerto For Clarinet And Orchestra in A (Major, K. 622) (Wolfgang Amadeus Mozart), 83

Could You Pass In Love (Mack Gordon-Harry Revel), 18

Dark Shadows (Shifty Henry), 97

Darktown Strutters' Ball. *See* At The Darktown Strutters' Ball

Darn That Dream (Jimmy Van Heusen-Eddie DeLange), 69

Deacon And The Elder, The (Nat Adderly), 97

Dear Old Southland (Henry Creamer-Turner Layton), 10

Dearest (Benny Davis-Harry Akst), 108

Dearly Beloved (Jerome Kern-Johnny Mercer), 120

'Deed I Do (Walter Hirsch-Fred Rose), 76, 90(2)

Deep Purple (Peter DeRose-Mitchell Parish), 22, 23

Dig(g)a Dig(g)a Do(o) (Dorothy Fields-Jimmy McHugh), 95, 96

Dinah (Harry Akst-Sam M. Lewis-Joe Young), 44

Dixieland Band, The (Johnny Mercer-Bernie Hanighen), 8, 10, 79

Dizzy Fingers (Zez Confrey), 77

Dizzy Spells (Benny Goodman-Teddy Wilson-Lionel Hampton), 17

Donna Lee. *See* Indiana

Don't Be A Baby, Baby (Buddy Kaye-Howard Steiner), 59

Don't Be That Way (Benny Goodman-Edgar Sampson-Mitchell Parish), 16, 34, 80, 88, 99, 103, 113, 114, 115, 116(2). *See also* Don't Be That Way/Stompin' At The Savoy—Medley

Don't Be That Way/Stompin' At The Savoy—Medley, 117, 119, 121

Don't Blame Me (Dorothy Fields-Jimmy McHugh), 91

Don't Worry 'Bout Me (Rube Bloom-Ted Koehler), 72, 74, 86

Down By The Old Mill Stream (Tell Taylor), 24

Down South Camp Meetin' (Fletcher Henderson), 88

Dreazag (Buddy Greco), 73

Earl, The (Mel Powell), 35, 87

East Of The Sun (Brooks Bowman), 109

Easy To Love (Cole Porter), 84, 94

Eight, Nine And Ten (Charlotte Mansfield), 65

Elmer's Tune (Sammy Gallop-Dick Jurgens-Elmer Albrecht), 34

Embraceable You (George Gershwin-Ira Gershwin), 112

Entertainer Rag (Scott Joplin), 119

Every Little Moment (Dorothy Fields-Jimmy McHugh), 8

Ev'ry Time We Say Goodbye (Cole Porter), 47

Ev'rything I Love (Cole Porter), 104

Ev'rything I've Got (Belongs To You) (Richard Rodgers-Lorenz Hart), 79

Exactly Like You (Dorothy Fields-Jimmy McHugh), 80

Farewell Blues (Elmer Schoebel-Paul Mares-Leon Rappolo), 8

Fascinating Rhythm (George Gershwin-Ira Gershwin), 104, 105, 115

Feelin' High and Happy (Ted Koehler-Rube Bloom), 17

Fiesta Time (Chico O'Farrill), 74

Fine Romance, A (Jerome Kern-Dorothy Fields), 85, 90, 91

First Rhapsody For Clarinet (Claude Debussy), 30

Fishin' For The Moon (Edward Seiler-Sol Marcus-Guy B. Wood), 56

Fly By Night (Jack Pleis), 60

Flying Home (Benny Goodman-Lionel Hampton-Eddie DeLange), 26, 29, 76, 88, 91

For Every Man There's A Woman (Harold Arlen-Leo Robin), 68

Four Once More (Benny Goodman), 110

Four Or Five Times (Byron Gay-Marco Hellman), 78(2)

Frenesi (Alberto Dominguez-Leonard Whitcup), 33, 49

Futuristic Rhythm (Dorothy Fields-Jimmy McHugh), 3

Gee, But You're Swell (Charlie Tobias-Abel Baer), 13

Get Happy (Harold Arlen-Ted Koehler), 81, 94

Get Thee Behind Me, Satan (Irving Berlin), 11

Gilly (Benny Goodman), 31

Give Me The Simple Life (Harry Ruby-Rube Bloom), 56, 58, 59

Goin' To Chicago (Jimmy Rushing-Count Basie), 90

Gone With What Draft (Benny Goodman), 32, 33

Gone With "What" Wind (Count Basie-Benny Goodman), 27

Good Enough To Keep, 34. *See also* Air Mail Special

Good-Bye (Gordon Jenkins), 82

Goodbye Sue (Louis Ricca-Jimmy Rule-Jules Lowman), 46

Goodnight My Love (Mack Gordon-Harry Revel), 12, 74

Gotta Be This Or That (Sonny Skylar), 99

Grand Duo Concertante For Piano And Clarinet (Carl Maria von Weber), 65

Great Lie, The (Andy Gibson-Cab Calloway), 42

Happy Session Blues (Bobby Gutesha-Benny Goodman), 95

Harry Pepl's Blues (Harry Pepl), 121

Harvard Blues (Count Basie-Tab Smith-George Frazier), 90(2)

Henderson Stomp (Fletcher Henderson), 29, 43, 44, 69

Here's That Rainy Day (Johnny Burke-Jimmy Van Heusen), 117, 121(2)

He's Funny That Way. *See* She's Funny That Way

Hi 'Ya Sophia (Mel Powell-Benny Goodman) (originally "Gulliver Travels"), 67

High Falutin' (Charles Lawrence-Otis Rene), 69

Honeysuckle Rose (Fats Waller-Andy Razaf), 43, 44, 82, 112, 114, 116, 117

Hora Staccato (Jascha Heifitz-G. Dinicu), 61

House Hop (Jimmy Mundy-Benny Goodman), 11

How Can You Forget? (Richard Rodgers-Lorenz Hart), 94

How Deep Is The Ocean? (Irving Berlin), 35

How High The Moon (Morgan Lewis-Nancy Hamilton), 80

How Little We Know (Hoagy Carmichael-Johnny Mercer), 53

Hunkadola (Jack Yellen-Cliff Friend-Joseph Meyer), 8, 9

I Ain't Mad At Nobody (Johnny White-Terry Nolan), 59

I Can't Get Started (Ira Gershwin-Vernon Duke), 64

I Can't Give You Anything But Love, Baby (Dorothy Fields-Jimmy McHugh), 71, 76

I Cried For You (Arthur Freed-Gus Arnheim-Abe Lyman), 22, 85

I Don't Want To Set The World On Fire (Eddie Seiler-Sol Marcus-Bennie Benjamin-Eddie Durham), 36

I Found a New Baby. *See* I've Found a New Baby

I Got Rhythm (George Gershwin-Ira Gershwin), 8, 23, 56, 86, 103

I Gotta Right To Sing The Blues (Harold Arlen-Ted Koehler), 91, 104

I Guess I'll Have To Change My Plan (Howard Dietz-Arthur Schwartz), 7, 113, 117

I Had Someone (Else) Before I Had You, 74

I Hadn't Anyone 'Til You (Ray Noble), 91, 92

I Know That You Know (Vincent Youmans-Anne Caldwell), 8, 64, 118, 119

I Know Why (Harry Warren-Mack Gordon), 104

I Never Knew (I Could Love Anybody) (Tom Pitts-Raymond Egan-Roy Marsh), 65, 66

I Only Have Eyes For You (Harry Warren-Al Dubin), 77

I See A Million People (But All I Can See Is You) (Robert Sour-Una Mae Carlisle), 34, 36

I Surrender, Dear (Gordon Clifford-Harry Barris), 8

I Thought About You (Johnny Mercer-Jimmy Van Heusen), 24

I Want A Little Girl (Billy Moll-Murray Mencher), 85, 91

I Want To Be Happy (Vincent Youmans-Irving Caesar), 96, 99, 116, 119

I Was Lucky (Jack Meskill-Jack Stern), 8

I Will Wait For You (Norman Gimbel-Michel LeGrand), 114

If Dreams Come True (Edgar Sampson-Benny Goodman-Irving Mills), 16

If I Could Be With You (One Hour Tonight) (Henry Creamer-James P. Johnson), 80

If I Had You (Ted Shapiro-Jimmy Campbell-Reg Connelly), 92, 121

If The Moon Turns Green (Paul Coates-Bernie Hanighen), 8

If You Build A Better Mousetrap (Johnny Mercer-Victor Schertzinger), 37

I'll Always Be In Love With You (Herman Ruby-Bud Green-Sam H. Stept), 62, 64

I'm Always Chasing Rainbows (Joseph McCarthy-Harry Carroll), 31

I'm Beginning To See The Light (Don George-Johnny Hodges-Harry James-Duke Ellington), 104, 105

I'm Comin' Virginia (Donald Heywood-Will Marion Cook), 90(2)

I'm Gonna Sit Right Down And Write Myself A Letter (Joe Young-Fred E. Ahlert), 11

I'm In A Crying Mood, 69

I'm Livin' In A Great Big Way (Dorothy Fields-Jimmy McHugh), 8

In A Mellotone (Duke Ellington) (Lyrics added in 1955 by Milt Gabler), 99

In De Ruff (Blue Six), 5

In My Arms (Frank Loesser-Ted Grouya), 43

In The Evening (in Thai, Yarm Yen). *See* Yarm Yen

Indian Summer (Victor Herbert), 26

Indiana (James P. Hanley-Ballard MacDonald), 70, 117, 121, 123

It Had To Be You (Gus Kahn-Isham Jones), 21

It Isn't Fair (Richard Himber-Frank Warshauer-Sylvester Sprigato), 72

It's A Most Unusual Day (Jimmy McHugh-Harold Adamson), 112

It's All Right With Me (Cole Porter), 94, 110

It's Bad For Me (Cole Porter), 85

It's Been So Long (Walter Donaldson-Harold Adamson), 68, 71, 78

It's Delovely (Cole Porter), 12

It's Only A Paper Moon (Harold Arlen-E. Y. Harburg-Billy Rose), 53

I've Found A New Baby (Spencer Williams-Jack Palmer), 12, 32, 44, 45, 80, 82, 109, 113

I've Got A Gal In Kalamazoo (Harry Warren-Mack Gordon), 104

I've Got The Sun In The Morning (Irving Berlin), 60

I've Got The World On A String (Harold Arlen-Ted Koehler), 5

I've Got You Under My Skin (Cole Porter), 91, 92

I've Grown Accustomed To Her Face (Alan Jay Lerner-Fredrick Loewe), 105

Japanese Sandman (Raymond B. Egan-Richard A. Whiting), 8

Jersey Bounce (Bobby Plater-Tiny Bradshaw-Edward Johnson), 104

Jingle Bells (Originally titled "The One Horse Open Sleigh") (James S. Pierpont), 12

Jumpin' At The Woodside (Count Basie), 104

June Is Bustin' Out All Over (Richard Rodgers-Oscar Hammerstein II), 50, 52

Just One Of Those Things (Cole Porter), 47, 51, 75, 108

Just You, Just Me (Raymond W. Klages-Jesse Greer), 53

Keep Me In Mind (Elliot Wexler-Adrian King), 68

King Porter (Stomp) (Jelly Roll Morton), 8, 26, 57, 86, 88, 103, 104, 111, 115, 116, 117

Kiss In The Night, A (I Sent You) (Martin Mayne-Elizabeth Ann Carroll-Yniguez Garcia), 60

Lazy Day (Gus Kahn-G. LeBoy Kahn-George Posford-A. Martin), 5

Let Me Be Alone With You (Harold Dixon-Irving Mills), 2

Let Me Off Uptown (Ray Evans-Earl Bostic), 76

Let The Doorknob Hitcha (Benny Goodman-Margie Gibson), 33

Let's Dance (Gregory Stone-Joe Bonime-Fanny May Baldridge), 15, 25, 33, 82, 88, 91, 99

Let's Do It (Cole Porter), 35

Let's Fall In Love (Harold Arlen-Ted Koehler), 47

Limehouse Blues (Douglas Furber-Philip Braham), 36, 45

Liza (All The Clouds'll Roll Away) (George Gershwin-Ira Gershwin-Gus Kahn), 57, 80, 110

Lonely Moments (Mary Lou Williams), 62

Look For The Silver Lining (B. G. DeSylva-Jerome Kern), 112

Louise (Leo Robin-Richard A. Whiting), 21

Love Doesn't Grow On Trees (Jack Palmer-Jimmy R. Dupre), 60

Love For Sale (Cole Porter), 104, 115, 117

Love Me Or Leave Me (Walter Donaldson-Gus Kahn), 11, 120

Love Sends A Little Gift Of Roses (Leslie L. Cook-John Openshaw), 108(2)

Love Walked In (George Gershwin-Ira Gershwin), 49

Lover Man (Jimmy Davis-Roger "Ram" Ramirez-Jimmy Sherman), 73

Lucky (Edgar Sampson-Benny Goodman-Jack Palmer), 57, 58

Lullaby In Rhythm (Edgar Sampson-Clarence Profit-Walter Hirsch-Benny Goodman), 79, 113
Lullaby Of The Leaves (Joe Young-Bernice Petkere), 76

Ma Belle Marguerite (A. P. Herbert-Vivian Ellis), 72
Macedonia Lullaby (Bobby Gutesha-Benny Goodman), 93
Madhouse (Earl Hines-Jimmy Mundy), 26
"Main Title Music" (Intro to Don't Be That Way, q.v.), 84
Make With The Kisses (Johnny Mercer-Jimmy Van Heusen), 24
Makin' Whoopee (Walter Donaldson-Gus Kahn), 120
Man Here Plays Fine Piano (Joe Bushkin-Peter De-Vries), 62
Man I Love, The (George Gershwin-Ira Gershwin), 23, 77, 103, 114, 115
Marchin' And Swingin' (Fred Karlin), 98
Margie (Benny Davis-Con Conrad-J. Russel Robinson), 79
Mary's Idea (Mary Lou Williams), 71
Maybe-Who Knows (John Aloyseus Tucker-Joseph Schuster-Ruth Etting), 3
Meadowlands (Meadowland) (Lev Knipper-Victor A. Gussev-M. L. Koor-Alice Mattullath), 104
Mean To Me (Roy Turk-Fred E. Ahlert), 82
Meet The Band (Bob Prince), 104, 105
Melancholy Baby. *See* My Melancholy Baby
Memories Of You (Eubie Blake-Andy Razaf), 82, 99, 103, 115, 116
Mexico Joe (Johnny Lange-Leon Rene), 43
Midnight Blue (Edgar Leslie-Johnny Burke), 12
Minnie The Moocher's Wedding Day (Harold Arlen-Ted Koehler), 14
Minnie's In The Money (Harry Warren-Leo Robin), 44
Mission To Moscow (Mel Powell), 44, 104
Mood At Twilight (Mel Powell), 38
Moon And Sand (Bill Engvick-Alec Wilder-Morty Palitz), 36
Moon Glow (Will Hudson-Eddie DeLange-Irving Mills), 11, 99
Moon Of Manakoora, The (Alfred Newman-Frank Loesser), 102
Moon River (Henry Mancini-Johnny Mercer), 114
Moon Won't Talk, The (Charlie Hathaway-Helen Bliss), 33
Moon-Faced, Starry-Eyed (Kurt Weill-Langston Hughes), 63(2)
Moonlight Serenade (Glenn Miller-Mitchell Parish), 104
More Than You Know (Vincent Youmans-William Rose-Edward Eliscu), 87
Mozart Concerto For Clarinet And Orchestra In A (K.622) (Wolfgang Amadeus Mozart). *See* Concerto For Clarinet And Orchestra In A (K.622)
Muskrat Ramble (Kid Ory), 38
My Baby Done Tol' Me (Jack Sheldon-Flip Phillips), 101
My Daddy Rocks Me (J. B. Barbour), 57
My Guy's Come Back (Mel Powell-Ray McKinley), 54, 55
My Kinda Love (Louis Alter-Joseph H. Trent), 3, 4
My Little Grass Shack (Tommy Harrison-Bill Cagswell-Johnny Noble), 102
My Melancholy Baby (George Norton-Ernie Burnett), 9, 117

Nagasaki (Harry Warren-Mort Dixon), 7, 67
Nice Work If You Can Get It (George Gershwin-Ira Gershwin), 80, 82, 104
No Name Blues, 84
No Way To Stop It (Richard Rodgers-Oscar Hammerstein II), 99

Not A Care In The World (Vernon Duke-John LaTouche), 37

Oh, Baby! (Owen Murphy), 59(2), 95
Oh, By Jingo (Albert Von Tilzer-Lew Brown), 84
Oh, Gee! Oh, Joy! (George Gershwin-Ira Gershwin), 92, 109
Oh, Lady Be Good! (George Gershwin-Ira Gershwin), 12, 44, 88, 113, 115, 116, 121(2)
On A Clear Day (Burton Lane-Alan Jay Lerner), 115, 116
On The Beach At Waikiki (Henry Kailimai-G. H. Staver), 102
On The Sunny Side Of The Street (Dorothy Fields-Jimmy McHugh), 80, 90, 99, 119
One O'Clock Jump (Count Basie), 16, 26, 80, 82, 88, 99, 104
One Sweet Letter From You (Harry Warren-Sidney Clare-Lew Brown), 24
Only Another Boy And Girl (Cole Porter), 47(2)
Oo-Bla-Dee (Mary Lou Williams-Milton Orent), 73
Oomph Fah Fah (Ellis Larkins), 48, 52
Opus 3/4 (Benny Goodman-Lionel Hampton), 23

Paradise (Nacio Herb Brown-Gordon Clifford), 18
Pardon My Love (Oscar Levant-Milton Drake), 8
Pardon My Southern Accent (Matty Malneck-Johnny Mercer), 7
Peace, Brother! (Eddie DeLange-Jimmy Van Heusen), 26
Pennies From Heaven (Johnny Burke-Arthur Johnston), 13, 90, 91
People (Jule Styne-Bob Merrill), 111
Play, Fiddle, Play (Emery Deutsch-Arthur Altman-Jack Lawrence), 119
Please Be Kind (Sammy Cahn-Saul Chaplin), 17, 67
Poor Butterfly (John Golden-Raymond Hubble), 103, 106, 114, 115, 116, 119, 121
Put That Kiss Back Where You Found It (Peter DeRose-Carl Sigman), 61
Put Your Arms Around Me, Honey (Albert Von Tilzer-Junie McCree), 43
Puttin' On The Ritz (Irving Berlin), 5

Rachel's Dream (Benny Goodman), 45, 46, 47(2), 51, 106
Rainfall (in Thai, Sai Fon) (Phumiphol Aduljej). *See* Sai Fon
Ramona (L. Wolfe Gilbert-Mabel Wayne), 39
Rattle And Roll (Count Basie-Benny Goodman-Buck Clayton), 58
Record Ban Blues, The, 70
Remember (Irving Berlin), 120
Rhapsody In Blue (George Gershwin), 41, 42
Ridin' High (Cole Porter), 14, 104
Right About Face (G. Whiting-N. Borton), 8
Roll 'Em (Mary Lou Williams), 88, 91, 115, 116, 117
Rollin' Down The River (Fats Waller-Stanley Adams), 4
Room Without Windows, A (Ervin Drake), 111
Rose Room (Art Hickman-Harry Williams), 42, 46, 76, 81, 99, 117
Rosetta (Earl Hines-Henri Woode), 97
Royal Garden Blues (Clarence Williams-Spencer Williams), 28
Runnin' Wild (Joe Grey-Leo Wood-A. Harrington Gibbs), 80, 82

'S Wonderful (George Gershwin-Ira Gershwin), 19, 85
Sai Fon (Rainfall) (Phumiphol Aduljej), 88(2)
St. James Infirmary (Joe Primrose), 100
St. Louis Blues (W. C. Handy), 11, 64, 106, 113

Santa Claus Came In The Spring (Johnny Mercer-Matty Malneck), 9

Satin Doll (Duke Ellington-Billy Strayhorn-Johnny Mercer), 118

Scarecrow (Benny Goodman), 33

Scatter-Brain (Johnny Burke-Frankie Masters-Kahn Keene-Carl Bean), 25, 26

Send In The Clowns (Stephen Sondheim), 119

Sensation Rag (Original Dixieland Jazz Band), 84

Sent For You Yesterday (And Here You Come Today) (Jimmy Rushing-Eddie Durham-Count Basie), 90

September Song (Kurt Weill-Maxwell Anderson), 107

Serenade For A Wealthy Widow (Reginald Foresythe-Dorothy Fields-Jimmy McHugh), 7

Serenade In Blue (Mack Gordon-Harry Warren), 40

Seven Come Eleven (Benny Goodman-Charlie Christian), 86, 117, 119, 122

Shady Lady Bird (Hugh Martin-Ralph Blane), 36

Sheik Of Araby, The (Harry B. Smith-Francis Wheeler-Ted Snyder), 23, 46

She's A Latin From Manhattan (Al Dubin-Harry Warren), 8

She's Funny That Way (Richard A. Whiting-Neil Moret), 48

Shine (Cecil Mack-Lew Brown-Ford Dabney), 54, 117

Shirley Steps Out (Mel Powell), 68

Show Me (Alan J. Lerner-Frederick Loewe), 104

Sing Me A Swing Song (Hoagy Carmichael-Stanley Adams), 11

Sing, Sing, Sing (Louis Prima), 15, 82, 84, 99, 100, 104, 119, 121

Singapore Sorrows (Jack LeSoir-Ray Doll), 2

Sleep (Earl Bunnett-Adam Geibel), 97

Slipped Disc (Benny Goodman), 48, 58, 81, 82, 119

Smoke Dreams (Arthur Freed-Nacio Herb Brown), 14

Smo-o-o-oth One, A (Benny Goodman), 34, 35, 36, 80, 117

Soft Lights And Sweet Music (Irving Berlin), 85

Soft Winds (Benny Goodman), 27

Solo Flight (Charlie Christian-Benny Goodman-Jimmy Mundy), 34

Somebody Loves Me (George Gershwin-Ballard MacDonald-B. G. DeSylva), 58, 110, 115, 119

Somebody Stole My Gal (Leo Wood), 31, 32

Someday, Sweetheart (John Spikes-Benjamin Spikes), 11, 80

Someone To Watch Over Me (George Gershwin-Ira Gershwin), 97

Something New (Negra Soy) (Albert Gamse-Nilo Menandez), 36

Sometimes I'm Happy (Vincent Youmans-Irving Caesar), 9, 90, 96

Song Is Ended, The (Irving Berlin), 90

Song Of The Islands (Charles E. King), 102

Soon (George Gershwin-Ira Gershwin), 90

Space, Man (Benny Goodman), 19

Spin A Record (William Conrad-Jack Wells), 74

Splanky (Neal Hefti), 97

Squeeze Me (Fats Waller-Clarence Williams), 27

Star Dust (Mitchell Parish-Hoagy Carmichael), 8, 26, 73

Stealin' Apples (Fats Waller-Andy Razaf), 23, 71, 80, 114, 115, 116, 117

Stompin' At The Savoy (Benny Goodman-Chick Webb-Edgar Sampson-Andy Razaf), 9, 10, 14, 23, 76, 82, 83, 88, 90, 99, 116, 117, 121. *See also* Don't Be That Way/Stompin' At The Savoy—Medley

String Of Pearls, A (Jerry Gray), 38, 104, 115, 116, 117

Sugar Foot Stomp (King Oliver-Louis Armstrong), 88

Summertime (George Gershwin-Ira Gershwin), 104, 105

Sunday, Monday And Always (Johnny Burke-Jimmy Van Heusen), 43

Superman (Eddie Sauter), 36

Sweet And Lovely (Gus Arnheim-Harry Tobias-Jules Lemare), 67

Sweet Georgia Brown (Ben Bernie-Maceo Pinkard-Kenneth Casey), 8, 46, 64, 103, 112, 113, 116, 117, 119

Sweet Leilani (Harry Owens), 102

Sweet Lorraine (Cliff Burwell-Mitchell Parish), 64, 106, 114

Sweet Miss (Bill Harris), 97

Sweet Sue-Just You (Will J. Harris-Victor Young), 17

Swift As The Wind (Tadd Dameron), 105

Take Another Guess (Al Sherman-Charles Newman-Murray Mencher), 12

Take It (Margie Gibson), 35

Take Me (Mack David-Rube Bloom), 40

Tea For Two (Vincent Youmans-Irving Caesar), 23, 97

Temptation Rag (Louis Weslyn-Henry Lodge), 76

Ten Bone (Al Cohn), 96

Ten Days With Baby (Mack Gordon-James V. Monaco), 46

That Lucky Fellow (Jerome Kern-Oscar Hammerstein II), 25

That's All That Matters To Me (Kenny Jacobson-Rhoda Roberts), 55

That's A-Plenty (Lew Pollack), 7, 67, 68, 76, 80, 119, 121

That's Life I Guess (Sam M. Lewis-Peter DeRose), 13

That's The Beginning Of The End (Joan Whitney-Alex Kramer), 61

Them There Eyes (Maceo Pinkard-William Tracy-Doris Tauber), 111

There Is No Greater Love (Marty Symes-Isham Jones), 113

There'll Be A Jubilee (Phil Moore), 46

There's A Small Hotel (Richard Rodgers-Lorenz Hart), 71, 73

There's No Fool Like An Old Fool (Joe McCarthy, Jr.-Joe Meyer), 90

There's Something In The Air (Harold Adamson-Jimmy McHugh), 12

These Foolish Things (Holt Marvell-Jack Strachey-Harry Link), 112

Things Ain't What They Used To Be (Mercer Ellington-Ted Persons), 48

Things I Never Knew Till Now (Walter Winchell-Al Vann-Sid Kuller), 4

This Is My Lucky Day (B. G. DeSylva-Lew Brown-Ray Henderson), 90, 91

This Is The Missus (Lew Brown-Ray Henderson), 4

Thou Swell (Richard Rodgers-Lorenz Hart), 117

Three Little Words (Bert Kalmar-Harry Ruby), 8, 12, 43(2)

Thrill Is Gone, The (Lew Brown-Ray Henderson), 104, 105

Tiger Rag (Original Dixieland Jazz Band), 13, 54

Till Tom Special (Benny Goodman-Lionel Hampton), 26

Time On My Hands (Vincent Youmans-Harold Adamson-Mack Gordon), 32, 96

Tin Roof Blues (w: Walter Melrose; m: New Orleans Rhythm Kings-George Brunies, Leon Rappolo, Paul Mares, Mel Stitzel and Ben Pollack), 115, 117

Toccata In E Flat (Reginald Foresythe?), 7

Together (B. G. DeSylva-Lew Brown-Ray Henderson), 107

Too Close For Comfort (Jerry Bock-Larry Holofcener-George Weiss), 117

Too Many Tears (Harry Warren-Al Dubin), 101

Trees (Oscar Rasbach-Joyce Kilmer), 73

Trigger Fantasy (Irv Manning), 88

Two Little Fishes And Five Loaves Of Bread (Bernie Hanighen), 49

Undecided (Charlie Shavers-Sid Robin), 21, 76

Under A Blanket Of Blue (Marty Symes-Al J. Neiburg-Jerry Livingston), 78

Untitled (later, Slipped Disc, q.v.) (Benny Goodman), 46

Vieni, Vieni (Vincent Baptiste Scotto-Henri Eugene Vantard-George S. Konyn-Rudy Vallee), 15

Walk, Jennie, Walk (Sam Wooding-Bob Schaffer), 8

Wardell's Riff. *See* Benny's Bop

'Way Down Yonder In New Orleans (Henry Creamer-Turner Layton), 44

What A Day! (Harry Woods), 3

What A Diff'rence A Day Makes (Stanley Adams-Maria Grever), 95

What A Little Moonlight Can Do (Harry Woods), 78

What's New-It's You, 33

When Buddha Smiles (Arthur Freed-Nacio Herb Brown), 77, 105

When I Go A-Dreamin' (Bickley Reichner-Clay Boland), 19

When My Baby Smiles At Me (Billy Munro-Ted Lewis-Harry Von Tilzer-Andrew B. Sterling), 8

When You're Smiling (Mark Fisher-Joe Goodwin-Larry Shay), 90(2)

Where Or When (Richard Rodgers-Lorenz Hart), 37, 62

Whispering (John Schonberger-Richard Coburn-Vincent Rose), 95

Whistle (Whistling) Blues (Mary Lou Williams-Milt Orent), 63

Who? (Jerome Kern-Oscar Hammerstein II-Otto Harbach), 94

Who Can I Turn To? (Alec Wilder-Bill Engvick), 36

Who Cares? (George Gershwin-Ira Gershwin), 90, 104, 105, 107

Wholly Cats (Benny Goodman), 28

Why Don't You Do Right? (Joe McCoy), 41

Why'd Ya Make Me Fall In Love? (Walter Donaldson), 17

Wild And Wooly Willy (John Redmond-Fred Meadow-Lee David), 3

Willow Weep For Me (Ann Ronell), 102

Winter Weather (Ted Shapiro), 37

World Is Waiting For The Sunrise, The (Eugene Lockhart-Ernest Seitz), 17, 22, 40, 70, 75, 78, 80, 88, 104, 116, 119, 121(2)

Wrappin' It Up (Fletcher Henderson), 105, 123

Yardbird Suite (Charlie Parker). *See* Rosetta

Yarm Yen (In The Evening) (Phumiphol Aduljej), 88

Yesterday (John Lennon-Paul McCartney), 111, 115

You And I (Meredith Willson), 36

You Can't Pull The Wool Over My Eyes (Milton Ager-Charles Newman-Murray Mencher), 77

You Couldn't Be Cuter (Jerome Kern-Dorothy Fields), 92

You Don't Know What Love Is (Don Raye-Gene DePaul), 37

You Got Me (Clay Boland-Bickley Reichner), 18

You Must Meet My Wife (Stephen Sondheim), 118, 119, 121

You Took Advantage Of Me (Richard Rodgers-Lorenz Hart), 69

You Turned The Tables On Me (Sidney Mitchell-Louis Alter), 22, 68

You're Dangerous (Johnny Burke-Jimmy Van Heusen), 33

You're My Best Bet, 12

You're Out Of This World (Jule Styne-Kim Gannon), 41

You're Right, I'm Wrong. *See* Lucky

Yours (Jack Sherr-Albert Gamse-Augustin Rodriguez-Gonzalo Roig), 33(2)

INDEX OF TUNE TITLES: THE SAVORY GOODMAN AIR CHECKS

This index applies solely to Bill Savory's transcribed acetates and tapes of Benny Goodman's air checks, whose chronological listings begin on page 139 of this work. As noted in the preamble to the index of tune titles for the text, these performances are not in *Legacy,* save for the few exceptions cited. Neither are they included in the text, nor in its index of tune titles.

It is emphasized that these air checks are unavailable to the collector at present. They are tabulated to provide accurate provenance for any of them that may be released in the future.

Absence Makes The Heart Grow Fonder, 150
After I Say I'm Sorry, (What Can I Say, Dear), 153
After You've Gone, 142, 145
Alexander's Ragtime Band, 140, 141, 147(2), 153
All Of Me, 148
All The Things You Are, 150
Always, 146, 148, 149, 153
Always And Always, 144
And The Angels Sing, 153
(I Would Do) Anything For You, 139, 153
Anything Goes, 139
At A Perfume Counter, 146
At Sundown, 147, 148
At The Darktown Strutters' Ball, 142, 148
A-Tisket, A-Tasket, 148
Avalon, 141, 144

Bach Goes To Town, 149(2)
Bei Mir Bist Du Schon, 143
Big John Special, 141, 143, 146
Blossoms On Broadway, 143
Blue Interlude, 147, 148
Blue Moon, 139
Blue Room, 153
Blue Skies, 143, 145, 153
Blues In My Flat, The, 148
Blues In My Heart, 148
Bob White, 143
Body And Soul, 144, 148
Bolero, 150(2)
Boy Meets Horn, 150
Bugle Call Rag, 140, 142, 144, 152, 153
Busy As A Bee (I'm Buzz, Buzz, Buzzin'), 151

Camel Hop, 140, 143
Caravan, 142
'Cause My Baby Says It's So, 141
Changes, 139
Cherokee, 150
Cherry, 153
China Boy, 139(2), 143(2), 153
Chlo-e, 140
Ciribiribin, 142, 145, 148
Clap Hands, Here Comes Charlie, 140
Clarinet Marmalade, 145, 149

Cocoanut Grove, 151
Cowboy From Brooklyn, 146

Dance Of The Russian Peasant, 147
Dear Old Southland, 147
'Deed I Do, 153
Deep In A Dream,149(2)
Dixieland Band, The, 153
Dizzy Spells, 144, 146(2), 148
Don't Be That Way, 144(2), 145, 148, 153
Don't You Know Or Don't You Care, 142
Down South Camp Meetin', 152, 153

Every Little Moment, 139

Farewell Blues, 148, 149
Farewell, My Love, 142
Flying Home, 150
From The Land Of Sky Blue Water, 148

Glory Of Love, The, 153
Good Evenin', Good Lookin'!, 151
Good-Bye, 147

Hallelujah!, 141, 151
Have You Forgotten So Soon?, 147
He Ain't Got Rhythm, 140
Heart And Soul, 148
Honey Chile. *See* Lullaby In Rhythm
Honeysuckle Rose, 140, 142, 147, 150(2)
Hot Foot Shuffle, 149
House Hop, 146
How'd Ya Like To Love Me?, 145, 146

I Can't Get Started, 139
I Can't Give You Anything But Love, Baby, 146, 147
I Can't Lose That Longing For You, 140
I Cried For You, 149
I Didn't Know What Time It Was, 150
I Got Rhythm, 139, 142, 145, 151
I Have Eyes, 149
I Know That You Know, 147, 149
I Let A Song Go Out Of My Heart, 145, 146
I Love To Whistle, 145
I Married An Angel, 146
I Must Have That Man, 146
I Never Knew, 146, 147(2)
I Surrender, Dear, 142, 150, 151
I Wanna Be In Winchell's Column, 143
I Want To Be Happy, 141
If I Could Be With You (One Hour Tonight), 145
If I Didn't Care, 149
If It's The Last Thing I Do, 143(2)
I'll Always Be In Love With You, 148
I'll Never Say "Never Again" Again, 153
I'm A Ding Dong Daddy (From Dumas), 143, 145, 146, 147

I'm Bidin' My Time, 152
I'm Getting Sentimental Over You, 142
I'm Hatin' This Waitin' Around, 141
In A Mist, 142
In The Mood, 150
In The Shade Of The Old Apple Tree, 142
Indian Summer, 151
It's Been So Long, 153
It's Easy To Remember, 139
I've Found A New Baby, 139, 141, 144
I've Got My Love To Keep Me Warm, 140
I've Got To Sing, 145
I've Hitched My Wagon To A Star, 143

Jam Session, 141
Joseph, Joseph, 146
Journey To A Star, A, 152

King Porter Stomp, 139, 144, 145

Lady Is A Tramp, The, 143
Let That Be A Lesson To You, 144
Let The Doorknob Hitcha, 151
Let's Dance, 140
Let's Go Slumming On Park Avenue, 139
Let's Have Another Cigarette, 142
L'Heure Bleu, 141
Life Goes To A Party, 142, 143, 149
Limehouse Blues, 139, 140, 142
Liza, 139, 140, 143(2), 144
Loch Lomond, 142
Love Me Or Leave Me, 145, 146
Lullaby In Rhythm, 144, 145(2), 146

Madhouse, 141, 148
Marie, 141
Me, Myself And I, 142
Melancholy Baby, 146(2), 147
Memories Of You, 151, 153
Milenberg Joys, 153
Minnie The Moocher's Wedding Day, 139, 140
Mission To Moscow, 152
Mr. Ghost Goes To Town, 141
More Than You Know, 140
Music, Maestro, Please, 146
My Blue Heaven, 149
My Heart Belongs To Daddy, 148
My Reverie, 147, 148

Nagasaki, 140(2), 141
Never In A Million Years, 141
Nice Work If You Can Get It, 153
Nobody's Sweetheart, 144, 147

Ode To A Cement Mixer, 149
Oh, Johnny! Oh, Johnny! Oh!, 150
Oh, Lady Be Good!, 140(2), 141, 145, 146, 148
Old Man River, 140
Once In A While, 142, 143(2)
One Alone, 148
One O'Clock Jump, 142, 143, 145, 151
oooOO-OH Boom!, 144
Opus 1/2, 149

Peace, Brother!, 150
Peckin', 141
Perfidia (Tonight), 151
Pick-A-Rib, 148, 150

Please Be Kind, 145
Pop-Corn Man, 142

Quintet For Clarinet And Strings—Menuetto, 151

Remember, 140, 150
Reverie, 147
Ridin' High, 139, 153
Roast Turkey Stomp (a.k.a. Seven Come Eleven), 150
Robins And Roses, 139
Roll 'Em, 140, 141, 142, 145, 150, 152, 153
Rose Room, 152
Roses In December, 142
Russian Lullaby, 147

'S Wonderful, 144, 147
St. Louis Blues, 142
Satan Takes A Holiday, 142
(I've Been) Saving Myself For You, 146
Scatter-Brain, 150
September In The Rain, 140
Serenade To The Stars, 144, 146
Shine On, Harvest Moon, 146
Sing, Sing, Sing, 153
Sing You Sinners, 147
Smiles, 148, 150
Smoke House (Rhythm), 149(2)
So Rare, 142
Soft As Spring, 151
Soft Winds, 151
Solid Mama, 144
Some Of These Days, 149
Somebody Loves Me, 140
Someday Sweetheart, 139, 143
Sometimes I'm Happy, 141, 153
Spring Song, 150
Star Dust, 139
Stompin' At The Savoy, 140, 149
Sugar, 145
Sugar Foot Stomp, 140, 153
('Way Down Upon The) Swanee River—comedy routine, 139
Sweet As A Song, 145
Sweet Georgia Brown, 144
Sweet Is The Word For You, 140
Sweet Reed, 151
Sweet Stranger, 143
Sweet Sue-Just You, 141, 144, 145, 146, 147, 148
Swing Low, Sweet Chariot, 139, 144
Swingtime In The Rockies, 150(2)

That Feeling Is Gone, 146
That Old Feeling, 142
There's A Lull In My Life, 141
They All Laughed, 141
They Say, 149
This Can't Be Love, 149
This Is My Last Affair, 139
Three O'Clock In The Morning, 148
Ti-Pi-Tin, 144(2), 145
Tuesday At Ten, 151

Vibraphone Blues, 143
Vieni, Vieni, 142, 143(2)

Wait 'Til The Sun Shines, Nellie, 149
Waitin' At The Gate For Katie, 148
Well, All Right! (Tonight's The Night), 150

What A Little Moonlight Can Do, 153
What Goes On Here In My Heart?, 147, 148
What Have You Got That Gets Me?, 148(2)
When It's Sleepy Time Down South, 143
Where Or When, 144, 146
Who's Sorry Now?, 147
Wolverine Blues, 153
World Is Waiting For The Sunrise, The, 144, 149, 153
Would You?, 139

Wrappin' It Up, 142, 147, 149, 151

Yam, The, 147
You Leave Me Breathless, 146
You Showed Me The Way, 143
You Turned The Tables On Me, 153
You're Here, You're There, You're Everywhere, 139
You're Laughing At Me, 140(2)
You're Lovely, Madame, 147